LIFE IN A WEST AFRICAN VILLAGE

KONKONURU: LIFE IN A WEST AFRICAN VILLAGE
The Impact of Socio-Economic Change on Rural Communities

MARGARET HARDIMAN

GHANA UNIVERSITIES PRESS
ACCRA
2003

Published by
Ghana Universities Press
P. O. Box 4219
Accra

PRODUCED IN GHANA
Typesetting by Ghana Universities Press, Accra
Printing and Binding by Assemblies of God Literature Centre Limited, Accra

CONTENTS

Introduction   1

Chapter

1. THE RURAL SECTOR IN WEST AFRICA   12
     The Dimensions of the Rural Situation   12
     Public and Social Services   18
     Policies for Rural Development   25
     Theoretical Approaches to the study of Socio-
     Economic Change   28

2. LIFE IN RURAL GHANA   36
     The Northern Savannah   37
     The Coastal Savannah   39
     The Forest Region   41
        Food Crop Production in Forest Areas   42
        Cocoa Farming   47
     Demographic Aspects   54
     Fertility and Mortality   55
     Public and Social Services   60

3. THE HISTORY OF KONKONURU   63
     Origins of the Settlement   65
     The Akwapim State   68
     Foreign Rulers, Missionaries and Cocoa   70
     Konkonuru's Position in the Akwapim State   72
     Missionaries in Konkonuru   77
     Cocoa in Konkonuru   78

4. KONKONURU TODAY   80

5 FOOD CROP FARMING   103

6. MIGRANT CITIZENS OF KONKONURU   132

7. THE EDUCATION OF THE YOUNGER GENERATION   152

8.   THE DOMESTIC GROUP   174
        Kwamena Asamoah's Compound   187
        E.K. Owusu's Compound   190
        Abena Boakyewa's Compound   192

9.   SUMMARY AND CONCLUSIONS   204
        Infrastructure   213
        Agricultural Systems   214
Appendices   217
References   233
Index   243

INTRODUCTION

In a world experiencing rapid social and economic change there is increasing concern about the consequences of these changes for rural communities in the Third World. Many aspects of change have tended towards increasing the gap between town and country. Investment has been concentrated in the urban sector, services in rural areas have not kept pace with those in towns, employment opportunities for the young have been lacking, leading to migration, which has deprived rural communities of working age population, particularly of men.

Social indicators are one way of demonstrating this gap. Death and morbidity rates, infant mortality, and illiteracy, particularly amongst women, are generally higher in rural than in urban areas. Villages are far less likely to have adequate water supplies, let alone the convenience of piped water; electricity services have been slow to reach rural areas, and those villages which ask to be connected are frequently asked to make a substantial contribution to its installation. In many parts of the world good access roads to villages are lacking, making it difficult to market their produce or to receive the goods they need from the town. It follows that the access to services is limited by these and other considerations. Even the services especially intended for rural areas tend not to reach the more remote or isolated communities. Extension workers are not only short of transport; they are also usually reluctant to visit locations where it means a long trek on foot. Rural communities have been disadvantaged by the price twists which depressed the returns to the products of rural areas, which generally were to the advantage of the urban elite, and as they were the dominant force in the government they tended not to be challenged. Recently, however, the evidence of mass urban poverty may to some extent have reversed the position, as prices for farm products have reached high levels.

There is now far greater recognition of the problems that these phenomena have caused (Chambers *et al.* 1989). National development plans and international agencies are giving higher priority to the rural sector, with greater emphasis, for example, on rural water supplies, electrification, and the delivery of health and education services. Agricultural research, which previously tended to be directed to the larger scale modernized type of farming, is now paying more attention to the possibilities of improving traditional agriculture, on which so many people in the Third World depend, not only for a living but also for the food eaten by the nation as a whole (Gubbels 1993).

Despite this recognition solutions still tend to be formulated at the macro-level, taking insufficient account, not only of local differences, but also of the perceptions of the rural people themselves about their situation. The attempt to get small farmers to adopt the "Green Revolution" package is a good example of the misunderstandings that can occur when there is insufficient recognition of the way in which the economy of traditional farming works.

This study of the impact of socio-economic change on rural communities, seen from the perspective of a particular village, considers the present situation in West Africa, with particular reference to Ghana. It illustrates the regional and local differences which have to be taken into account when formulating policies for rural development. These differences concern not only the climatic and topographical variations between different areas, but also the historical and cultural backgrounds of the people themselves. For example, the role of women and their position in society are important ingredients, as was demonstrated some years ago by Esther Boserup (1970), when she referred to areas of female farming; West Africa in general, and Ghana in particular, afford examples of this phenomenon. My own experience in Northern Nigeria revealed a contrasting situation to my studies in Akwapim, Ghana, although I had already come across similar situations in the Northern Region of that country. This was in part due to different systems of cultivation, although the cultural differences were also significant. Women in the north, even in villages, were in house purdah, and as a result did not work in the fields. Exceptions to this were cases where families were too poor to dispense with the labour of their women members. This was considered an undesirable and hence a slightly shaming situation. The women themselves were no doubt happy not to have to toil out of doors in the heat of the sun. To what extent their absence led to their economic dependence on men is a debatable question. In my household survey of Maiduguri in Northern Nigeria it was evident that many women carried out trading and other occupations, such as embroidery, from their home base, often unknown to their menfolk. These illustrations serve to emphasize the importance of understanding in depth the particular characteristics of different communities. Too often policy makers prescribe solutions without regard to the likely reactions of the people concerned. My own work, not only in Ghana and Nigeria, but also in Sierra Leone, Swaziland, Zambia and Uganda, as also in India, testifies to this tendency to overlook vital factors which are likely to affect the success of policies.

This study first takes an overview of the rural sector in West Africa, with some comparative data on other countries of the World. The first section of this chapter, on the dimensions of the rural situation, relies heavily on statistics collected for and by national and international organizations. Although reservations about the reliability and use of such data are frequently mentioned in the text, it is important at the outset to strike a cautionary note. The question of how statistics are collected should always be asked. Whenever one has personal knowledge of these operations one realizes how unreliable they can be. In my own days as a small farmer in England keeping pigs and chickens, I was obliged to submit a quarterly return to the Ministry of Agriculture and Fisheries which included details, not only of the total number of chickens and the eggs that they produced, but also how many eggs the family had consumed. The form was long and complicated, and a penalty was incurred by lack of return. It therefore had to be completed, inevitably with a certain amount of guesswork. There have certainly been great improvements in methods of data collection and every year significant adjustments are made in the way in which they are presented and evaluated. It is interesting to look through subsequent annual reports, such as the World Development Report, published by the World Bank to note the differences this makes in the relative position of countries in terms of their social and economic indicators.

Despite these deficiencies it is useful to look at aspects of the economic and social life of a country, which are of undoubted importance to the welfare of the people. Of particular importance is what can be gathered about trends over the years. It is depressing that in the poorer countries of Africa per capita growth rates have not only declined, but have also shown negative growth in many cases, to an extent that has not been experienced in the poorer countries of Asia or Latin America. Moreover this decline is reflected in social indicators.

The first chapter goes on to consider policies and plans for the rural sector and suggests some of the reasons for the failure that many of them have experienced. It concludes with a brief account of some of the theoretical approaches to the study of socio-economic change.

The second chapter looks more specifically at the rural economy of Ghana. Once again a word of caution is necessary about the reliability of statistical data. This is particularly so where questions of opinion are involved. When interviewed, the respondent has perceptions of the interviewer, which may lead to answers that are not an expression of true feelings. For example, in considering women's views on the desired number of children, or the advisability of using contraceptives, it has often been found by those closely connected with respondents that what they have said is very different from their real views. A good example of this phenomenon was analyzed many years ago by Mamdani (1972), who found that the village people involved in the Khanna project in India accepted the idea of family planning when it was put to them by the project team, because they were too polite to refuse the offer being made. They did not, however, have any intention of taking the prescribed pills, and this accounted for the fact that the expected fall in the birth rate did not occur. Despite these reservations some of the more questionable data have been included in several of the Tables.

The overview in Chapter 2 of policies and programmes in Ghana has been brought as up to date as possible. Information on many relevant aspects was difficult to find; many years of political unrest and economic decline meant that ongoing research, which had been strong in the 1960's and early 1970's was curtailed. It is only recently that the situation is beginning to improve, but a serious gap has been left in tracing changes and trends over the past twenty years.

After the first two chapters, this study looks at socio-economic change in a particular community in Ghana, over a period of twenty-eight years. It may seem a long step from the more general considerations of the first two chapters to this particular case. But it is in accordance with the point made above that more account needs to be taken of the way in which the traditional sector operates if valid solutions are to be found to rural development. It is through intensive studies that a better understanding can be gained of the impact of socio-economic changes on rural communities. All villages are in a sense unique, but many common features exist, so that even from one case study lessons can be learnt. A major factor is that still, in many rural areas in developing countries, particularly in Africa south of the Sahara, the main occupation of the people is agriculture and value systems are based strongly on the claims of the community and the individual to the use of land. Traditional systems centering around land usage are still observed in many parts of the world. In Akan society today alienation of land to outsiders is still not normally acceptable. Traditional leadership retains its importance, despite the erosion of its functions by central and local government activities.

Konkonuru is in the Akwapim Hills of Ghana, and only thirty miles from Accra. Although off the main road from the capital to Aburi, it is a community which for many years has been in close touch with the world outside. The people of Akwapim have played an important part in the development of the country. As a result of the activities of the Basel Mission they have been influenced by western style education for over 150 years. Their farmers were quick to seize the opportunity to cultivate cocoa when it was introduced to the country by the missionaries in 1879 (Hill 1963). So they were not only better formally educated than most, but also more prosperous, and much of their new found wealth was invested in the education of their children. As a result they have played a crucial part in the civil service, the professions and in trade.

The citizens of Konkonuru have been represented in all these fields, and some have even emigrated to Britain and the United States of America to pursue their occupations. It is, therefore, of particular interest to observe to what extent these wider experiences have affected the more traditional patterns of behaviour. So, while the study of this community exemplifies some general aspects of the situation in rural communities in Ghana today, it also looks more closely at the impact of socio-economic change on traditional practices in communities that have over a long period been subject to outside influences.

I have known Konkonuru since 1970 and worked there intensively in 1970–1971. I returned in 1972 to continue my research and again for a brief period in 1977. In 1990, I was working on a project at the University of Science and Technology in Kumasi. During the 4 months I spent there I was able to make several visits to Konkonuru and was also able to meet citizens from the community in Accra and Kumasi. All the time that I have been away from Ghana since 1971 I have been kept in touch with events by Isaac Ohene Osae, who has conscientiously answered my many questions and himself volunteered information which he thought would be of interest to me. It was a great pleasure to meet him again after so many years of absence. Details of how the study was made and why Konkonuru was chosen are given in Appendix I.

While working at the University of Ghana at Legon, Accra from 1968–1971 I had the opportunity to visit many rural communities throughout the country, supervising students on fieldwork assignments during the long vacation. Many of these assignments consisted of research projects on topics formulated by the students themselves.

In choosing topics the Department of Social Welfare and Community Development was consulted with a view to suggesting subjects that were considered important. These research projects formed a basis for ongoing discussions, both with the students themselves and with staff in the Department of Sociology, in which I worked. All the students on the non-graduate Diploma course which I taught had worked for many years in Government Departments, mainly in Social Welfare, Community Development and Rehabilitation, but also in others, such as the Prison Service or Education. They mainly came from rural backgrounds and were still in close contact with their communities through their kinship networks. They had a wealth of knowledge and experience, from which I gained much insight.

The people of Konkonuru belong to the twentieth century as much as we do, and in more senses than that they just happen to inhabit the same earth. I start with this premise, rather than that of cultural difference, because I believe that it is a more fruitful approach to the analysis and explanation of their present situation and outlook. They are conditioned by traditional patterns of behaviour, of prejudices, of beliefs, but so are we all, though some of us are too ethnocentric to apply it in our own case. Like us they are struggling to adjust to a new situation, and in doing so experience new doubts and inconsistencies. The setting is different and so are many of the problems. But there is a similarity in the recognition of change that could not be said of preceding centuries.

This model may not yet apply to all communities in the world; some are still sufficiently isolated to operate outside the parameters of rapid social change. But this is no longer true, if it ever was, of Konkonuru and for this reason I choose to use this as a starting point. I shall attempt to look at their way of life, their institutions as they see them. I shall not wholly succeed, any more than any anthropologist has in the past. But because Konkonuru is not an isolated community, is in constant touch with the capital city and contains many articulate citizens in every generation it has at least been possible to discuss and cross-check the views formulated. Attitudes are a notoriously dangerous field of study; what informants say does not necessarily correspond to what they do. The inconsistency may reveal a real incompatibility; it may on the other hand indicate a lack of understanding due to an incomplete knowledge of their conceptual framework. We are all inconsistent, we all rationalize some of it away and learn to live with the rest.

This study, therefore, is not based on a model of a functionally integrated social system. This model, based on before and after comparisons, has its uses; it informs us theoretically which elements of pre-industrial social systems cannot persist in an industrialized economy and the new modes of social organization required. But it has little to say about the range and temporal duration of tolerable variations and the sequential connection between primal cause and ultimate effect. It is these relationships which are the subject of this study, because they are particularly relevant to the present position in Konkonuru.

Consciously and unconsciously individuals and groups are wrestling with these problems, expressed in such forms as "it was not so in the past," in such contexts as the relationship between parents and children, or the older and younger generations; or in more material forms "next time you visit us we shall have a new Middle School, an electricity supply, a decent road to the town. This will improve our way of life and provide better opportunities for our children." They see these opportunities in terms of more contact with the world outside the town, more participation in the modern sector of the economy. They still have a fierce pride in their home town, but they want to see it a better place in which to live. They may not see clearly how this can be done or what the consequences will be, but the desire exists and is an important factor in their lives(Firth 1966). Unfortunately this increased contact with the modern sector of the economy has produced much frustration, not least because of the expectations aroused as a result of education, and the devaluation of the educational currency. In colonial times a seventh grade qualification could lead to a clerical job or employment in such occupations as community development. Now such employment requires considerably higher qualifications, and even Middle School leavers are unlikely to be engaged. Education has not been seen by the people themselves as a preparation for improving the life of rural communities; rather it is considered as an investment which hopefully will give access to the cash economy.

Meyer Fortes once said that it was not change that surprised him, but the persistence of traditional patterns of behaviour. My first concern when I went to Konkonuru was to look for evidence of this persistence, particularly in relation to the domestic group and the matrilineal system. Although no specifically anthropological studies existed of the southern Akwapim, Osae Djan's account of their customs in *The Sunlight Almanack* (1936) suggested that they corresponded to the central Akan model. These people did, after all, originate from Akwamu, and Akwamu was more consistently Akan than many of the traditional states of the Ashanti fringe areas. It, therefore, seemed justifiable to use, at least to some extent, the work of R.S.Rattray, Fortes and others as base data. In any case it appeared to agree with the people's own accounts of past practices. Meyer Fortes visited Ghana in 1970–1971, which enabled me to discuss these aspects, drawing, not only on his published accounts, but also on additional material gathered during the Ashanti survey in 1946–1947.

Konkonuru, since its inception was never a functionally integrated social system, as will become apparent in the chapter dealing with its history. In so far as its origins and development can be traced it has always been in a process of constant change. In this it is not unusual, as all communities in this area have been in a state of flux as far back as records are available. Many of the links with the outside world are old, going back for as long as anyone in the village can remember,such as relations with the traditional authority, with lineage members living elsewhere, and with other communities connected through myths of origin. Migration has for long been a feature of life in Ghana, (Johnson 1972) and although its present form may have different characteristics from those in the past, the idea of mobility is not new,.either for communities or for individuals. To seek work outside the village, to acquire land in far off places, or to develop trading contacts with strangers are well established activities; they have increased in scale and type, but are not altogether unfamiliar, and in consequence may not in themselves be as disruptive of traditional values as might be supposed. The village retains its importance as the "home town" for every member, however long he or she may spend away from it. Kinship obligations remain strong however troublesome they may be found in practice.

Of the newer relationships, the contact with the outside world through education, Christianity and public services, these too have existed throughout the lifetime of most village people in Ghana today. But the quality of these relationships is recognized as different by the people themselves in that they are not considered as "having existed from time immemorial", but are looked upon as distinct from their traditional culture, and are judged as such. They may be welcomed as opening out new opportunities and insights, they may be accommodated in various ways, but they are not confused in their minds with their own traditions, even though they may have affected their perception of these traditions. Changes, in short are part of the "tradition" of Konkonuru. In talking, therefore, about what is traditional one is speaking in relative terms. Even when looking at agricultural practices, which may appear to have persisted over many hundreds of years, there is evidence of change in the form of new crops or the use of imported cutlasses. The introduction of cocoa as a cash crop is a striking example of the relationship between its cultivation and the social structure and institutions of the community.

My last letter from Konkonuru, written by Isaac Ohene Osae, was dated 26 April 2000. I also spoke recently to Edmund Asamoah, younger brother of Nana Addo Mensah II, who happened to be in Konkonuru at this time. So I was updated on recent developments. These developments illustrated the impact of a new generation of farmers who had had better opportunities for formal education, and were better able to make use of the services available to them.

The Institute of Statistical and Economic Research at the University of Ghana had been asked to come to Konkonuru to test the farm soil.   Samples were collected to find out how much acid there was. Most land turned out to have a pH between 5.5 and 6.8. Pineapple grows best in soil with a pH of 4.5 to 5.5 and oil palm with one between 5.0 and 6.0.   These are good crops for marketing to provide income. It was recommended that for land which fell below the desired pH levels it could either be dressed with lime or left fallow for some time. The amount of organic matter in the soil was also tested. Most land in Konkonuru measured between 3.0 and 4.0 OM, which is satisfactory. If it falls below 3.0 OM the land should be left fallow for longer periods, although cassava might grow well enough.

Other information, apart from news of those I had known, concerned the building of improved housing and the better condition of the approach road, although it is still not tarred and subject to problems in the rainy season. Electricity was still not connected, but sufficient poles had been bought and it was hoped that this would soon be achieved, as it would make a great difference to life.

These are encouraging developments and illustrate how, without inter-
fering with existing structures of land tenure and agricultural practices, increases in productivity can be achieved. This is of great importance, as Ghana
still relies for most of its food on traditional systems of agriculture.

Konkonuru, a village in the Akwapim Hills of Ghana was first written in
1977 as a mimeo. As this edition was primarily intended for the citizens of
Konkonuru it was written in two parts. Part I contained a straightforward
account of my findings, what I had learnt from the people themselves, based
on living in the town and sharing in its activities, supplemented by more detailed studies of household size and composition, farming practices, domestic
roles and the school. Part II described methods of data collection, and more of
the detailed quantitative findings of the supplementary studies. It discussed the
theoretical implications of the account in Part I, comparing the data with other
Akan studies. It was arranged as notes to Part I with cross-references in the
text. The present edition does not draw this distinction. Only in a few cases,
such as methods of data collection, are these relegated to an appendix. The
chapters on Konkonuru follow the same pattern as in the first edition, with the
inclusion of material collected more recently.

I am greatly indebted to the people of Konkonuru who made me so
welcome and did so much to help me to carry out my studies. Their enthusiasm
to know more about their own home town made my task not only easier, but
more interesting. For example, when I asked the chief how many people were
living in the town he replied that he did not know, but would very much like to
have this information. I offered to collect this if he could provide me with some
helpers, whereupon he allocated some Middle School leavers to work with me.
I had not intended to carry out a household census so early in my time there,
but this was an opportunity not to be missed. The Gyasehene (a sub-chief)
gave it his full backing and called a meeting of the whole community so that
we could explain the purpose of the exercise and consult them on appropriate
terminology, such as the distinction between households and compounds.
Moreover the Gyasehene asked us to include all the citizens of Konkonuru in
our census, whether or not they were resident at the time. He wanted to know
the strength of his community. This made the task of collection more complicated, and to some extent who was and who was not included must have been
arbitrary, probably based on matrilineal lines. But it did yield very interesting
material, particularly on patterns of migration.

The possibility of carrying out a second household census in 1990 was
discussed with the Chief, Nana Addo Mensah III, who gave it his enthusiastic
support. He said that he had been thinking of seeking to find out the present
strength of his citizenship, and this would provide a good opportunity. He took

a close interest in every stage of the operation, and also read and commented on *Konkonuru 1977*. He had not read this before as the original text left in the town had been destroyed when Kwasi Osae's House was burnt. His comments have been incorporated in the present version. Since I was last in Ghana in 1990 we have been in constant touch; he has not only answered my many questions, but has himself volunteered a great deal of information on his own.

Of the original five Middle School leavers chosen to help me three have assisted with subsequent studies, namely Isaac Ohene Osae, Jacob Ayesu and Stephen Asamoah and all these three took part in the household census in 1990. Since 1970 they had all sought jobs in Accra, and had been employed there off and on. But the economic depression had not only resulted in loss of work; it had also raised the cost of living in the city to such an extent that it was impossible for low-waged workers to survive. As a result these three returned to farm in their home town and they seemed to be doing well. Their presence, along with others of their generation helped to redress the age and sex imbalances of the population that was such a striking feature in 1970.

Several of those whom I wish to thank are unhappily no longer in this world. Nana Kwadjo Bediako, the Gyasehene, died on 15 August 1989; his linguist, Kwaku Ahwireng had already died on 29 October 1983. The Asafosupi, Kwamena Asamoah, in whose house I had a room, was still alive when I returned to Konkonuru in 1990; he was then in his nineties and has since died. E.K. Owusu, the Methodist Catechist was a great source of information and a good friend; he died on 27 February 1983. It was Godfried Addo who first introduced me to Konkonuru and I am greatly in his debt. I knew him as a Social Welfare Officer in the Department of Social Welfare and Community Development in Accra, and he suggested that his home town might be a suitable place for my studies. His mother still lived in the town and he was connected by marriage with the Gyasehene. His good offices smoothed my initial entry, and I also gained much from subsequent discussions with him, both in 1970–1971 and when I returned to Ghana later. Sadly he too has died, as has his mother.

There are many more to thank. Kate Asare adopted me as her sister soon after my arrival and was a constant mentor of my behaviour. She made sure that I was well looked after, saw, for example that ample supplies of water were brought to my room. We developed a close relationship. The Head Teacher, and other teachers of the Primary and Middle Schools spent many hours in discussion and co-operated with a survey of the eating and sleeping practices of schoolchildren. There are so many others with whom I used to pass the time of day, who accompanied me to their farms and taught me how to farm, who brought little delicacies to my room, and who always welcomed me when I arrived. To all these I extend my thanks and assure them that they will always live in my memory.

At the University of Ghana I received help from both staff and students. Dr. Nelson Addo and Dr. Stephen Gaisie, of the Demographic Unit, both of whom had extensive experience of household surveys, were of great value in discussing possible pitfalls in data collection. Dr. Addo also made available the facilities of ISSER for analyzing the material, including the assistance of Mr. Odai of the Statistical Service. On my return to Ghana in 1990 I was able to meet, once again, members of the Department of Sociology at Legon. Dr. G.K. Nukunya gave me a copy of papers on *The Social Structure of Ghana* which he had recently written, based on lectures to students; these were particularly valuable in bringing me up to date with what he perceived as the present situation. I also benefited from the discussions with staff and students at the University of Science and Technology, Kumasi.

April 2000

Chapter 1

THE RURAL SECTOR IN WEST AFRICA

This chapter first looks at the dimensions of the rural sector, with particular reference to West Africa. It examines this sector's contribution to the economy and employment, and the differences between the economic and social indicators of urban and rural areas. It then considers policies and plans for the rural sector and reasons why so many of these have proved disappointing. Finally it discusses some theoretical approaches to the study of the impact of socioeconomic change on rural communities.

The Dimensions of the Rural Situation

In the poorer countries of the World, the majority of the population still live in rural areas and depend on agriculture for their livelihood. Although the proportion of those living in towns has increased, the comparatively high birth rates in these countries means that in most of them there has been an increase in the total numbers living in rural areas. This is in marked contrast to the situation in the industrialized countries today; whereas in 1800 only 3 per cent of the people in these countries lived in cities and the vast majority were employed in agriculture, 80 per cent now live in urban areas and less than 5 per cent depend on agriculture for a living. Although agriculture only accounts for a small proportion, both of employment and of the GNP (Gross National Product) in most of the industrialized countries yields have increased to such an extent that agricultural production provides for a high proportion of consumption needs. In some of these countries there are even considerable surpluses for export, a very different situation from that in many of the poorer countries where despite a large percentage of the labour force being engaged in agriculture, they are not able to satisfy the food requirements of the country (Todaro 1989, FAO 1997).

Before looking specifically at the rural sector there are some basic indicators which need to be borne in mind. Table 1 gives some general information about countries in West Africa, and, for comparative purposes, a few other countries in Africa and further afield. Methods of data collection have been greatly improved, but statistics still need to be viewed with caution. However, it is clear from this Table that West African countries have low per capita incomes, and the situation has not improved during the 1990s. The GNP per capita in 1992 had already fallen as a result of low growth rates; between

1980–1992; of the West African countries listed in Table 1, ten had negative per capita growth rates. The 1996–1997 data showed positive growth rates, but in many cases these had not raised the GNP pc. above 1992 levels. Life expectancy continued to be low, compared to richer countries; in Sierra Leone, Togo and Zimbabwe it had even declined since 1992, and illiteracy rates continued to be high, especially for women.

Although the various ways of life of people living in rural areas may be well adapted to local conditions, they are beset by the problems of a harsh material environment. West Africa is hot, extremely humid in the coastal and forest regions and dry in the interior. The people suffer from endemic diseases which in some cases, such as river blindness, impair the productivity of whole communities. Soils are light and easily leached by heavy rains and the forest is dense (UNECA 1998). Rivers are not conducive to navigation and overland transport has been slow and difficult to develop. The forest communities have few domestic animals and on the savannah trees are scarce. These conditions, which lasted almost unchanged for several millenia, are still relevant (Dickson & Benneh 1969, Todaro 1989). They are fundamental to an understanding of the struggle to overcome the limitations of a hostile environment, and are factors which have contributed to the economically backward state of countries in West Africa.

For the past five hundred years West Africa has had contacts with Europe and these have profoundly influenced the development of different regions. The arrival of the Portuguese in the late fifteenth century led to an Atlantic trade in slaves, which continued until the 1830s. Before this, any influences from the north came across the Sahara and mainly affected the savannah regions. The slave trade did not lead to European penetration into the interior and although it had a profound effect on West African commerce it did not disturb indigenous politics. It was only towards the end of the nineteenth century that imperialist expansion reached beyond the coastal areas, and direct colonial rule lasted for not more than sixty years (1900–60). Trade in raw materials, such as vegetable oils, developed in the nineteenth century in response to the demands of the newly industrializing nations. It introduced a new dimension into rural communities which had previously concentrated on the production of food crops to meet subsistence needs. The production of cash crops for export continues to play an important part in the economies of countries which are only minimally industrialized (Fei and Ranis 1961, FAO 1997; Ray 1998). The following account of the current rural situation needs to bear in mind these considerations.

Table 1

Basic Statistical Indicators for Africa and rest of the World

	Population (millions)		GNP per Capita US$ Av, growth p.a			LE at birth		Adult Illiteracy	
	1997	1992	1997	1980–92	1996–97	1996		1995	
						M	F	M	F
WEST AFRICA									
Sierra Leone	5	160	200	-1.4	n.a	35	38	55	82
Chad	7	220	240	3.4	4.2	47	50	38	65
Guinea-Bissau	1	220	240	1.6	5.0	42	45	32	58
Niger	10	280	200	-4.3	0.1	44	49	79	93
Burkina Faso	11	300	240	1.0	4.0	45	47	71	91
Nigeria	118	320	260	-0.4	1.2	51	55	33	53
The Gambia	1	370	350	-0.4	2.2	53	53	61	61
Togo	4	390	330	-1.8	2.1	49	52	33	63
Benin	6	410	380	-0.7	2.3	52	57	51	74
Ghana	18	450	370	-0.1	0.5	57	61	24	47
Guinea	7	510	570	n.a.	4.6	46	47	50	78
Mauritania	2	530	450	-0.8	3.2	52	55	50	74
Cote d'Ivoire	15	670	690	-4.7	4.2	53	55	50	70
Senegal	9	780	550	0.1	1.6	49	52	51	77
Cameroon	14	820	650	-1.5	5.3	55	58	25	48
OTHER AFRICA									
Mozambique	19	160	133	-3.6	5.7	44	46	42	77
Tanzania	31	110	210	0.0	n.a.	49	52	21	43
Uganda	20	170	320	n.a.	2.3	43	43	26	50
Kenya	28	310	330	0.2	-0.1	57	60	14	30
Zimbabwe	11	570	750	-0.9	0.0	55	57	10	20
REST OF WORLD									
Malaysia	21	2790	4680	3.2	5.2	70	74	11	22
India	961	310	390	3.1	3.2	62	63	35	62
China	1227	470	860	7.6	7.8	68	71	10	27
Sri Lanka	18	540	800	2.6	5.8	71	75	7	13
UK	59	17790	20710	2.4	3.2	74	80	Trace	
USA	268	23240	28740	1.7	2.9	74	80	"	

Note: After the 1998 Report the statistics format was changed. Making it impossible to make direct comparison with earlier years.

Source: World Development Reports. 1994 and 1998

The Human Development Report (UNDP 1994), gives the proportion of the population living in rural areas as 72 per cent for the countries with the lowest human development scores, and 80 per cent for the least economically developed countries. In comparison with 1965 the proportion of those engaged in agriculture had fallen by 1996, but was still high, as can be seen in Table 2. These figures reflect the dependence of these countries on the agricultural sector for a significant proportion of the Gross Domestic Product (GDP) as is shown in Table 3. This sector also makes a major contribution to exports. In some countries, such as Sierra Leone, Togo, Benin, Burkina Faso, Guinea Bissau, Senegal, Cameroon, Nigeria and Cote d'Ivoire in West Africa, and Mozambique and Zimbabwe in other regions of Africa, the proportion of the GDP from agriculture had increased since 1980. Although this could indicate increased productivity in the agricultural sector, this is unlikely, as is shown by the small or negative growth rates of food production in these countries. It is therefore more probable that it reflects low or negative growth rates in the economy as a whole (IFAD 1994).

Table 2

Rural Population and Sectoral Employment

	Rural Population * as % of Total Population	Distribution of Labour Force (%) Agriculture		Industry		Services	
WEST AFRICA	1992	1965	1996	1965	1996	1965	1996
Sierra Leone	69	78	61	11	17	11	22
Chad	66	92	72	3	7	5	21
Guinea-Bissau	80	87	79	6	5	7	16
Niger	81	95	86	1	2	4	12
Burkina-Faso	83	90	84	3	5	7	11
Nigeria	63	72	64	10	13	18	23
The Gambia	76	n.a.	86	n.a.	9	n.a.	11
Togo	71	78	67	9	12	13	21
Benin	60	83	54	5	10	12	36
Ghana	65	61	52	15	19	24	29
Guinea	73	87	74	6	13	7	13
Mauritania	50	89	45	3	21	8	34
Cote d'Ivoire	58	80	49	5	14	15	37
Senegal	59	83	77	6	7	11	16
Cameroon	58	87	n.a.	4	n.a.	9	n.a.
Liberia	53	79	n.a.	10	n.a.	11	n.a.

Table 2 contd.

| | Rural Population as % of Total Population | *Distribution of Labour Force (%) | | | | | |
		Agriculture		Industry		Services	
WEST AFRICA	1992	1965	1996	1965	1996	1965	1996
OTHER AFRICA							
Mozambique	70	87	81	6	10	7	9
Tanzania	78	91	79	3	7	6	14
Uganda	88	91	n.a.	3	n.a.	6	n.a.
Kenya	75	86	75	5	9	9	16
Zimbabwe	70	79	n.a.	8	n.a.	13	n.a.
REST OF WORLD*							
Malaysia	55	58	26	13	28	29	46
India	74	73	62	12	11	15	27
China	72	81	73	8	14	11	13
Sri Lanka	78	56	49	14	21	30	30
UK	11	n.a.	2	n.a.	20	n.a.	78
USA	23	n.a.	3	n.a.	26	n.a.	71

Source.   Human Development Report 1994 and 1998. African Development Report 1998
*   1996 figures not available.

Comparable data on the average growth of food production and cereal imports are not available for all the countries listed in Table 3 but the latest report of the UN Economic Commission for Africa (1998) indicates that food indices in many countries have not kept pace with population growth and that agricultural output has been lacklustre.

The high proportion of the service sector in many of these countries is significant, particularly when it is not accompanied by a corresponding increase in the industrial sector. As an economy develops the balance shifts from the primary to the secondary and tertiary sectors. But when the indicators show a decline in food production, without a compensating increase in industrial production, this can lead to serious economic consequences for poor countries (Fei & Ranis 1961, UNECA 1998). The increasing service sector in these countries is more likely to benefit the better off members of the society, both through the provision of services, on which more is spent in urban than rural areas, and through for example, the salaries of bureaucrats (Castro-Leal *et al.* 1997).

Table 3

The Structure of Production

	Agriculture		Industry		Services		Food Production Average growth	Cereal Imports Thousand tons	
	1980	1997	1980	1997	1980	1997	% per annum 1979–1992	1980	1992
WEST AFRICA									
Sierra Leone	33	44	21	24	47	32	-1.2	83	103
Chad	45	39	9	15	46	46	0.3	16	61
Guinea Bissau	42	54	19	11	39	35	1.1	21	82
Niger	43	38	23	18	34	44	-2.0	90	105
Burkina-Faso	33	35	22	25	45	40	2.8	77	145
Nigeria	21	45	46	24	34	32	2.0	1828	1126
Togo	27	40	25	22	48	38	-0.7	41	124
Benin	35	38	12	14	52	48	1.8	61	212
Ghana	58	47	12	17	30	36	0.3	247	319
Guinea	n.a.	26	n.a.	36	n.a.	38	-0.5	171	338
Mauritania	30	25	26	29	44	46	-1.5	166	290
Côte d'Ivoire	26	27	20	21	54	51	0.1	469	568
Senegal	16	18	21	18	63	63	- 0.2	452	585
Cameroon	29	41	23	20	48	39	-1.7	140	424
OTHER AFRICA									
Mozambique	37	39	35	23	27	38	-2.1	368	1164
Tanzania	n.a.	48	n.a.	21	n.a.	31	-1.2	399	252
Uganda	72	44	4	17	23	34	0.1	52	22
Kenya	33	29	21	17	47	54	0.1	387	669
Zimbabwe	16	28	29	32	55	41	-3.3	156	1493
REST OF WORLD									
Malaysia	22	13	38	46	40	41	4.0	1336	3198
India	38	27	26	30	36	43	1.6	424	3044
China	30	20	49	51	40	41	2.9	12952	11661
Sri Lanka	28	22	30	26	45	52	-2.2	884	1055
Japan	4	2	42	38	54	60	n.a.	n.a.	
USA	3	n.a.	33	n.a.	64	n.a.	-0.2	194	3718

Source: World Development Report 1998 and Human Development Report 1994

Statistics relating to agricultural production have to be regarded with reservation for countries where there is a large degree of subsistence agriculture, as the data depends on calculations of the value of crops consumed by the producers themselves a reservation which is discussed more fully below. Despite this, the degree of self-sufficiency in staple foods for a country as a whole is obviously of great importance where exports are insufficient to cover the cost of importing such foods. Table 3 shows calculations of the average growth of food production between 1979–1992. Although, as mentioned above, more up to date comparable figures are not available, the latest UNECA Report indicates that the situation is no less serious. If taken alongside the rate of population growth over this period, which for Sub-Saharan Africa has averaged 3.0 per cent per annum in the period from 1980–1992, it can be seen that for many countries food production did not keep pace with this increase. This resulted in the need to import essential foods, such as cereals, the payment for which has not been made up by increased exports. Even in Ghana, where agricutural production has done better than in most West African countries a figure of 22 kg of cereal imports per head of population was given for 1997 (UNECA 1998). As it is, a high proportion of the foreign exchange earned has been absorbed by debt repayments, a subject which will be further considered below.

Public and Social Services

There is a marked disparity between services in urban and rural areas, as is shown in Table 4. for three such services. The data in this Table are incomplete, especially regarding health services, and the comparability of provisions in different countries has to be viewed with caution, as they are dependent on records submitted, which are collected in various ways. Looking back to reports for earlier years there are big differences in the figures. For example, the figure for the provision of sanitation in rural Tanzania is given as 62 per cent in the 1994 report and 77 per cent in the report for 1993. Both figures seem improbably high. The difficulty of collecting reliable data is reflected in the fact that recent Human Development Reports do not include a breakdown between urban and rural areas. Undifferentiated data for sevices in some of the countries are given in Table 5.

A good water supply is of special importance for health and for a general improvement in the standard of living. The lack of adequate, readily available water is keenly felt by rural people. In many villages in Africa the position has deteriorated, due to a fall in rainfall, resulting in the drying up of streams or the failure of springs, and the increase in the rural population (Buller & Wright 1990).

A survey carried out in Sierra Leone in 1978–1979 (Hardiman and Midgley 1982) illustrated how lack of access to services affects rural communities. This survey covered thirteen villages in all the major administrative areas, and one provincial town. Details were collected abut the knowledge and utilization of Government services by the 2500 individuals in the sample. Although undertaken some years ago, indications from more recent information suggest that it is unlikely that there has been much change. Sierra Leone, since then, has suffered severe economic, political problems, resulting in less money being available for public and social services. One of the results has been a fall in life expectancy in recent years.

The Sierra Leone village survey dealt primarily with services provided by the Ministries of Health, Education and Social Welfare and Rural Development. At that time the services of the Ministries of Labour and Housing and Country Planning were not accessible to the country's rural population, so they were not included in the study. A few examples of the findings will illustrate the situation. All the villages in the sample were served by Government assisted schools, which provided free primary education, although only four had them in their own villages; seven were within five miles and the remaining two within eight miles. Although there was some relationship between distance and school attendance, it was rather ambiguous as in one village where there was a school only 25 per cent of the children of school going age attended. Overall 74 per cent of the more than 500 children in the sample households had never attended school. Only five children were attending secondary school. In contrast, the provincial town had four secondary and ten Government assisted primary schools,and in addition several private schools. Of the town children in the sample between 5–14 years about 60 per cent were attending primary school and about 17 per cent were in secondary schools.

None of the sampled villages was served directly by a Government Health Centre or Dispensary, and on average the distance away was about twelve miles. None was in easy reach of a Government Hospital. So it was perhaps surprising that as many as 27 per cent of the sample said that they had used a Government Health service. Local traditional practitioners were resorted to in the first place, mainly because of ease of access, not because of lack of faith in modern medicine, as a majority expressed a preference for it when it was readily available.

Only one village in the sample had piped water, another had a deep well sunk by the Government, and two had wells dug by the villagers themselves. The remaining nine villages obtained all their water from rivers or streams. In the provincial town 80 per cent of the sample had access to piped water.

Table 4

Rural Urban Gaps

	Rural Population as % of total 1991	Health Urban	Health Rural	Water Urban	Water Rural	Sanitation Urban	Sanitation Rural	Underweight under 5s 1990–97%	HDI Rank 1995
WEST AFRICA									
Sierra Leone	69	88	13	n.a.	33	39	3	29	174
Chad	66	—n.a.—		n.a.	25	—n.a.—			163
Guinea-Bissau	80	—n.a.—		56	35	27	n.a.	n.a.	164
Niger	81	86	17	98	45	39	3	36	173
Burkina-Faso	83	—		78	70	77	6	n.a.	172
Nigeria	63	87	62	81	30	30	5	30	142
Togo	71	60	n.a.	77	53	56	10	19	144
Benin	60	—n.a.—		73	43	60	31	n.a.	145
Ghana	65	n.a.		93	35	64	32	27	133
Guinea	73	—n.a.—		87	56	84	5	n.a.	167
Mauritania	50	n.a.		65	n.a.	34	13	23	149
Cote d'Ivoire	58	n.a.		70	n.a.	62	n.a.	24	148
Senegal	59	n.a.		84	26	85	36	22	158
Cameroon	58	n.a.		95	27	100	64	14	132
OTHER AFRICA									
Mozambique	74	n.a.		44	17	61	11	27	166
Tanzania	78	94	73	65	45	74	62	27	150
Uganda	88	n.a.		43	12	63	28	26	160
Kenya	75	n.a.		74	43	69	5	23	137
Zimbabwe	70	90	80	95	14	95	22	16	130
REST OF WORLD									
Malaysia	55	n.a.		96	50	94	94	n.a.	60
India	74	n.a.		n.a.		53	n.a.	n.a.	139
China	72	n.a.		87	81	100	95	16	106
Sri Lanka	78	n.a.		100	64	73	58	38	90
Nicaragua	39	n.a.		78	21	78	16	n.a.	126
SUMMARIES									
All developing countries	65	90	n.a.	85	62	75	45	30	—
Least developed countries	79	85	n.a.	60	30	61	25	39	—
Sub-Saharan Africa	70	87	n.a.	74	31	55	23	n.a.	—

1.   Underweight under 5s refers to the country as a whole.
2.   The Human Development Index has been developed by the UNDP. It combines indicators of real purchasing power, education and health, including life expectancy, and is claimed to be more comprehensive than GNP alone. The top country in 1995 was Canada, the bottom Sierra Leone. All the top 22 were industrialized countries.
3.   As so many indicators are missing summaries must surely be viewed with caution!

Source: Human Development Reports 1994 and 1998. UNDP New York.

Although the survey did not collect data on fertility or infant and child mortality the general impression was that both these indicators were high. A survey in the Western Area during 1969–1971 gave an infant mortality rate of 130 : 1,000 live births. The Western Area, with its close proximity to the capital city of Freetown, is the most economically developed part of Sierra Leone, and it was believed that the rate in the provinces at that time was somewhere in the region of 182: 1,000.

The lack of services in rural areas, illustrated by this example from Sierra Leone, undoubtedly contributes to poorer social indicators (UNICEF 1997; WHO 1997). Data relating to these indicators are less reliable than those relating to services, although recent work by the Demographic and Health Surveys programmes (1994) has shed more light on the situation. In the past twenty to thirty years there has been a marked decrease in most countries in infant and child mortality, and a corresponding increase in life expectancy, but progress has been uneven and there are recent indications that in some countries the trend has been reversed particularly since the onset of IFD, AIDS. The 1994 DHS studies, which used a sample of 26 countries, found that the decline over a period of 15 years preceding the survey showed that the decline in child and infant mortality was less in Sub-Saharan Africa than in other continents, as can be seen in Table 6.

Table 5

Access to Services in Selected Countries

Country	Safe Water % 1990–96	Population without Health Services % 1990–95	Access to Sanitation % 1990–96	Human Development Index 1995
Sierra Leone	66	62	89	174
Chad	76	70	79	163
Nigeria	50	49	43	142
Ghana	35	40	45	133
Tanzania	62	58	14	150
Uganda	54	51	42	160
Malaysia	22	n.a.	6	60
Sri Lanka	43	7	37	90
China	33	12	76	106

Human Development Report   1998

Our concern in this chapter is with the differentials between urban and rural areas. The DHS surveys, conducted between 1985–90 were particularly valuable because they distinguished within urban areas between households with piped water supplies and those depending on public taps, wells, springs, lakes and trucked water. The latter were classified as poor urban areas. The findings bore out references, later in this chapter, to the importance of disaggregating urban figures, in order to make meaningful rural/urban comparisons. A few of the DHS findings are given in Table 7.

Table 6

Mortality declines in 15 years by Regions. 1978-1993

Region	No. of countries %	Under 5 mortality %	Infant mortality %	Child* mortality %
Sub-Saharan Africa	11	-22	-20	-27
Near East/N.Africa	3	-43	-35	-59
Asia	3	-33	-29	-40
Latin America/Caribbean	9	-31	-27	-43
All countries	26	-29	-25	-38

*Child mortality: deaths between 1-5 years.

Source: Demographic and Health Surveys. Comparative Studies 15. 1994 .

There are, of course, factors other than rural/urban to take into account in assessing differences in mortality. Of these the education of the mother is critical (King & Anne 1993). The DHS studies found that in those 23 countries where comparisons were possible six of them had differences in under five mortality of over 100 deaths per 1000 children in the age group, between mothers with no education and those who had completed some post-primary education, the largest difference being for Senegal with 151: 1000. The overall average for these 23 countries showed a difference of 76 deaths per 1000 children in this age group. Unfortunately in Ghana only 4 per cent of the sample of mothers had post-primary education, so the figures were not a reliable indication of differences. However, differences were shown between mothers with no education and those who had completed primary school. Infant mortality of children born to mothers with no education was estimated as 87:1000, whereas for those whose mothers had completed primary school it was 62:1000.

For child mortality the figures were 96:1000 for children whose mothers had no education and 64:1000 for those whose mothers had completed primary education.

Table 7

Infant & Child Mortality by urban-rural residence and type of water supply in selected countries, 1992–1993

Region/Country	Infant Mortality per 1000 live births			Child Mortality per 1000 children 1–5 yrs		
	Urban		Rural	Urban		Rural
	Piped water	No piped water		Piped water	No piped water	
SUB-SAHARAN AFRICA						
Liberia	135	142	161	89	90	94
Senegal	56	78	102	45	89	165
Uganda	93	107	106	n.a.	74	93
Ghana	49	73	87	36	85	83
Kenya	45	68	59	23	45	34
Botswana	38	39	39	8	23	17
OTHER COUNTRIES						
Indonesia	52	49	83	22	30	42
Sri Lanka	40	32	32	4	11	48
Bolivia	65	87	107	33	55	69
Brazil	54	118	106	9	22	15

Source: Demographic and Health Surveys. Comparative Studies 15. 1994

As the proportion of women who have no formal education is high in rural areas of Sub-Saharan Africa it follows that they are more likely to suffer the loss of their children. However, once again, figures for urban areas, if disaggregated by education might well show little difference from rural areas.

Mortality is also affected by occupation, and the DHS surveys showed that in many countries where the father's occupation is in agriculture infant and child mortality is likely to be greater than for the children of blue collar, technical or professional workers. Children whose fathers were in agricultural occupations were found to have twice the level of under five mortality than those in the other categories in 9 out of 25 countries, and at least 50 per cent higher mortality on 18 countries. So the figures for rural areas reflect these differentials.

Although recent work, such as that quoted, has thrown more light on the rural situation, the difficulties of obtaining reliable data on sensitive indicators is still considerable, and means that both urban/rural and inter-country comparisons have to be viewed with caution. Even the excellent work done under the DHS programmes can be questioned in this respect. Great reliance is put on respondents, who will judge their responses by their perceptions of the role and status of the interviewer. The more educated the respondent the more they are able to manipulate the situation, and the same applies to locally recruited assistants,who are not beyond inventing answers in order to complete a schedule as quickly as possible.

It is only by intimate knowledge of the communities being studied that any degree of accuracy can be obtained. An interesting example of this was a follow-up fertility study of the 1961 census in Ghana. The initial findings revealed a significantly lower birth rate in the Northern Region. Rational explanations were suggested for this phenomenon. It then occured to one of the team that this might be accounted for by the practice of burying the dead within the compound. This had been declared as prohibited by the Medical authorities. The people, despite this edict, continued to practice their traditional custom. But when interviewers, who were perceived to be Government servants, came along the respondents naturally concealed any evidence of this practice. As infant mortality rates were known to be high this alone could account for the apparently lower birth rate. Subsequently locally known community development workers were sent to conduct interviews in the area; the results, as expected, produced a birth rate not dissimilar from that in the rest of Ghana.

A great deal of published data relates to the stream of services rather than to the impact that these services have made. For example, school attendance figures, even if they have not been rigged, do not indicate educational attainment. Unfortunately many of the schools in developing countries are inadequately funded or staffed and even after ten years attendance a child may emerge very poorly educated. His or her education may instead prove counterproductive in terms of the contribution it could make to the improvement of rural life. Education in rural communities is seen as a way of escaping from the village, rather than as a means to becoming more effective countrymen or women. This problem is considered in detail in the case study of Konkonuru (Chapter 7).

This brief consideration of the dimensions of the rural situation has painted a gloomy picture. However, those of us who frequently spend time in rural areas find that in many respects the way of life is not as bleak as might be supposed from bald statistics. Rural people enjoy amenities such as fresh air, freedom from crowding, and a full community life; the lot of the urban poor is often far worse, and statistics showing urban-rural differences are seldom disaggregated by income group, or other relevant factors, such as education and access to public services. So although the indicators for rural areas may be unfavourable, as recorded by such organizations as the World Bank, one needs to look more closely at the reasons for these discrepancies. Services are certainly less available, and some health indicators appear to be worse, although there is far too little information available on impact factors; once again, comparisons need to take account of the situation of the urban poor. But indicators are misleading because many of the tasks for which money has to be paid in towns, such as the carrying of water where piped supplies do not exist, or help with the building or maintenance of houses, are embedded in reciprocal relationships in village communities and do not involve monetary transactions. Therefore, talk by economists about the growth or decline of incomes in rural areas and their relationship to urban incomes frequently fails to paint an accurate picture.

Policies for Rural Development

It follows, from this consideration of the situation in West African countries, that the health of the rural sector is of vital importance to their economies. Arthur Lewis's (1955: 75) statement, although made some years ago, still holds good. He wrote that "the most important item on the agenda of development is to transform the food sector, create agricultural surpluses to feed the urban population and thereby create the domestic basis for industry and modern services. If we can make this domestic change, we shall automatically have a new international economic order." Hence, if standards of living are to be improved for the majority rural development policies are of central importance.

This importance is recognized in the texts of National Development Plans, although when they are examined critically the indication, in many cases, is that this recognition amounts to lip-service in the face of other more appealing priorities (Lipton 1977, Lipton and Longhurst 1989, Hardiman 1974b, UNECA 1998). Even where priority is given to the rural sector there has been a high incidence of failure of these plans to reach their targets. To what extent has this been due to the inappropriateness of the plans themselves, to inadequate funding, or to lack of implementation (Bardhan 1997)? In analyzing planning documents it can be seen that too frequently insufficient attention is paid to the ways in which proposed programmes and projects are to be carried out. Plans have to be implemented by people, at all levels. What may seem logical and feasible to the planner, sitting at his or her desk in the capital city, may look very different to the farmer who is ultimately the person who is expected to carry out the plan. The success or failure of the plan will, in the end, depend on the farmer.   The planning process must, therefore, take into account the reactions of those who will be concerned at the operational level.

In some parts of the world the "green revolution" has succeeded in significantly increasing the production of crops, and this has been of widespread benefit, despite social problems concerning the distribution of gains. But these developments have tended not to benefit the smaller farmer, and in no way apply to those farming on traditional lines. In many African countries these farmers still make up the majority of those in the agricultural sector, and their produce is vital to the economy, as even in the so-called "subsistence sector" marketable surpluses are produced to feed the urban population. For example, a study in Ghana (Republic of Ghana and UNCF, 1990) estimated that 20 per cent of food crop farmers marketed over 50 per cent of their produce; this figure was borne out in the study of farming in Konkonuru (chapter 5).

It is still insufficiently recognized by governments that the key to the development of predominantly agrarian states lies in the countryside and not in the cities (Hart 1982). These countries suffer from "an overcentralized political system, with the state as principal entrepreneur in an economy that is still based on a dispersed population of small agricultural commodity producers" (Hart 1982: 46)

Following from this it is easy to say that "West African States must revolutionize their agricultural sectors if they wish to escape from permanent backwardness and poverty"... and that "no single factor is more important" (Hart 1982: 51). The question is what are the practical steps that can be taken to make this a reality?

A first step, undoubtedly, is to develop a greater understanding of the traditional agricultural sector upon which most countries still depend for their food supplies (Murinde 1993). Projects for agricultural improvement tend to ignore the validity of systems of production used by traditional farmers (Brush & Sabinsky 1995). These farmers, as my own experience in Ghana showed, possess an enormous fund of knowledge of local soil conditions, which crops will best grow in which situations, when is the best time for planting, and what account should be taken of variations in rainfall. Shifting cultivation has its own criteria. For example, as a result of fallow periods there is no need for artificial fertilizers, which may indeed be harmful. Instead of improving a crop they may actually lead to its destruction, as was demonstrated to me by a farmer in Konkonuru. He agreed, experimentally, to apply fertilizer on part of a farm growing cassava. It grew excessively quickly, sporting a splendid array of leaves, but when lifted it was found that most of the tubers were rotten. Another example, again from Konkonuru, was the farm made by the local Primary School. The headmaster, who was not from the village, decided to plant pineapples on the school plot, despite the fact that he was told that the ground was not suitable. It was not surprising to the people that his endeavours failed.

Most traditional farmers these days are conscious of the world outside the village. They want to share in the fruits of increased consumption. They are anxious and willing to try out measures to improve their productivity. But, unfortunately, too little attention has been paid to steps that can be taken in the traditional sector to increase yields and to introduce and market alternative products. Several projects initiated by voluntary organizations (NGOs) have worked in these directions, but they have been on a small scale and appear, even when successful, to have had little influence on government policies, which tend to operate at the macro-level. For example, in Sierra Leone a great deal of effort and resources went into bringing in Chinese experts to develop the production of paddy rice in the river valleys. But more dry rice was still produced by farmers in hilly districts. No research had gone into how these farmers could increase their yields.

This then is one essential way in which policies for rural development could be more realistic and effective. Another consideration of great importance is the recognition of the division of labour between sex and age groups. Much of West Africa lies in the area described by Boserup (1970) as one of "female farming", and although men do play a significant part it is women who, in many areas, bear the greatest burden, particularly in the production of food crops. Yet very few projects are specifically addressed to women, or are so planned as to ease their burdens.

Apart from measures directly addressed to agriculture the general upgrading of levels of living in rural areas is of crucial importance. It is ironical that in industrialized countries many people express a preference for rural living. If an appointment to a General Practice in a small country town is advertised there will be many applications from well qualified doctors, compared to those for an appointment in an inner city area. People in the richer countries are not disadvantaged by living in the country, as they have electricity, piped water and equally good health and social services. The situation found in the poorer countries is very different. The younger generation especially, who are more knowledgeable about the outside world, feel keenly about the lack of electricity, which can in many ways transform village life. There are, it is true, schemes to connect electricity supplies to villages, such as those in the Brong-Ahafo and Ashanti regions of Ghana. But still in many areas village people are told that if they want to be connected they must bear a substantial portion of the cost themselves. For example, the people of Konkonuru have been struggling for years to contribute to the costs of installation, such as buying the poles for electricity cables over a distance of nearly one and a half miles; despite their efforts, in 1998 they are still without electricity. Likewise with water, at a time when rural supplies have diminished and become less accessible in many communities. Women and children are having to walk long distances to meet their needs and lack of adequate supplies is detrimental to health. Better rural services would also encourage more professional people, such as doctors and teachers to work in small towns, thus providing much needed services to rural populations.

So, if substantial progress is to be made, much greater priority needs to be given to the rural sector, both in terms of research into agricultural improvement and consideration of how such improvements can be implemented, and in the general enhancing of rural levels of living. It is many years since Lipton (1977) drew attention to the urban bias in development, yet this phenomenon still exists. If this bias is not reversed the brain drain from rural areas will continue to perpetuate the situation. It is significant that in those countries where positive rural policies have been adopted by governments there has been a dramatic reduction in poverty, bearing out the contention of Arthur Lewis, referred to above. A good example of this can be found in Malaysia, where investment in the rural sector has contributed to the overall success of the economy in raising per capita incomes to a degree not experienced in most developing countries.

Theoretical Approaches to the Study of Socio-Economic Change

A great many studies have been made of the impact of socio-economic change on rural communities by economists, sociologists, anthropologists, experts in the fields of health and education, and others (Jaffee 1998). Some of these have been mainly descriptive, and the accurate recording of the life and work of the people in these communities still forms a necessary basis for research. But the favoured approach, at least by academics, is to collect and present material within a theoretical orientation. Malinowski maintained that there were no facts without theories or theories without facts, and his development of the functionalist approach testified to this belief. Malinowski was not the first person to use the concept of function in a society. The term was previously used by Herbert Spencer (1820–1903), who saw close parallels between human societies and biological organisms. Their existence, he argued, was maintained by the "functional dependence of parts" (Spencer 1862: 1396 ff.). Later, when Durkheim (1858–1917) elaborated his principles of sociological method (1893) he said that in order to explain a social phenomenon one must seek both the cause that produced it and the function that it fulfilled. But it was Malinowski who developed the concept of function to its greatest elaboration, and even (according to Lucy Mair, partly in joke) gave himself and his students the title of "the Functional School" (Mair 1965).

Functionalism had a profound influence on a generation of anthropologists, who, through its methodology, gained significant insights into the social structure and functioning of societies. The approach has been criticized on various counts. An exaggeration of the theory could lead to the assumption that because every social institution has a function a society is so perfectly balanced that any change will be resisted as disfunctional. Although it may be preferable to look for function in social usages, rather than assuming, as earlier anthropologists did, that if they are hard to understand they must be anachronisms, the possibility that certain customs have survived without retaining much meaning must be faced. This can, in particular, be the case with rituals. Another question concerns the contrast of synchronic and diachronic studies. Malinowski approached his work with the assumption that what he was looking at was "a going concern"; he hesitated to look at a society in terms of survivals. This has led to the criticism that this approach takes too little account of the changing nature of all societies, even of those designated as the most 'traditional'. The anthropologists of Malinowski's generation were certainly not so concerned about the processes of social change as is the case today, and this is understandable in terms of the historical context, which is reflected in more recent theoretical approaches.

It is significant that Mair (1965) discusses social change under the heading of "Related Subjects" and says that the subject falls into a different category from the topics so far discussed. In the following chapter on another "Related Subject", namely Applied Anthropology, she describes these two subjects as two sides of a penny, saying that "anthropologists first became interested in social change as a problem that needed to be solved; in Britain very few of them have thought of it as a subject for explanatory generalizations." (1965: 253). And although many more anthropologists are now pursuing research into the impact of socio-economic change, the main theoretical developments have come from economists and sociologists. The question as to how anthropologists view these approaches will be discussed later in this chapter.

Economists took the lead in formulating the modernization approach, in the search for a macro-theoretical framework to explain the processes of economic development and social change. Rostow (1960; 1963) is probably the best known exponent of this approach, with his account of the five stages of economic development, ranging from the traditional to the mass consumption society, progression from stage to stage depending on the fulfillment of certain conditions. His concept of the 'take off' into self-sustaining growth was influential in the early plans for developing countries, stressing, as it did the need for capital formation. It led to a concentration on the development of industries in a modern sector of the economy, and contributed to the neglect of agriculture.

The achievement of independence by ex-colonial countries, with their aspirations to improve the level of living of their people, stimulated interest in the processes of social change. This led sociologists, as well a economists to a revival of interest in evolutionary theories, and the study of development processes, raised much earlier by writers such as Spencer, Tyler and Durkheim.

The concept of modernization put forward by Moore (1963: 89) indicated a 'total' transformation of a traditional, or pre-modern, society into a type associated with the so-called 'advanced' industrialized society. In terms of the social structure of traditional communities, economic measures would fail unless traditional social institutions and cultural values were modified. Goode (1963) argued that the extended family impeded economic development, because the large number of dependents hindered labour mobility and limited a family's capacity to save. Modern bureaucracy, with its insistence on merit, could not easily co-exist with kinship obligations.

Moore's view assumes that the general features of both traditional and modern societies can be clearly described. A more complex approach to these questions is provided by other exponents of modernization theory, such as Smelser (1963), Parsons (1971), Hoselitz (1960) and Eisenstadt (1963). These sociologists take account of the diversity of social types subsumed under Moore's concepts of traditional and modern. They distinguish between the different processes by which change may occur.

Long (1977) provides a critical account of modernization theory, which, at the time that he was writing, had gained considerable popularity, not least in its influence on the policies of the World Bank and other donor agencies. In evaluating its usefulness to an understanding of the processes of socio-economic change he explores two different problems. Firstly, "does it single out the crucial sociological variables and relationships associated with development in contemporary rural situations, and thereby help us to understand more fully the dynamic of social change? And second, are the underlying assumptions of the model adequate for comprehending the complexities involved?" (Long 1977: 15). In order to look at this question he discusses selected empirical work, such as Epstein's study of "Economic Development and Social Change in South India". Epstein (1962) sought to analyze the effects of technical innovation and economic change on the institutional structures of two villages. She found that in the case of the village which had benefited from irrigation and had therefore expanded its agricultural economy, developments were in line with the existing organization, and that little structural change ensued. The nearby village, which had not benefited directly from the new irrigation scheme, experienced greater structural changes as its members responded to increased employment opportunities, as a result of the project,in a neighbouring town. Epstein examined the functional relationship between different types of structural change in the light of these findings and showed how "economic development may occur without change in traditional economic roles and relationships." (1962: 318).

Long considers that structural analysis, such as this, "cannot adequately deal with the variability and flexibility of social systems, with the problem of isolating the factors responsible for changes, nor can it handle the question of the differential responses to change shown by different social groups or categories within a given population" (Long 1977: 18). My own research in Maiduguri, Nigeria (Hardiman 1975), for example, found that whereas changes occured readily in the economic domain, the domestic domain retained much of its traditional beliefs and values, particularly in relation to customs associated with birth, marriage and death. The case study of Konkonuru also demonstrates such differential responses in the economic, domestic, political and jural domains. Many examples of such differentials can be found in our own society today, so this is not a phenomenon confined to the so-called developing world (Appiah 1992).

Modernization theory's stress on the increase in the scale of social relations, and the trend towards the formation of more differentiated institutions, is borne out in a general way by many empirical studies. But its tendency to take a deterministic stance on the unilinear nature of development limits its usefulness, particularly as it takes a somewhat ethnocentric view about the directions of change. A debate which frequently occured amongst my students at the University of Ghana was to what extent modernization was necessarily equated with Western style economic and political institutions. Economic and social change were seen as inevitable in the world today, but how could traditional values and beliefs be incorporated in this process? This, to the students, was a question of critical relevance, as they perceived a great deal in Western civilization that to them seemed undesirable, and they cherished much in their own culture which they desired to preserve. The modernization approach did not to them address this question adequately, a subject discussed by Appiah with particular reference to Ghana (Appiah 1992).

Structural Dependency theory emerged as a challenge to modernization theory. It was first formulated by Latin American economists, notably Prebicsh and his colleagues on the United Nations Economic Commission for Latin America (Prebisch 1950). He argued that the reliance of non-industrialized countries on the export of primary commodities did not lead to economic growth, but to an increasing dependency on the richer industrial nations of the world. Faced with the continuing import of manufactured goods the trade deficit of poor countries had increased, due, in addition, to the manipulation of prices by the industrial countries. Underdeveloped countries have, therefore, been dominated economically and politically by external centres of power, and thus have become satellites. Moreover, within these societies this dependency has resulted in striking inequalities between different groups in the population and the rural-agricultural sector has been worse affected.

Leading proponents of the dependency school were Furtado (1970), Cardoso (1972), Dos Santos (1973), and Frank (1967). Their writings received much attention in academic circles in the 1970s and succeeded in displacing the supremacy of the modernization school. Notably, they drew attention to the problems of international inequality and unequal trade, stressing that an analysis of the causes of poverty cannot be undertaken at the national level, but is rather a product of the unequal relationship between interdependent economies. As Hardiman and Midgley (1982) put it, "This is another way of saying that mass poverty in the Third World is the direct consequence of colonial and neo-colonial exploitation and the impoverishment of the Third World, or in Frank's phrase 'the development of underdevelopment'." (1967: 55).

Most of the empirical studies using this model have been made in Latin America, many of them amongst rural populations. In the context of the Latin American situation they represent a considerable advance on modernization approaches in the analysis of rural development. However, they also have limitations in terms of their contribution to the understanding of social processes. For example, in the case of a study in Peru it is argued that the pattern of external domination established by Spanish colonization and continued by advanced industrial countries, is repeated in a multiplicity of ways at the level of the nation and its differentiated social sectors, leading to the concept of a plural society. Little attention, however, is given to how these systems are interrelated economically and politically or of the ways in which the region is tied into the wider politico-economic structure. The discussion of dominant and dependency relationships is restricted to the analysis of the internal organization of settlements.

The structural dependency approach does not sufficiently take account of a situation where, despite domination, elements of co-operation exist. This is well illustrated by Gluckman (1955) in his analysis of the South African situation where "a policy of apartheid forces an extreme form of domination by whites over blacks in economic, political and social matters" but "despite the inequalities certain blacks and whites tacitly collaborate in the pursuit of common political and economic goals". (1955 Ch. VI: 21).

Participation in any relationship involves a degree of dependence, which may or may not be accompanied by domination; the concept of reciprocity developed by anthropologists well illustrates this point. Dependency theory tends to oversimplify and overgeneralize the complexity of social relationships, whereas the work on modes of production by Meillasoux (1972) and others, addresses some of the analytical difficulties, by looking in greater detail at the problem of interrelations between different modes of production. This is in line with work done by anthropologists on the analysis of different systems of economic and social exchange, which has thrown valuable insights into the functioning of social institutions.

Although studies using the modernization and dependency approaches have produced much of value, both these theories tend towards a centralist view of development, and pay too little attention to the ways in which local groups and processes contribute to and modify patterns of development. In this respect all macro-level theories are flawed. The attempt to formulate sound propositions of a general nature fail, because counter evidence can always be produced.

We need, therefore, to move the analysis to a different level. Long considers this in relation to different responses to entrepreneurship, asking "why it is that in particular development situations persons possessing certain social and ideological characteristics are apparently more strategically placed for successfully engaging in new forms of economic activity" (Long 1977: 105). He maintains that we need a model that looks closely at the mobilization of resources. He discusses the contribution made by economists to the study of entrepreneurship, both through their work at the macro-level, providing data concerning the parameters in which entrepreneurs operate, and at the micro-level, as in the theory of the firm.

Anthropologists have, ever since the work of Malinowski, studied exchange processes, mainly in rural situations, analysing the different types of exchange that operate in a society, such as monetary and non-monetary transactions (Firth 1970). Bohannan (1959), in his study of the Tiv in Nigeria, found that there were three spheres of activity within the traditional system of the economy. Firstly there was the subsistence sphere, where gifts of agricultural and craft products were exchanged. These exchanges were accompanied by a good deal of bargaining. Secondly, there was the prestige sphere, consisting of the exchange of cattle, houses, ritual offices, imported cloth, medicines, magic and slaves. This sphere was not associated with the market economy, and there were no prices, although a rough idea existed of equivalent values. The third sphere was concerned with rights in people other than slaves, notably dependent women and children.

Barth developed the analysis oi˙   .eres of exchange further and related it to a study of the commercialization of local economies. He maintained that a true representation of the structure of an economy must relate to all forms of circulation and transformation of value, whether by exchange, production, inheritance or other means (Barth 1967). Such analysis is relevant to studies such as that of Konkonuru, where exchanges take place at different levels and are governed by different criteria. A critical question in Akan society is, for example, to what extent traditional patterns of inheritance affect the distribution and value of resources, and the ways in which the introduction of cocoa introduced new forms of transaction and entrepreneurship.

Another fruitful field of study lies in the examination of interpersonal relationships. This takes the analysis of exchange systems a step further in that it looks at what actually happens as a result of face-to-face interaction, rather than what is described as a system governed by traditional values, norms and social conventions. Such studies face the problem of distinguishing between the 'ideal norm' and the 'actual' what people tell you should happen and what happens in practice. All field workers must experience this dilemma, where it is all too easy to fall into the trap of taking what one hears at face value. It is only by long term immersion in the life of the community that a more authentic picture can emerge. Moreover, people's perceptions of the 'ideal norm' is of importance as it is an expression of the values attached to certain patterns of behaviour. An example of this was the contention of the people of Konkonuru that all citizens returned to their home town for the Odwira festival, although in practice only a small minority appeared.

The type of research outlined above works at the micro-level. It may look at the interaction between local communities, regions and the nation state. But it does not lead to the formulation of macro-theories. This in itself has advantages, as it counteracts the danger of generalizing about the characteristics of rural people and the communities in which they live.

The growth of planning in developing countries has provided sociologists and anthropologists with new problems for analysis (Grillo and Rew 1985; Hobart 1993) The governments of newly independent nations in the Third World have set out to develop their countries through planned social change. All development plans include attention to the rural sector, although, as mentioned above, resources for implementation have usually not matched up to the proposals. Long (1977) distinguishes between two approaches to planned development in the rural sector, which he describes as the improvement approach and the transformation approach, pointing out that in most countries there may be a combination of the two. The improvement approach does not seek radically to change social institutions, but aims at encouraging development within existing production systems, whereas the transformation approach attempts to establish new forms of agrarian and social organization, making a break with existing social structure. A major concern of the transformation approach is systems of land ownership and tenure. The debate on this question in Ghana is discussed in Chapter 5. Circumstances vary so much between countries that very different strategies are appropriate. An overall lesson, however, that can be learnt from the experience of planned change is that too often there is a fatal lack of attention, not only to differences between areas, but to the views of the people who will be affected and are being asked to implement the change. The value of micro-studies, apart from their intrinsic worth in furthering knowledge, is that they can act as a salutary reminder of the importance of taking account of how existing systems operate. They can provide guidance on the way in which planners should set about their task.

Chapter 2

LIFE IN RURAL GHANA

The economy of Ghana is still primarily based on agriculture, as is shown in the Tables in Chapter 1, and 64 per cent of the population still lives in rural areas. It is significant that there has been virtually no change since 1970 in the proportion of the Gross National Product that comes from agriculture, which stood at 47 per cent in 1970 , 1980 and 1997. The proportion of the labour force in this sector has decreased since 1965 but still accounts for 52 per cent of the working population. It is the agricultural sector that makes the largest contribution to exports, as cocoa alone has accounted for 45 per cent – 70 per cent of all commodity exports since the early 1970s, the wide variations being due mainly to fluctuations in world market prices. On the food front Ghana has still not reached self-sufficiency in staple crops, as can be seen in Table 3, which shows an increase in imported cereals in 1992 in comparison with 1980. Since then there has been an improvement in agricultural production; nevertheless cereals are still being imported,amounting to 22kg per head in 1997 (UNECA 1998, Sahn 1996),

The well-being and development of rural areas is influenced by the over-all economic situation of Ghana (Brown 1986). Among the many factors involved, the deterioration in terms of trade for primary products has added to the country's difficulties in recovering from the economic problems of the 1970s and 1980s. The export of cocoa is of crucial importance and falls in world prices, when they occur, have serious consequences. External debt stood at US$ 5.9 billion in 1995, a total amounting to 95 per cent of GNP, resulting in a debt service ratio of 23 per cent of the GNP for that year. This is a crippling burden for a country to bear, with grave consequences for its development programme. Development aid in 1995 amounted to US$654 million, or 10.8 per cent of GNP, considerably more in value than net foreign direct investment which accounted for only 3.7 per cent of GNP.

This chapter first looks at the different geographical regions of Ghana, the types of farming practised, their contribution to the economy, and policies and programmes that have been introduced in the past fifty years in order to improve agricultural production. Special consideration is then given to cocoa farming, as this affects not only the economy but the whole structure of the communities involved, and raises important issues regarding the impact of economic development and entrepreneurial activities on traditional social structures. Finally, demographic data are discussed with particular reference to rural areas, and within these to the women and children of Ghana.

In considering the rural economy of Ghana a broad distinction must be made between the coastal savannah, the forest areas, and the northern savannah. Before the 20th century the forest was an inhospitable area compared to the more open stretches of savannah country, where domestic animals could be kept and used for haulage and meat and milk, and where plough cultivation was possible. The northern savannah areas faced north across the Sahara to the Mediterranean, and were influenced by the spread of Islam, although the penetration into Ghana was less extensive than into many other countries of West Africa, such as Nigeria, or Mali, and there were no urban centres comparable to Timbuctoo, Gao or Kano. The southern coastal savannah was in early contact with traders and missionaries from overseas, and was the first part of the country to come under colonial rule (Dickson & Benneh 1969).

The Northern Savannah

Although two-thirds of Ghana is designated as savannah much of the northern region is more characteristic of a middle belt between savannah and forest, with moderate rainfall and scrub woodland. The north east corner of the country suffers from the interrelated problems of population pressure, over cultivation, soil erosion, seasonal hunger, hyperendemic diseases, such as river blindness, and emigration,resulting in sex ratios as low as 52 males to 100 females. Annual rainfall is in the region of 40 inches, 90 per cent of it falling between May and October. The remainder of the year has very low humidity and the countryside suffers from drought. Much of the natural vegetation of savannah woodland has been destroyed (Nsiah-Gyaboah 1994).

There is little nucleated settlement, as most families live in the middle of their lands, and cultivate intensively the same patches of land around the compound. In addition to these fixed home farms they also grow crops from bush farms in unsettled areas, where a rotation system is practiced. The most common crops are millet, guinea corn and groundnuts, and some vegetables are grown, mainly tomatoes for sale. A factory for canning tomatoes was opened in Bolgatanga in the 1960s and nearby another factory produced corned beef and frozen meat. It was still operating when I visited the region in 1970, but its dependence on imported cattle and refrigerated trucks to deliver its products to the south of the country ran into difficulties during the recession of the 1970s and 1980s. Cattle are raised for ritual purposes and bride price; their manure is vital for agricultural purposes. But they are only sold in cases of extreme need, and are not normally eaten; hence the need to import meat for the factory at Bolgatanga.

The overpopulation of this part of Ghana has been exacerbated by land falling out of use and reverting to bush, as a result of river blindness. Because there is not enough land to allow for fallow periods many areas have been stripped of top soil. Yields are insufficient to provide adequate nutritional levels and seasonal hunger is chronic. Confronted with these problems an interdisciplinary approach is needed in the formulation of policies to improve levels of living in the savannah areas. Proposals for land planning were put forward as a possibility before Independence. In 1950 the Gonja Development Company was set up with a share capital of 1 million. One of the aims of the project was village settlement, bringing together the dispersed compounds in which people traditionally lived. As with the similar objective of Nyerere's ujamaa villages in Tanzania, too little account was taken of the preferred life style of the local people, and in 1956 the company was disbanded having achieved "nothing except extravagant expense for the government" (Chambers 1969: 7).

In the 1960s the country around Navrongo, Bolgatanga and Bawku was constituted a land planning area in an attempt to improve rural conditions. Contour bunds were laid out to reduce erosion and earth dams were constructed to irrigate vegetables and rice and provide water for domestic use and livestock (Groves 1978). Some success was achieved but the scheme failed significantly to improve rural conditions in this area and emigration continued to reduce the working age population, particularly of men.

Nkrumah in 1960 started to establish State farms, as a possible solution to improving agricultural production, and most of these were situated either in the northern savannah or in the coastal region. By 1964 there were 9600 hectares under cultivation, but of these 2240 were under rice, mainly on the Volta Plain. From the outset State farms ran into difficulties and losses occured. At their peak between 1962–1965 they produced less than 0.5 per cent of the total food supply of the country at prohibitively high costs (La Anyane 1969: 9). By the end of the 1960s all but one or two were no longer viable and were abandoned. La Anyane maintained that a more effective alternative policy would be to enlarge existing peasant holdings, through the reform of land tenure systems, accompanied by a programme to assist farmers to invest in improved methods of production.

The northern savannah region was more suitable for mechanical cultivation, but the model co-operative scheme, involving hundred families, which was created in Damongo, by the Gonja Development Corporation, made little progress in modernizing agriculture, and the scheme was discontinued in 1956, as already noted. Lack of viable solutions to the problems of the northern region resulted in a situation where emigration was the main outlet, initiated by the people themselves. As mentioned earlier this led to marked imbalances in the population. Even today, the bulk of agricultural production, here as elsewhere in Ghana (Republic of Ghana 1989), remains in the hands of the small scale farmer, using mainly traditional systems of cultivation. It was estimated that in 1988 ninety percent of local food production still came from the traditional sector and that 84 per cent of farm households cultivated less than 1.6 hectares.

The Coastal Savannah

The most important part of this region from the agricultural point of view is in the southeast. The Volta delta, occupied by the Ewe people is probably more productive than anywhere in Africa. One of the most striking features of this densely settled area, between Keta and Anloga, is the intensive production of shallots, maize and vegetables, grown in irrigated plots along the edge of the Keta lagoon (Nukunya 1969; 1992). Crops are watered from shallow wells, manured with crop residues, fish manure and bat dung; as many as three crops a year can be produced. A great deal of the produce is sold, much of it in Accra, which is about 130 miles to the west. Fishing is also an important activity of the Ewe people, not only in the south east area, which is their base, but also all along the coast of Ghana and into the Ivory Coast. Traditional dug out canoes are used, many of them now fitted with outboard motors. Women are actively engaged in processing and selling the fish, which is a major source of income in the coastal region.

The Volta Dam, built in the 1960s, has had a great influence on this area, and illustrates the problems connected with attempts to change rural life styles. Below the dam the Volta plain has 180,000 hectares of land potentially suitable for irrigation. The plan was to irrigate this, principally for growing sugarcane and rice, both of which were needed to offset the necessity to import foods which were major items in the balance of trade. However, the terrain is difficult, both in terms of its topography and soil. Over thirty years later substantial progress has not been made, although this is no doubt due to some extent to the overall economic situation of the country during much of this period, rather than solely to the specific problems involved.

North of the dam the task was to resettle the people displaced by the newly formed lake. The evacuation of about 80,000 people began in 1964, organized by the Volta River Authority (VRA). In designing the programme account was taken of the experience in resettling Tema fishing families when the villages were incorporated in the new port. The new approach was intended to be more benevolent and permissive. But the waters rose more quickly than anticipated, and the social survey of households to be affected was not completed before the plans were prepared.

There was no formal local participation, and the planners worked on the basis of quasi-urban values, prevalent in West Africa at the time. Over 700 villages or hamlets were to be resettled, and it was decided that they should be moved to 52 "new towns". It was considered that these would form more effective economic units, which could develop mechanized agriculture and co-operative forms of organization. A standard of housing was built which was thought to be superior to that found in the former villages. The responsiblity of negotiating for land, selecting sites, and managing welfare was given to the Department of Social Welfare, which already had experience with the Tema resettlement. The Department seconded its Mass Education Assistants (MEAs) to carry out these tasks. The District Commissioners were deliberately not involved as they were political appointees, were thought not to have sufficient commitment to the programme, and would in any case not welcome direction from the VRA.

The MEAs became town managers and formed town development committees. But they were young and junior in status, and thought by the local people to be intruders in their environment. Displaced persons were offered compensation as an alternative to resettlement, but only 13 per cent took up this offer. In Tema a similar offer was taken up by only two households out of a population of 12,000, as the terms of compensation were considered too poor. So most of the displaced households took up housing in the "new towns", though subsequently they may have regretted their decision. Because there the problems started. These people were not primarily farmers; they were fishermen, and this had been their main source of livelihood. They were reluctant to learn new farming skills, despite the assistance of the Ministry of Agriculture, which posted staff to develop the newly acquired land. This in itself led to a conflict situation with the MEAs, quite apart from the fact that negotiating for land with local communities had proved more difficult than anticipated. Given the traditional customs of land tenure it is surprising that this difficulty had not been appreciated. The bureaucrats seemed to have forgotten the roots to which most of them must have belonged in their "home towns" in rural areas.

The housing, although perhaps structurally sounder than those in their previous villages, did not meet the needs of the settlers, as they were of a standard size, inadequate for larger families. Building extensions to the houses was strictly controlled. They were not allowed to use swish or wattle and daub, which were the traditional methods of construction, and relatively much cheaper.

All this dissatisfaction led to migration from the new towns. The aim of creating modern agricultural organizations which would make rural life more profitable and more attractive, and stop the drift of school leavers to the older, larger towns, was thwarted. Instead there was large scale migration. Many went back to live on the shores of the newly formed lake in improvised dwellings; others, particularly the young, sought their fortunes in Accra and other urban centres. The new towns became ghost towns, as I found when I visited them in 1969–1970. They were mainly occupied by old women and children. What had been thought of as an opportunity to wean farmers from their traditional shifting cultivation and substitute settled, improved farming, had failed. Fortunately fish soon populated the new lake and fishing once more became a viable occupation. The development of river transport also assisted in the marketing of their produce.

The experience of Volta resettlement is a good example of the importance of taking local lifestyles and systems of production into account (Diaw *et al*, 1990). Although a social survey was planned, not only was it carried out too late, but few lessons seemed to have emerged from its findings. As with the building of all dams which involve extensive flooding of existing communities, there is bound to be resentment. The question is to what extent this can be mitigated by more meaningful consultation with the people concerned.

The Forest Region

By contrast with the northern savannah and parts of the coastal region agriculture in the forest areas, which in the early days were considered backward, has expanded in scope, greatly influenced by the introduction of cash crops, and by the greater accessibility to markets. Ghana was one of the first countries in West Africa to develop crops for export. The trade in palm oil products began in a small way in the late eighteenth century, and became more important in the nineteenth century when the Krobos were amongst those who made plantations for this purpose. Palm oil production is still important, but since the introduction of cocoa in the late nineteenth century it is no longer the main export crop.

In those parts of Ghana where it can be grown cocoa has had a profound effect on the way of life of the people and, as has been seen earlier, a great influence on the economy as a whole. It was first introduced in Akwapim in 1879, and was rapidly taken up by local farmers. The soil and climate were ideal and extensive areas of forest were felled in order to plant the new crop. From Akwapim cultivation spread to other parts of Ghana, mainly in those areas occupied by the Akan people (see Map, Fig. 1). In 1970 cocoa cultivation occupied 3.6 million acres, or 56 per cent of the cultivable area of Ghana. In southern Ghana it accounted for 70 per cent of the cultivable area. Since then there have been changes in the distribution and techniques of cocoa cultivation and there may have been some reduction in acreage; it still forms, however a vital part of the economy. Before looking at cocoa farming in greater detail the production of food crops will be considered, as it is from the forest areas that most of the food needs of the nation are met (Sahn 1996).

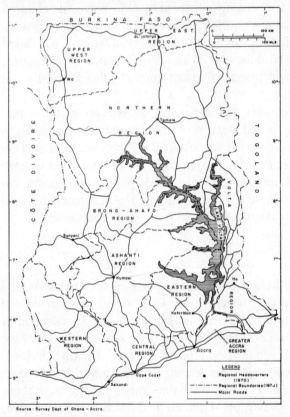

Source: Survey Dept. of Ghana — Accra.

Fig. 1: Map of Ghana

Food Crop Production in Forest Areas

The forest areas not only produce the staple food crops of cassava, yam, maize and plantain, but also provide citrus fruits, oil palm, pineapples and vegetables. Although often described as subsistence agriculture most farmers manage to sell some of their crops. It was estimated (Republic of Ghana & UNCF 1990) that 20 per cent of food crop farmers marketed over 50 per cent of their produce. As will be seen in Chapter 5 my own findings in Konkonuru were that nearly all farmers sold some of their produce. In a sample of 28 men and women farmers only three marketed no produce, and in all these cases they provided for eating groups of between eighteen and twenty-four people.

Concern about the quantity of output has already been expressed. There have been considerable fluctuations during the past twenty years and different estimates vary widely. The general conclusion, however, is that production declined substantially between 1970 and the 1980s, but has since improved. A survey undertaken by the Republic of Ghana and the United Nations Children's Fund (1990), using indices of per capita food production as 100 for 1970 arrived at figures in 1986 as 70 for cereals, 84 for cassava and 34 for cocoyam. This represents a serious decrease, and was reflected in the same survey's study of nutrition, which found that the 1986 calorie intake of pre-school children was only 40–70 per cent of their requirements. The study reckoned that this represented twice the level of shortfall to those recorded in 1961–62.

A more hopeful picture is painted in the Quarterly Digest of Statistics for March 1993 (Republic of Ghana, Statistical Service 1993), which shows a steady increase in production from 1986–1992. For example, the production of cassava more than doubled during this period and maize increased by over 50 per cent. Since then recent harvests have been good, assisted by adequate rainfall, so the improvement has continued.

Before considering appropriate policies to improve output, systems of production will be described. As the forest region is vast there are obviously variations between areas in the crops grown, and the systems used, due to differences in topography, soil, rainfall and local customs. But in the vast majority of cases the main system of agriculture is by shifting cultivation. Every year a farmer makes a new farm, or, more commonly, farms by clearing the bush, which has lain fallow for up to ten years. The fallow period varies considerably, and there are now decreasing intervals where population pressures are greatest. In some places as little as three or four year intervals have been observed. The by-product of bush clearance is firewood, which apart from its use as a cooking fuel for the family is a highly marketable commodity. The system of clearance is described more fully in the Chapter on food farming in Konkonuru. It is a highly laborious task and a problem for older men and women, who have to employ young men to carry it out for them, and they must pay them accordingly. Chapter 5 also describes methods of planting and the close attention that is given to differences in soil and location. Having walked many miles through the bush I was impressed by the detailed knowledge of the terrain possessed by all those who accompanied me. Farms in Konkonuru are mostly in hilly country, as is the case throughout Akwapim, and the traditional methods of cultivation help to prevent the erosion that would occur if more radical ways of clearance, involving mechanical equipment, were used. Different conditions prevail in less hilly areas, although at present there is not a great deal of variation in the system described. The main food crop in Akwapim is cassava, although considerable quantities of maize are grown, and some white and yellow yams. Tools and methods of cultivation throughout the forest region are almost completely non-mechanical, relying on the cutlass, the axe and the hoe. In 1990 less than one in ten farmers in the whole of Ghana owned any other equipment (Republic of Ghana & UNCF 1990).

In the forest region only 12 per cent of the total area is permanently cropped; most of this is accounted for by farms of cocoa, citrus or oil palm (Myers 1991). Some land is still occupied by primeval forest, which has never been felled, but most of it is subject to shifting cultivation. There is increasing concern about deforestation, trees being felled both for commercial purposes and for firewood for domestic use. The increase in population in rural areas has greatly exacerbated this, and the rate of depredation of forest is now running at 2 per cent per annum. The Ministry of Finance and Economic Planning prepared an investment programme in 1991 for forest resource management, the implementation of which was to be under the Department of Game and Wild Life. This plan concentrated on thirteen conservation areas which had suffered from inadequate funding over the years, reducing the capability of the Department to manage the protected areas, resulting in illicit exploitation of animals and encroachment of timber and forest exploitation (Republic of Ghana: Ministry of Finance and Economic Planning 1991). Due to limited means no action was planned outside these areas, but it was intended to obtain data on fauna and other forest reserves for the production of bush meat on a sustained yield basis. My own observations over a period of twenty years confirms the seriousness of deforestation. Travelling along the road from Accra to Kumasi in the 1990s much of the country was barely recognizable compared with the 1970s, and the approach to the Akwapim hills from Accra revealed that large areas of the hillsides were bare. In Konkonuru the people told me that yields had been affected by drought, and suggested that one cause might be lack of vegetation. Apart from exploitation for timber, trees are being felled for use as fuel as population pressures increase.

The forest region is mainly occupied by Akan people with matrilineal systems of inheritance and succession. The rule of matrilineal descent is a key to Akan social organization. Rattray (1923, 1929) was greatly impressed by the influence of this system. He wrote that "It is not easy to grasp what must have been the effect on West African psychology of untold generations of acting and thinking, not in terms of oneself but in relation to one's group. The

Ashantis' ideas of what we should term 'moral responsibility for his actions' must surely have been more developed than with peoples where individualism is the order of the day" (Rattray 1929: 62.). This view was reflected in a discussion I once had with a woman in Konkonuru who said that "in your society you do not care about the individual". This seemed strange to one brought up in a society which attached so much importance to individualism. When questioned as to why she thought this she replied that "in Konkonuru every individual matters as a member of the group as a whole (the concept of a cog in the wheel), whereas in your society the individual is isolated". This is an interesting example of one of the traditional values that so many Ghanaians wish to retain in the face of socio-economic change (Appiah 1992).

The Akan system is based on the principle of reckoning kinship on the basis of matrilineal descent (Assimeng 1981). All Akans are members of a local lineage organization, which consists of a unilateral group of descendants from a specified ancestor or ancestress, through the female line. Every person of free matrilineal descent is by birth a member of his or her mother's lineage (abusua), and a citizen of the chiefdom in which his or her lineage is legally domiciled. The clan is a wider group, whose members claim descent from a common, extremely remote ancestress. According to Rattray a clan shared totemic and other taboos, but there is little knowledge of this by people today, or even when Fortes was in the field. The rule of exogamy lays down that intermarriage between members of the same abusua is forbidden, and this ruling extends to the wider membership of the clan, although there are exceptions and variations to this rule, as is demonstrated in the case study of Konkonuru.

As far as political organization and property rights are concerned it is the lineage that is important, because it is this that determines rules of inheritance and succession. Every citizen at death must have an heir and a successor, appointed on the 8th or 40th day after burial by the lineage, under the presidency of the lineage head (abusua panin). Male heirs take precedence over females, unless the particular property or office was occupied by the woman who died. Women are jurally autonomous as citizens and capable of owning property, incurring debts and holding any of the offices allocated to women, but it is generally felt that property is better controlled by men (Fortes 1950: 261).

Land is vested in the lineage, not the stool, which is the seat of the chief to which citizens owe allegiance. The chief safeguards the territory of his chiefdom and must agree to any alienation of land, but it is the lineage that bestows usufructuary rights on individuals. In general in Akan society, even today, there is a strong feeling against the permanent alienation of land held by the lineage; there is in theory no question of selling what we should call the freehold, although, as will be seen later in the discussion of cocoa farming, the distinguishing line is often hard to draw (Uchendu 1969: 17). Further consideration of the ways in which the matrilineal system works, and how it affects the social structure is dealt with in a later section. Its significance here is with regard to land tenure and how the individual acquires usufructuary rights.

Although straightforward in theory, practices attaching to usufructuary rights are more flexible than might be imagined. For example, a widow who has been farming on her husband's land (the husband, according to the marriage rules of exogamy, being of a different abusua) may continue to be allowed the use of this land after his death. Land, customarily, is not sold, but usufructuary rights can be hired out to people who are not of the abusua. There has been much discussion of to what extent this system of land tenure inhibits agricultural development, and this again is considered in more detail in Chapter 5. The lack of freehold ownership of land has meant that it cannot be used as a collateral for credit. Even if there were to be a greater recognition of usufructuary rights, which may be envisaged in the latest MTADP, this may not altogether solve the problem. This is an important consideration, particularly for women, as in many forest communities women form the majority of farmers. They tend to be left with the main responsibility for providing for their children, as many of their husbands have migrated, either to towns or to cocoa farms in other parts of the country.

Women in Akan society have always been independent, frequently heading their households, but socio-economic change has increased the burdens they bear (Hardiman 1974a). The consequences of structural adjustment have fallen particularly heavily on women and children. An IFAD study (1994) estimated that 3.8 million smallholders fell below the poverty line, whereas this applied to only 1.95 million in 1970. More recent data on this particular measurement are not available, but the Human Development Report of 1998 estimated that between 1989–1994 31 per cent of the population as a whole fell below the income poverty line. The Programme of Action to Mitigate the Social Costs of Adjustment (PAMSCAD) was set up in 1988 to mitigate the results of structural adjustment, but the situation continues to cause anxiety.

Government policies to improve agriculture under the MTADP are cited on page 53. Unfortunately too little research has been directed towards methods of improving production in the traditional sector, although some more fruitful steps have been taken recently, as policy thinking has begun to realize that support of the small farmer is vital for the country. One report (Republic of Ghana 1989) considered that the main obstacles to new techniques being adopted were lack of access to credit, deficiencies in the supplies of inputs and difficulties in marketing produce. This may be true, particularly as far as marketing is concerned, but my own observations suggest that too little is understood about traditional systems by those in authority, and that there are, as yet, too few viable alternatives. It would, for example, be of great benefit to farmers if they could use their cleared farms for more than one year without loss of fertility. Inorganic fertilisers are put forward as one answer, but they are expensive and not always effective, as was demonstrated by the experiment of a farmer in Konkonuru, cited in Chapter 1. A more promising development might be the cultivation of *Leucaena*. This is a shrub which is planted in rows, between which crops are grown. It is a potent source of nitrogen, so acts as a fertiliser. The leaves can be used as fodder for livestock and the branches eventually as a source of fuel. Although developed in the 1980s it has not yet been widely adopted, so its effectiveness cannot be fully evaluated. In Konkonuru and in other villages I visited in 1990 no one had heard of it , the experimental plots that I were shown in Ashanti were poorly kept, and the agricultural assistants did not seem to be energetic in its promotion.

In addition to addressing directly the improvement of agriculture much else needs to be done to enhance levels of living in rural areas and thus to attract the younger generation to remain in, or return to their home towns (Mikell 1989). Chapter 1, looked at this problem in general and at some of the consequences of urban bias, which will be further considered in the section on demographic aspects of the rural situation in Ghana. Rural people are increasingly aware of what is happening in the outside world, and are dissatisfied with their lot. They are willing to adopt new techniques if they are convinced of their value, but they need guidance as how best to do this. They also need to know how to deal with modern bureaucracy (Ewusi 1978).

Cocoa Farming

Compared with the production of food crops the Government has paid a great deal of attention to policies on cocoa, as it is still the mainstay of the economy, and particularly of exports. The relatively high proportion of Government expenditure allocated to agriculture, compared with other African countries, which was 9 per cent in 1979 (World Bank 1980) was largely accounted for by cocoa programmes. Cocoa farming has also been the focus of much academic research. It is an excellent example of the rational economic behaviour of farmers, a fruitful source of analysis in assessing the significance of customary property relations in Akan society, and in considering in what ways the introduction of this crop has affected social institutions. Hart (1982: 8) questioned whether the conversion of farmers to cash crops unleashed a capitalist revolution in the heart of rural society, resulting in the erosion of traditional values, as some had asserted. He pointed out that the penetration of the market into subsistence agriculture occurred a long time ago in West African village societies, as surpluses were always sold. Even where the circulation of commodities was minimal, complex social organization intervened systematically in the economic affairs of households (Hart 1982: 9). He also maintained that a distinction must be made between commodity production that depended on wage labour and production dependent mainly on family members; in other words, the difference between the production of goods for sale and the direct sale of wage labour to capitalist production units.

Cocoa was first introduced into what was then the Gold Coast in 1879. It was initially grown in Akwapim, but its cultivation rapidly spread to the rest of the forest areas, and by the time of the first World War the Gold Coast had become the world leader in production. The cocoa farms of Akwapim were the first to be struck by swollen shoot disease, and many of them have now been abandoned in favour of better sites in other parts of the country. As is seen in the study of Konkonuru, the Akwapim farmers themselves have continued to hold considerable interest in the crop as a result of their acquisition of land elsewhere. In 1957, the year of Independence, Ghana accounted for 40 per cent of world production. The forest population, at that time about four million, enjoyed a higher standard of living than most countries in Africa south of the Sahara. The distinctive feature of cocoa production is that from the outset it was in the hands of indigenous farmers,who showed a remarkable initiative in its development. These farmers needed resources to plant a tree crop that would take up to six years to yield and 10 to 12 years to reach maturity, so they had to rely on sufficient income from food crop production and other resources, such as the sale of palm oil, in order to establish their farms. In the first place they relied mainly on family labour, but as their farms developed and they acquired virgin land away from their home bases, they began to hire labour, much of which was supplied by migrants from the savannah region of Ghana and from abroad.

Profits from cocoa were invested in acquiring more land, in building houses, trading, developing transport and other services, and in education, which led to considerable social mobility. A survey in 1973 of the children of early Brong Ahafo cocoa farmers in the Sunyani District (Mikell 1989) revealed that only 40 per cent were still farming; 24 per cent were in the civil service, or in clerical jobs, 18 per cent were in crafts and trades, 15 per cent were trading and 2 per cent were in advanced professions. Many cocoa farmers became rich and resided in towns, leaving the management of their farms to others on some sort of share-cropping arrangement, known as an *abusa* contract. Such a manager could not be referred to as a tenant because of the ambiguous territorial rights held by farmers away from their home towns.

Cocoa farming is still an industry contained within the matrix of indigenous family life, despite the fact that the bulk of cocoa for export is produced by a small percentage of farmers with large land holdings. Hart (1982: 63) suggests that one reason why the industry has remained largely unmodernized is that the State has skimmed off much of the wealth produced, through state controls, monopsonistic marketing arrangements and revenue extraction. The Cocoa Marketing Board was set up by the colonial government after the Second World War. The stated aim was to maintain production prices at secure levels (Bauer 1954), but the government was able to skim off a large surplus from export sales, part of which was used to pay off Britain's war debts. After Independence the CMB continued to prove a valuable source of revenue, and the colonial trading monopsonies were taken to new extremes, milking even more revenue from the Board. The slump in cocoa prices in the mid-1960s drastically reduced earnings, and led Ghana into a state of indebtedness resulting from the failure to meet the cost of large scale developments, such as the Volta Dam. The plans for these projects had relied on paying back the funds borrowed out of export earnings. The fall of Nkrumah's government was not unrelated to this situation.

The extent to which earnings from cocoa production were transferred to the State carried the danger of killing the goose that laid the golden eggs. At times the price paid to growers was little more than what would cover their production costs. A comparison of cocoa prices and real wages, carried out in the 1960s is shown in Table 8.

Table 8.

Cocoa Prices and Real Wages, reckoned as indices of real value

	Cocoa Producer Prices	Minimum Wage/Accra	Average Earnings/Accra
1956	100	100	100
1960	72	120	130
1965	33	69	86

Source: Mikell, Gwendoline 1989: *Cocoa and chaos in Ghana*

This poor rate of return certainly had its effect. One response of farmers was to sell their cocoa over the border to Togo or the Ivory Coast, where prices were higher, despite efforts by the government to control these operations. Statistics showed a fall in cocoa production in the mid-1980s, which, because of these activities may have been misleading (Buhr 1998). Some farmers, it is true, had taken farms out of production when the trees had reached the end of their useful life, and used the land for other crops, such as citrus fruits, cereals or vegetables, all of which commanded good prices. Replacement of trees was considered too expensive an exercise in relation to the uncertainty of cocoa prices in the future.

In 1985 the CMB was reorganized as the Ghana Cocoa Board (COCOBOD) and strenuous efforts were made to stimulate increased production. Over 3 million hybrid cocoa seedlings were distributed, but still many farmers chose to plant food crops, for which the market prices had increased substantially. The Cocoa Research Station at Tafo is still actively promoting the replanting of exhausted farms and the present government seems to be relaxing its monopoly on the sale of cocoa. World prices continue to fluctuate, but cocoa exports are still vital to the Ghanaian economy. Christine Okali is currently studying the situation, so more information, not only on the progress of government policies, but also on trends in the impact of cocoa on rural relationships should soon be available. New techniques have been developed, with strains that do not require shade, dramatically altering the appearance of cocoa farms.

The question of the extent to which customary principles of land tenure and inheritance have been eroded by socio-economic change is wider than that of the possible influence of cocoa farming. Nevertheless, the changes that have occured as a result of the introduction of cocoa are undoubtedly significant, particularly under the matrilineal system, to which the majority of cocoa farmers belong. Differing views have been expressed as to whether or not traditional systems of inheritance have inhibited development. Okali and Kotey (1971) considered that it had probably affected the long-term care of farms. Hill (1963), on the other hand, in an earlier study, considered that corporate land holding acted as a spur to expansionary enterprise. This question is still debated, although it is probably now of less importance, in view of changes that are taking place, albeit gradually, in the way that farms are acquired.

The question of the impact of cocoa on rural relationships is important as an indicator of the direction of socio-economic change, and has been of great interest to scholars. Some studies have pinpointed the ways in which cocoa production led to matrilineal conflicts. For example Fortes (1950) reported an increase in witchcraft, due to claims based on lineage ties; Busia

(1951: 209–210) stated that "cocoa destroys kinship and divides blood relations", and Field (1960) expressed concern over the extent of insecurity and anxiety generated by disputes over the inheritance of cocoa farms. Okali researched this question further between 1971–1974 (Okali 1983), collecting field material in order to analyze the significance of customary property relationships in determining the distribution of cocoa farm ownership by age, sex and status, and its effects on relations between spouses, parents, offspring and matrikin. More recently Mikell (1989), in looking at the effects of cocoa at the local level, considered that it altered the production dynamics of rural economies, generated domestic tensions between husbands, wives and children and contributed to the fragmentation of lineages. She affirmed that this had repercussions at regional and national levels, where ethnic and regional political alliances emerged to gain control of cocoa resources. She reckoned that cocoa dealt a crushing blow to subsistence production, and that access to, and control of, land for cocoa farms commercialized and corrupted traditional land relationships. She found that there was a growing conflict between cocoa migrants and the local stool chiefs from whom they had acquired land for farms.

The debate continues. Unquestionably the acquisition of cocoa farms has changed the balance between matrilineal and patrilateral inheritance. It has always been possible in Akan society for an individual to leave privately owned property according to his or her wishes, so long as this is made clear before death. In the old days, before land was acquired away from home, specifically for growing cash crops, there was very little private property for an individual to distribute. But as the new generation of farmers sought out new fields for their entrepreneurial activities privately acquired property grew in importance. These farmers were enabled to extend their economic enterprises, backed by the existence of a conjugal work unit, which meant that they could leave food farming to their wives and children. In return they wished to reward their nuclear families, who were not members of their abusua, for their assistance. A farmer could either hand over his privately acquired cocoa farm during his lifetime, or will that this should be done after his death. The first mentioned method was safer, as it was less likely to cause claims by the matrikin. Examples of this are described in the case study of Konkonuru.

Hill (1963) maintained that the ownership of cocoa farms reverted to the abusua after the second generation. This may have been so at the time of her research, but it now seems more likely that patrilateral inheritance can endure over several generations. However, the matrilineage still has a strong hold over its members, and a significant proportion of farms are still being inherited in this line. There are no recent data on this question. Mikell (1989) quotes a study of inheritance patterns of cocoa farms previously belonging to men in the Sunyani District, which produced the results shown in Table 9.

Table 9

Inheritance of Cocoa Farms from Men Farmers

Relation of Inheritor	Sunyani		Nsuatre		Odumasi	
	No.	%	No.	%	No.	%
Brother	49	42	59	46	19	68
Nephew	8	7	21	16.5	5	18
Children	29	25	23	18	2	7
Wives	19	16	11	8.5	1	3.5
Abusua	7	6	5	4	1	3.5
Sister	2	2	5	4	0	0
Mother	2	2	4	3	0	0
Total	116	100	128	100	28	100

Source: Mikell (1989) p.115. Based on a survey in 1973.

Assuming that the nephew was a sister's son, overall 69 per cent of farms were inherited by the matriliny, whereas 31 per cent passed to members of other *abusuas,* that is the farmer's wife or children. This study was made over 20 years ago, but it indicates that changes were already taking place. Beckett's study of Akokoaso in 1932 (Beckett 1944) was in a different region, namely Akim, so that direct comparisons are not possible, although, in these studies a common feature is that they all inherit matrilineally. Beckett's study does, however, show a very different picture of inheritance. In Beckett's account of 41 farmers, only one inherited from his father and even in this case two-thirds of the property reverted to the matrikin. Okali and Kotey (1971) resurveyed Akokoaso in 1969. Their study of inheritance patterns was confined to the ten farmers intensively studied by Beckett. Four of these farmers, who had sons farming in Akokoaso, had given some cocoa farm land to them. Three of the sons were only given part of their fathers' holdings, the remainder going to nephews and grandnephews. Only one son received all the farm of his father, but the acreage involved was only three acres. So most cocoa farm land had still been transmitted in the matrilineal line. As far as this small sample was concerned inheritance patterns had not shown a substantial change over the period of nearly thirty years. Unfortunately, there has been little recent empirical research to quantify these relationships, so that the extent to which there has been an acceleration of change cannot be verified. Change in societies today is both rapid and uneven.

In the 1920s women began to enter cocoa farming in their own right. Women in Akan society have always been able to exercise usufructuary rights over land, so this did not represent any great change in principle. But in practice it was less easy for a woman to accumulate the necessary capital to establish a cocoa farm. As mentioned above, men had an advantage in being able to rely on the support of the conjugal unit, which would continue to produce the food crops for survival while they waited for their cocoa farms to yield. As a result the women who do own cocoa farms tend to be older and frequently widowed or divorced. Their holdings tend to be on a smaller scale.

In conclusion, this brief account of cocoa farming has demonstrated the significant part it has played in the life of the forest people, and beyond them to the economy of Ghana as a whole. The changes that this has brought about in rural areas is further reflected in the demographic aspects discussed below.

The Government introduced a Medium Term Agricultural Development Programme (MTADP) for 1990-1995 with the following objectives:

1. Provide all Ghanaians with food security by way of adequate, nutritionally balanced diets at affordable prices, both now and in the future.
2. Promote increased smallholder productivity and ensure that all efficient agricultural producers earn incomes that are comparable to those outside agriculture, thus making agriculture an attractive employment alternative to industry, trade and commerce.
3. Ensure that agriculture contributes effectively to the country's balance of payments position through export diversification and import substitution.
4. Establish effective linkages between agriculture and industry.
5. Promote balanced regional development and growth based on comparative advantages and resource endowments.

It was acknowledged that the country still faced a formidable task in exploiting its production potential, with a view to satisfying a higher percentage of food requirements from local output (Republic of Ghana 1989: 119). The MTADP has now been revised to cover the years up to 2000. Farmers are to receive subsidized loans to purchase high yield seeds and fertilisers. The attempts to organize them on a communal basis, either through State farms or co-operatives seems to have been abandoned. But although the aims of the MTADP are admirable, compared with the efforts that the Government has put into the promotion of cocoa production, policy in the food sector has been weak (Abbey 1996, pers. com.). Policies in themselves are not enough; they must be supported with strenuous efforts at grass roots level. This question has already been discussed in the section on food production in the forest region.

Demographic Aspects

The population of Ghana has doubled in the past twenty-five years, and although migration to towns has greatly increased their size, the majority of people still live in the country, and depend for their living on agriculture. Caldwell (1969), in his study of rural-urban migration, predicted that by the 1990s over half the population would probably be living in towns, as a result of economic development. This estimate was based on trends in the 1960s. Since then the shift in the rural-urban balance has slowed down (Singh 1985). This has happened for a variety of political and economic reasons which have affected most countries in Africa South of the Sahara. In the 1960 census 77 per cent of the population was recorded as rural,and an estimate in 1968 gave a figure of 70 per cent. The Human Development Report (UNDP 1998) gave a figure of 64 per cent for the rural population, and estimated that by 2015 it would still account for 52 per cent.

The rural-urban migrations have had a profound influence on village communities. More men than women left for the towns, leaving imbalances in sex-ratios, particularly of working age groups. The extent and nature of this migration varied according to differences in the pull-push factors. Some of the migration was seasonal, and was directed not only to towns, but also to other rural areas where casual labour was required for harvesting crops, such as on cocoa farms in the forest areas, which drew migrants from the Northern and Upper Regions, as well as from other countries. The outflow of men from these regions, where economic conditions were harsh, has already been mentioned. In the south the increase in formal education of the younger generation probably exerted a greater influence than the economic situation of the rural communities themselves. Data on sex ratios are patchy. Although the research of Caldwell and others in the 1960s, collected a lot of information on differences between men and women migrants there were no country wide studies specifically directed at measuring sex ratios, either in rural or urban communities. Caldwell, in an article in Ghana Population Studies No. 2. (Caldwell 1989) with reference to the 1960 census, stated that there was a surplus of males in urban areas, amounting to an overall rate of 16 per cent, reaching a figure of 32 per cent in Accra. However, he went on to say that the deficit in all rural areas was only 2 per cent, although it was as high as between 12–20 per cent in the north. This was over forty years ago,and even in the period from 1960 to 1968, referred to previously, there had been a considerable increase in migration to towns, which must have led to increased imbalances. The unsettled situation since then has probably worked in two directions. The serious economic situation of the 1970s and early 1980s, may to some extent have reversed the trend, as was found in the case of Konkonuru, and borne out by a Demographic and Health Survey in 1988 (Republic of Ghana 1989) which showed a slight increase in the proportion of people living in the countryside.

Demographic data on these questions are significant in relation to policies for rural development. The case study of Konkonuru highlighted the results of sex imbalances, one of which was the prevalence of women household heads. Although this is not unusual in Akan society, where many women have always lived with their matrikin, the circumstances in communities experiencing changes in sex ratios place these women in a different position from that in the past. Previously their husbands were likely to live in the same settlement, whereas, as a result of migration many of them have moved away. This has left women with a greater responsibility for the support of their children and older relatives.

Another result of migration has been the brain drain from rural areas. Those migrating have mostly been the younger , better educated members of the community. They are the ones who should, by their efforts be able to improve productivity and living conditions. Some assistance, it is true, is given by these migrants through their home-based societies in Accra and other large towns, but nevertheless their absence is felt by those that they have left behind. The need for leaders in rural areas who are able to understand modern bureaucracy is greater than ever. One outcome of this has been the phenomenon of "commuting chiefs" as was found in Konkonuru. This question is considered in more detail in the case study.

Fertility and Mortality

Chapter 1 dealt in general with some of the differences in fertility and mortality between urban and rural areas. The difficulty of obtaining reliable data on issues which are highly sensitive, was discussed. So when considering the more detailed information that is now available for Ghana this reservation must be borne in mind. A great many population studies were made in the 1960s and 1970s, notably by members of the Demographic Unit of the Sociology Department and the Institute of Statistical Social and Economic Research (ISSER) at the University of Ghana. Ghana's knowledge of the country's demography was at the forefront in Africa at that time, and the 1960 census showed a marked improvement on previous ones as a result of advice from the demographers. Although there was a census in 1971 the results were never fully analyzed owing to the prevailing political situation. The continuing political and economic troubles of the 1970s and 1980s restricted the amount of in depth research ; as a consequence so the considerable changes that occured during those years have not been documented to the same extent.

The main recent sources used in this Chapter are the Demographic and Health Survey of 1988 (Institute for Resource Development and Ghana Statistical Service 1989), Children and Women of Ghana: A Situation Analysis 1989-90 (Republic of Ghana and UN Children's Fund 1990) and the Demographic and Health Surveys Comparative Studies No. 9. (DHS 1994). The field work for all these studies was carried out between 1988-89, and represents the most recent information available at the time of going to press. Later data does not distinguish between urban and rural areas, which is vital to our discussion. It is recognized that the years since 1989 have seen many changes, including an improved economic situation, which has no doubt affected social indicators, although such overall indices as infant and child mortality have not greatly altered since then (UNICEF 1997). The Human Development Report (UNDP 1998) gave figures for 1996 of an IMR of 70:1000 and an under 5s mortality of 164:1000, which shows no improvement since 1988–89 (see Table 10).

In Africa South of the Sahara as a whole demographic indicators show higher levels of fertility, infant and child mortality, earlier marriage, a greater desire for more children, and less use of contraception than in other parts of the world. This applies to both rural and urban areas, but rates are usually higher in the rural sector. Some overall comparisons are given in Tables 10 and 11.

In Table 10 it can be seen that Ghana's high fertility rate was recorded as marginally lower in rural areas than in the other Sub-Saharan countries listed in the Table. The differences, however, between rural and urban were not so great. The percentage of women not wanting any more children showed similar differences between rural and urban to all the other countries listed, with the exception of Kenya, where there was a surprising reversal of the situation. This could be due to an active family planning programme, which seemed to have reached more women than in Ghana, Senegal or Uganda. Opinions recorded on these questions are notoriously unreliable, as they can be affected by the respondents' perceptions of the answers expected by the interviewers, especially when they are thought to be Government agents.

Table 10

Some Demographic Indicators in Selected Countries.   1988-1989

Country	Women Married by age 20yrs. %		Total Rate of Fertility 15–49)		Woman wanting no more children %		Women using any contraceptive %	
	Urban	Rural	Urban	Rural	Urban	Rural	Urban	Rural
AFRICA								
Ghana	54.3	68.2	5.03	6.59	28.0	20.6	19.6	9.9
Kenya	47.1	53.2	4.49	6.81	39.6	51.2	30.5	26.2
Togo	45.2	74.9	4.74	7.00	28.9	23.2	32.3	34.5
Senegal	48.7	85.9	5.42	7.02	28.5	14.4	14.2	9.9
Uganda	55.4	75.6	5.55	7.36	20.9	19.3	18.0	3.6
OTHER COUNTRIES								
Sri Lanka	19.4	29.6	2.18	2.84	6.72	6.47	65.0	61.1
Thailand	23.7	42.1	1.63	2.45	64.1	66.2	67.8	65.0
Indonesia	32.5	65.9	2.77	3.53	58.3	48.7	54.3	45.3
Brazil	36.3	49.5	3.09	5.33	66.1	64.0	69.8	56.7
Peru	29.8	51.1	3.13	6.47	69.4	71.0	58.5	24.0

Source: DHS 1994

Another factor in the desire for more children is the infant and child mortality rate, shown in Table 11, which was recorded as higher in Ghana than in Kenya; the Senegal data also suggests a relationship between mortality and the desire for more children, as there was an exceptionally high under 5 years mortality rate in rural areas, which was reflected in only 14.4 per cent of women not wanting any more children. This would bear out the birth survival hypothesis regarding fertility.

Table 11

Breast Feeding and Infant and Child Mortality in Selected Countries 1988-89

Country	Breast-feeding Median no. of months		Infant Mortality per 1,000 live births		Under 5 Mortality per 1,000 of 0-5s	
	Urban	Rural	Urban	Rural	Urban	Rural
AFRICA						
Ghana	18.3	22.2	66.0	86.6	131.0	162.5
Kenya	17.8	19.9	56.7	59.2	88.5	91.6
Togo	20.7	23.8	74.7	87.3	131.7	169.6
Senegal	16.8	20.4	70.1	101.9	137.2	250.3
Uganda	14.6	19.1	103.8	106.2	164.3	189.4
OTHER COUNTRIES						
Sri Lanka	13.9	21.6	34.4	32.2	39.9	42.8
Thailand	5.6	15.8	25.9	40.8	34.3	51.7
Indonesia	20.7	24.0	49.9	83.3	76.1	122.0
Brazil	4.8	6.8	72.9	106.0	84.4	119.6
Peru	11.3	19.0	55.8	106.1	76.5	159.6

Source: DHS 1994

The Ghana data reflect the high value still placed on marriage and children. A survey in 1988 (Institute for Resource Development 1989) found that only 1 per cent of women at 30 years of age had never been married, and that in the previous 10 years the median age of marriage had only increased from 18.0 to 18.5 years. There are educational and social differentials in age at marriage, which, as would be expected, tends to be higher in towns and amongst those with secondary schooling or above. In most traditional areas there is no social role for single women after they leave school. Both men and women continue to desire large families; women in rural areas with no education wanted, on average, at least ten children. This fell to an average of 6.5 children for those with Middle school and 5.2 for those with higher education. Young couples are still urged to have many children. In Akan society a girl used to be told that when she had borne ten children a special ceremony would be arranged in her honour, which included the sacrifice of a sheep. Fortes (1949) wrote that " the fate of a childless woman is reported to be a miserable one" and this still holds true. In rural communities children are still an economic asset, as they assist in farming and other activities from a very early age, and are a support to their parents in old age. When out farming one day in Konkonuru I was asked how many children I had. I realized that in answering "two" I would be pitied. But my questioner kindly remarked: "It must be difficult to feed many children in London as you have no farms".

Although the DHS survey collected data for different regions in Ghana , the numbers in urban areas, other than in Greater Accra, were too small to make meaningful distinctions between rural and urban for fertility indicators. There were, however, significant differences for other indicators in the sample where sufficient numbers made comparisons meaningful.

The literacy of women has proved a significant indicator of fertility and infant and child mortality (Greenstreet 1981). The urban-rural differences in literacy are therefore critical. Particularly relevant is the very low level of women's literacy in the Northern and Upper Region, where infant and child mortality rates are high. In the 1988 survey (DHS 1994) 218.8 out of every child born alive had died by the age of five, whereas in Greater Accra the rate was 95.7:1,000. Literacy , of course, is not the only factor accounting for these differences, but it must be of importance. The maternal and child health indicators, shown in Table 12, also reflect differences between urban and rural areas.

Table 12

Maternal and Child Health in Urban and Rural Areas of Ghana – 1988

Indicator	Urban %	Rural %
DPT* vaccinations 12–23 months	61.3	33.9
Under 5s with diarrhea in last 2 weeks	27.9	26.9
Treated with oral rehydration system	44.1	29.4
Births treated with tetanus toxoid vaccination	81.3	65.3
Professionally assisted births	70.3	28.9

Diptheria, Polio and Tuberculosis

Source: DHS 1994

Public and Social Services.

Turning to the provision of services, of which some are shown in Table 13, the gap between rural and urban areas is clear. The low proportion of the population living in households with electricity, which was only 7.4 per cent for Ghana as a whole in 1988, could largely be accounted for by the complete absence of this service in the majority of villages. Since 1988 efforts have been made in some regions, notably Brong Ahafo and parts of Ashanti, to install electricity, although in most cases the mains supply is to public places rather than to individual households. This limits its usefulness. For example, radios are owned by many village people, but they have to use batteries, which are expensive. As a result they are out of operation for much of the time. When visiting Konkonuru one of the chief requests was for me to bring them spare

Table 13

Socio-Economic Characteristics Of Urban and Rural Areas in Ghana 1988

Region	Literate Women (15-49)		electricity		Households with radio		refrigerator	
	Urban	Rural	Urban	Rural	Urban	Rural	Urban	Rural
All Ghana	63.4	40.5	65.9	7.4	54.8	34.3	21.1	1.6
Western	62.0	35.6	74.0	18.5	38.0	33.6	9.0	2.7
Central	53.5	36.4	44.2	11.9	42.6	40.9	15.5	1.8
Greater Accra	71.3	32.4	80.6	n.a.	59.8	29.4	29.1	n.a.
Eastern	62.4	52.8	55.1	5.5	64.6	42.3	10.7	1.1
Volta	49.5	49.4	25.2	1.3	36.4	35.9	8.4	0.5
Ashanti	65.1	52.5	80.1	11.7	64.7	35.2	32.5	4.0
Brong Ahafo	68.9	42.3	44.5	3.7	39.5	27.6	6.7	0.0
Northern & Upper	29.4	9.8	48.5	3.4	51.5	24.3	10.3	0.9

Numbers of women aged 15–49 in sample for Ghana as a whole: Urban 1523

Rural 2965

Total 4488

Source: DHS 1994

batteries. Much of the desire for electricity is thus unsatisfied. Rural people, these days, know of its benefits, and that it is readily available in towns. However, except in specially designated areas, they are told that they will themselves have to make a substantial contribution to the cost of installation. In Konkonuru they have been wrestling with this problem for many years, as mentioned in Chapter 1.

The effects of the years of recession in Ghana were particularly severe for women and children. A situation analysis in 1989–1990 (Republic of Ghana & UN Children's Fund 1990) found that in 1986 the per capita calorie intake of pre-schoolchildren was only 40–70 per cent of their requirements. Twice as many children than in a sample in 1961–1962 fell below the weight for age standards. No detailed analysis was given of urban/rural differences, but an IFAD study, made in 1988 was quoted, which had found that 3.8 million smallholders fell below the poverty line threshold, whereas in 1970 this had only applied to 1.95 million. The trough came in 1983, and non-cocoa producers were the most disadvantaged group. But since 1983 overall output in Ghana has increased by 4.5 per cent per annum; after taking population growth of approximately 3 per cent into account this amounts to a per capita increase of 1.5 per cent.

A measure of relative poverty (Abbey 1996, pers. com.), using a classification of the poor as those with a consumption of less than 2/3 of the national average and the very poor as those with less than half the national average, indicated that between 1988 and 1991–1992 there had been some alleviation of poverty. On this basis in 1983 37 per cent of the population were classified as poor and 22 percent as very poor; in 1991–1992 the figure for poor fell to 32 per cent and for very poor to 15 per cent. Since then there are worrying signs that the position may not have improved, as inflation in 1994 once again began to accelerate, public debt was rising and domestic debt accounted for 15 per cent of GDP (Abbey 1996, pers. com.). The measure of poverty referred to above found that rural poverty had decreased more than urban poverty. In Accra especially, there had been a rise in the overall figure of those below the poverty line. Another finding concerned the incidence of poverty in relation to the gender of household heads. Those living in female headed households were more likely to suffer from poverty, although during the period 1988–1992 their position had improved to a greater extent than that of male headed households. Much more information is needed on this subject in order to assess the present situation.

My own observations in 1990 of rural communities in Ashanti and Akwapim suggested that standards of living in villages were certainly no worse, and in many cases better, than in the poorer districts in towns. There was a great advantage in being able to produce food for the family when market prices were high, and surpluses for sale could bring good returns. So that except in those areas which had suffered badly from drought, the lot of rural people compared favourably with their counterparts in towns.

The case of Konkonuru, which is described in the following chapters, provides an illustration of how the economic situation in Ghana has affected rural communities. For example, the greater decrease in rural, as against urban poverty may to some extent be due to the return of able-bodied men to their rural home towns. One of the striking features of the comparison between the household censuses taken in Konkonuru in 1970 and 1990 was the significant shift in the proportion of males in the over 18 years age group. In 1970 it accounted for only 36 per cent of over 18 year olds, whereas in 1990 the figure had risen to 43 per cent. Moreover, many more of these men who had returned, by now in their forties, had received formal education up to Middle School level, and had experience of living in urban environments. They were more conscious of the need to improve conditions in their home towns.

Chapter 3

THE HISTORY OF KONKONURU

The people of Konkonuru attach great importance to the history of their home town. Despite the effects of socio-economic change Konkonuru is still a close community, bound by traditional values of kinship, and they take great pride in their senior position in the Akwapim traditional area or paramountcy.

The National Archives in Accra contained few references to Konkonuru, and all of those that existed were connected with the Aburi stool. The Colonial Government evidently experienced a lot of trouble with the Aburi Chief (the Akwapim Adontenhene). The first record was in a report written in 1910 by the District Commissioner, saying that Chief Djan (who had been enstooled on 9 July 1886) had been a continual source of trouble, that he would not co-operate with the Government, for example, in cleaning the roads. Chief Djan died in 1918 and was succeeded by Osae Mensah, who was enstooled in 1919. Osae Mensah's mother came from Konkonuru and he was born there. The installation was reported to the Assistant District Commissioner by five signatories, including Addo Kwaku, at that time Odikro (Chief) of Konkonuru. Addo Kwaku had already been mentioned on 6 December 1917 as Odikro in a document from the Abrade family (probably a reference to the Abrade abusua, or clan), concerning a meeting held to consider the sale of Abrade land for the building of the Nsawam road. It said that Addo Kwaku was not present at the meeting because of sickness.

Between 1923-25 trouble blew up again, but the Colonial Government was reluctant to intervene. A letter dated 16 November 1923 referring to the destooling of Osae Mensah on 31 August 1923 was sent to the Governor of the Gold Coast by "members of the Abrade Stool Family residing at Nsakye, Konkonuru, Agyemanti and Aburi", objecting to what they called the "illegal" destoolment by the Omanhene (King) of Akwapim. A reply from the Governor, dated 4 January 1924, said that he had confirmed the destoolment and that he considered "them ill-advised in carrying their grievances to a court of law". It was a case that caused much feeling. Osae Mensah had been charged by the police for indecent assault on a young girl and had been sentenced in the civil court to three months hard labour. A minority of the Oman (the Council of the Omanhene), three out of sixteen members, did not consider that he should have been destooled on this account.

A Police Report in 1925 recorded that a coroner's jury at Accra found that "the death of Osae Mensah II (late Ohene of the Aburi Stool) was caused, on or about 14 May 1925, by strangulation caused by hanging himself to a tree by a rag at Kun Kunu in the Akwapim District". He was buried at Agymanti.

As late as 1945 a report by the District Commissioner refers to continuing "internal difficulties in the political relationship of the Akwapim". Some reference to these difficulties had already been made in a report of the Commonwealth Council, at Aburi in 1937, in which it was said that 33 years of litigation between the Asona and the Agona clans had finally been settled. The Commonwealth Council had been set up in 1927 as the successor to the Aburi- Nsawam Road Committee. There is no record of membership and my informants in Konkonuru had no recollection of its activities. Most of its work, apart from the completion of the Nsawam road, seemed to centre on the improvement of Aburi itself rather than the surrounding villages.

The Akwapim Handbook (Brokensha 1972), for which the material was collected in the 1960's, was an ambitious undertaking, the result of a suggestion by Thomas Hodgkin, at that time the Director of the Institute of African Studies at the University of Ghana.

At that time several members of the University were engaged in research in Akwapim, which had attracted scholars from different disciplines. The Handbook proved to be a formidable task, so it took many years to produce. In many cases the writers were in the middle of their research, so it was decided that it would be better to wait until they could produce fairly comprehensive accounts. The five main sections dealt with ecology, history, society, economy, and recent developments, and there were several chapters under each of these headings. The Handbook as a whole has provided useful background to this study, although the only reference to Konkonuru is in Appendix XVI., where it is included in the statistical data for 1968. This data was collected by K. Asare Opoku of the Institute of African Studies. Although it is now over twenty years since this material was collected, there is little to replace it, as there has not been much recent research in this area.

So the history of Konkonuru related here is based on what was told to me by the elders. It was only after I had spent many months in Konkonuru that it was decided, quite suddenly one day, that I should be entrusted with this information. But when later I asked the Gyasehene whether I could include it in the story of Konkonuru he generously agreed. It should perhaps be mentioned at this point that the Chief, the elders and all the people of Konkonuru were very keen that their story should be told. They felt that far too little attention was paid to the situation of the rural citizens of the country. As is inevitable in the absence of written documents it is a mixture of recalled historical events and myth. Dates are notoriously difficult to establish and are not considered of much importance by the people. As in the Bible's "forty days and forty nights" specified times are used to signify long or short durations, and the actual figures have little significance. In oral tradition all that is carried on is carried on in memory; there are no records. This means that oral culture cannot and does not demand the kind of consistency that literacy permits. As Goody (1977) says "write down a sentence and it is there, in principle, for ever, and that means if you write down another sentence inconsistent with it you can be caught out."

Origins of the Settlement

Konkonuru was founded at a time of considerable movements amongst Akan speaking people, as is described later in this chapter. This is reflected in the account given to me by the elders. According to them it was founded by Nana Takyi Aprokyewah of the Abrade *abusua* (clan), who at that time was living at Aburiamanfo, a village on the hills to the north of the Aburi-Nsawam road. Konokonuru lies on the hills to the south of this road; the distance through the forest between Aburiamanfo and Konkonuru is about eight miles, and close ties are still maintained between the two communities, as I found on my visit to Aburiamanfo.

Nana Takyi Aprokyewah had originally come from Nyanawase and before that from Akwamu, which is in another district some distance from Akwapim (see Map, Fig. 2). He was out one day on a hunting expedition in the forest when he killed an elephant in the area known as Kokoduru. At the time the forest was not owned by anyone, but came under the jurisdiction of the chief at Aburi. It was the custom that anyone who killed an elephant, and buried it in a deep hole where it was killed, had a right to the surrounding land, and this frequently is given as an explanation of the way in which acquisitions were made and later confirmed by the paramount chief of the area. At the time of these settlements there was much unclaimed land in the forests, so that there was plenty of scope for migration of those who for one reason or another wanted to leave their place of origin.

After his successful hunting expedition Nana Takyi Aprokyewah went back to Aburiamanfo to fetch his wife and he told her to come and live with him at the place where the elephant had been killed; this she did and together they built a hut in which to keep their belongings on the site of what is now one of the present cemeteries of the Abrade clan. The place is known as Amanfo meaning "the House that was washed away ". After a few years he discovered the spring "obo Kofi"; *obo* means stone and Kofi is the day-name for Friday. The spring gushes out of a large slab of rock at the bottom of a hill covered thickly with forest. Because it was found on a Friday he dedicated it to the god of that name-day, so he moved his dwelling nearer to the spring, building

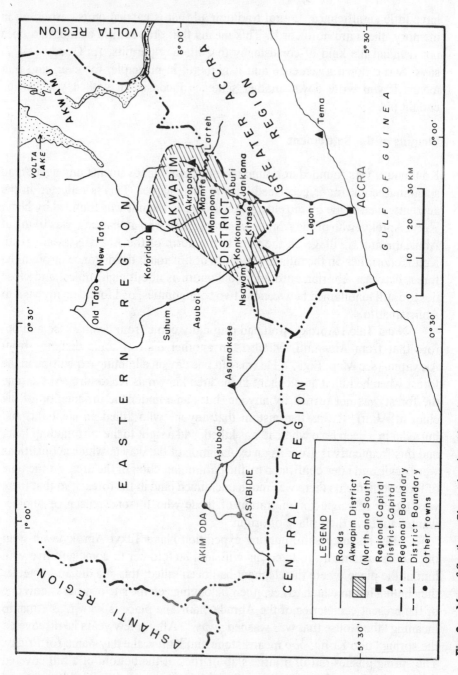

Fig. 2:   Map of Southern Ghana showing Akwapim

himself a house on a site above the present Osofo shrine. This is where he spent the rest of his life.

Meanwhile his family had grown in size and he had been joined by relatives. There was some friction between the settlers, and his sister's son, Obuobi, who later became chief, moved to the site by the lower cemetery and built his house where an *onya* tree (a silk cotton tree) now stands. Another settler, Anokoma, built a hut beyond Obo Kofi, but these sites were abandoned after the deaths of those who founded them and their children moved to the present site of Konkonuru in the vicinity of where Nana Takyi Aprokyewah had finally built his house, and this is certainly the oldest part of the town. Although in the telling of this history great importance was attached to the successive moves and locations of their forebears all these sites are really in quite close proximity.

At the time of Konkonuru's founding there was thick forest all around the settlement, full of evil spirits and wild animals, which made it difficult for strangers to enter. Anyone who came to the settlement and returned to his home safely was, therefore, considered to be a valiant person (Kokoduru means valiant in Twi), hence the original name of the settlement, which is now known as Konkonuru. According to the elders the name was not changed deliberately but gradually as a result of usage, as Konkonuru is easier to say than Kokoduru.

These events according to the elders, happened a very long time ago, at least 300 years, perhaps even 1,000 years. It is, however, safe to assume that the settlement was made after the battle of Aburi in 1733, as it was shortly before this that Ansa Sasriku, Chief of the Akwamu, came to Akwapim on his campaigns. It was only after his downfall at the battle of Aburi that the Aburi Stool went to the Abrade clan, the first settlers in Aburi having been Agona.

Since Nana Takyi Aprokyewah there had in 1971, according to the elders, been five chiefs:

Obuobi
Addo Kwaku I
Yaw Anofo
Obeng Kwaku
Addo Mensah II – known as Gyasehene Bediako

Gyasehene Bediako died on 15 August 1989 and was succeeded by Addo Mensah III.

The elders explained that the small number of chiefs recorded was because "in the olden days people lived a very long time, up to two hundred years; they just got very old and curled up in baskets like cats and went on and on and on and on... Nowadays they die much younger, perhaps because there are too many people, and one elder jokingly remarked, because they drink akpeteshie, which was not known in those days." Akpeteshie distilling was started in the town by Yaw Mensah before the time that any of the present elders can remember. "It was a long time ago," they say. Later the Colonial Government made it illegal to distil akpeteshie so the stills were hidden in the forest; now it is legal under licence and the first building one sees on entering the town is the distillery.

The only relevant references in District records are for the years between 1917–1923, which mention Addo Kwaku I as being on the Konkonuru stool. As he was very old when he died it is possible that he had been on the stool for 40 years before these dates, but no evidence can be found in the archives. Even if Obuobi and Nana Takyi Aprokyewah had each ruled for 40 years this would only date the settlement to the beginning of the 19th century, unless there were other chiefs whose names have been forgotten. Nana Owuku Denkyera II, the Mankrado of Aburi in 1971 when I spoke to him, considered that Konkonuru was not much more than 100 years old. He traced his own line of succession back to the Aburi war of 1733, and he was the 15th in line since that time. In smaller settlements, however, it is quite usual for there to be a gap in recall between the founding fathers and later chiefs.

The Akwapim State

Before looking at Konkonuru's position in the Akwapim State today it is necessary to know something about the history and political structure of this State. It was established as a State in 1733 after the Aburi war, in which the Akwamu were defeated. The history of the period before 1730 when Akwapim first became a political unit is confused. Previously it was thought that there was no Akan influence on the ridge, but recent research suggests that it is possible that a Twi speaking stool, either of Akim or Akwamu origin had been founded before 1730, perhaps by the middle of the seventeenth century.

Between 1680 and 1730 Akwamu power was unchallenged on the Accra plain and they were constantly engaged in wars with the surrounding peoples. During the latter part of this period they established their capital at Nyanawase and virtually ruled over the Akwapim ridge, as well as over the greater part of the Kwahu scarp and the left bank of the Birim river. But the Akim, another Akan group, were pressing down from the north-west and by 1700 were competing for ownership of the Pra and Birim valleys; they were joined in their opposition to the Akwamu by Fante groups, the Ga of Accra, the Guan and Kyerepon of the Akwapim ridge, and even by the Dutch from Crevecoeur, a fort on the coast. It was as a result of the part played in this campaign by the Akwapim that a separate Akan State (Akwapim) was founded after the Aburi war in 1733, sponsored by the then ruler of the Akim Abuakwa, Nana Odokyi, who was himself killed in the war. The royal lineage of Akim Abuakwa was of the Asona clan and as it was the Asona who were considered to have been the chief victors this determined the structure of the new Akwapim State. The Omanhene, paramount chief of the state, was, therefore, an Asona and established his capital at Akropong, which is some miles north of Aburi (Konkonuru is about three miles south of Aburi through forest paths, but considerably further if approached by the main Accra-Aburi road to Jankama and thence by the dirt road to the settlement). The organization of the State was on the Akan military pattern, divided into wings. The second in command, the Adontenhene, appointed from the Abrade clan, with his stool at Aburi, held delegated responsibility for affairs in the Aburi District. The commander of the left flank, the Benkumhene, was a Larteh and came from the patrilineal Guan peoples (Kwamena Poh 1972), and the commander of the right flank, the Nifahene, was at Adukrom. This pattern has been maintained to this day, and still operates in the traditional sector of the society. The Adontenhene at Aburi has his own second in command, the Mankrado, or Osomanyawa, who is of the Asona Clan, and his own Gyasehene, or head of the royal household, who is an Abrade like himself, and in 1971 was the chief of Konkonuru, Nana Bediako or Addo Mensah II, which was his stool name. The Gyasehene is an important person among the electors of the Adontenhene and has command of the paraphernalia of the ruling dynasty. Nana Bediako, at that time, made frequent visits to Aburi in fulfillment of his duties.

Although the main features of the traditional structure of Akwapim are still maintained some further developments took place in 1994, which have affected the status of Konkonuru. There are now four paramountcies. The first is still at Akropong, headed by Nana Addo-Dankwa II. The seat of the Nifa (Right Wing) Division has become the Okere Paramountcy, headed by Nana Asiedu Okoo II. Aburi, which was the seat of the Adonten Division, is now the seat of the Akuapem Anafo Paramountcy, and is headed by Nana Djan Kwasi II. Konkonuru still maintains its Gyasehene status, but has been elevated to the status of a wing. This means that the present chief of Konkonuru is now among the seven most senior chiefs of the Akuapem Anafo Traditional Area or Paramountcy. Such details may seem unimportant at a time when traditional leaders do not exercise political power. They are, however, still of great significance to the people themselves not only because they retain a fierce pride in their home towns, but also on account of the considerable role that traditional leaders play in settling disputes within their communities and generally maintaining law and order in the virtual absence of police in many rural areas.

Until the establishment of the Akwapim State there was a great deal of movement of tribes in this area, often as a result of conquest. For a time, in the 17th and early eighteenth centuries, guerilla war was waged in the hills and there was a general lack of unity, which to some extent continued after the foundation of the Akwapim State. As Kwamenah-Poh (1972) points out, the Akwapim State was composed of different groups with individual characteristics, which kept their own stories of origin, customs and beliefs. Moreover as Wilks (1964) has shown, "the nineteenth century account of Akwapim origins (recorded by Reindorf with the help of his close associate, Christaller) has been reabsorbed into local tradition in present day Akuapem (so that) there appears to be no surviving corpus of traditional historical lore that is independent of the influence of the nineteenth century historiography."

The original occupants of Akwapim are considered to have been Guan communities which had arrived in the hills from the coastal plain by the beginning of the seventeenth century, probably as a result of various pressures from the Akwamu and Ga people. Later Twi speaking people arrived on the ridge and gradually gained power. The Akan peoples of Akwamu and Akim were better armed than the Guans and had a more highly organized political system, which comprised the concepts of centralization and territorial and secular leadership. They did not, however, alter the inheritance and succession patterns of the Guans, which remains patrilineal, even though some of the communities changed to Twi speaking in the late eighteenth century. It has already been mentioned that the people of Larteh have retained a patrilineal system and this is also the case in some other areas of Akwapim. It is a significant factor in considering the present operation of patterns of inheritance and succession in the area as a whole, as the close proximity of the two systems may have had its own influence, quite apart from the effects of socio-economic change.

Foreign Rulers, Missionaries and Cocoa

Shortly after the formation of the State in 1733 hostile relations developed with the Ashanti. By 1742 Akwapim was brought under the suzerainty of the Asantehene and was forced to accept an Asante resident who was stationed at Mamfe. A Dane, Dr. Isert, who visited the ridge in 1786, remarks on this; Dr. Isert's visit appears to have been a result of Akwapim's alliance with the Danes in the campaign against the Anlo in 1784, an alliance which lasted until 1835 when the Danes refused help against the Krobo. Already by this time the British had begun to seek Akwapim help against the Ashanti, and at the battle of Akantamansu, near Dodowa, in 1826 they had played an important part in the Ashanti defeat and as a result gained their independence, which was confirmed in the Treaty of 1831. This independence, however, only lasted until 1850 when the Akwapim State was made part of the British colony of the Gold Coast, although the British did not really exercise full jurisdiction over the area until the end of the nineteenth century (Ward 1967). In the meantime, much of the peace and security that was achieved in Akwapim was due to the Christian Mission (Arhin 1968).

Akwapim was one of the first inland areas to be significantly influenced from overseas. One reason for this was its relationship with the Danes in their opposition to other tribes. But a greater permanent influence was that of the missionaries, who first arrived in Akwapim in 1835, having abandoned their mission station on the coast because of sickness and death (Smith 1966). The first Basel missionary was Andreas Riis, who established a mission at Akropong. In 1847 a second station was opened at Aburi. The missions not only spread the gospel and provided Western-style education; also, as the result particularly of the work of Widmann, Christaller and Zimmerman, they developed Twi and Ga as written languages and produced primers, dictionaries and translations of the Bible (Christaller 1881). These dictionaries are still used to-day. The high standard of literacy in Akwapim, at an earlier date than in most of the rest of Ghana, was a legacy of the Missionary Societies. Not only has Akwapim produced many teachers, but also the Civil Service owed much to scholars from this State.

The missionaries also encouraged the growing of new crops The most important of these was cocoa, which they were responsible for introducing to Akwapim; other crops introduced included avocado pear and coffee. They taught the people how to build in stone. Converts moved to new houses round the missions and these parts of the town are still known as Salem; they are distinguished by the continued existence of many of the houses built at that time. They also established workshops for blacksmiths, locksmiths, wheelwrights, carpenters and other artisans. Another significant contribution to the social, economic and political development of Akwapim was the construction of roads. In 1861 the Basel Mission built a road from Accra to Akropong. In 1877 the construction of the Accra-Aburi road was started, to be completed in 1880. The amount of £300 was voted for its maintenance by the Colonial Government, in order to facilitate the flow of trade, particularly in palm oil. In 1891 a telegraph line reached Aburi from Accra. Aburi had become an important centre as a result of the establishment of the Botanical Gardens, where cocoa was being developed as a new cash crop.

The missionaries' influence on traditional culture is more difficult to assess as there have been, since then,many other influences which have impinged on an area which is so close to the capital city and the original centre of production of the cash crop of cocoa. But it is significant that in Aburi the traditional matrilineal patterns of inheritance have been modified to a greater extent than in most Akan communities, although these modifications have not been applied to the rules of succession.

The coming of cocoa was an important historical event. It led to an economic revolution unprecedented in the history of Ghana, and brought with it many social and political consequences. These consequences began to appear in Akwapim before the end of the nineteenth century. It led to the intensification of migration into many new areas. The achievement of these migrant farmers was not recognized in the literature until the 1960's (Hill 1963, Johnson 1972), earlier writers assuming that the great increase in cocoa production had resulted from the initiative of non-migrant farmers who introduced this crop into their food farms. Later research has shown that by 1911, when the Gold Coast became the world's largest cocoa exporter, most of the cocoa was grown by migrant farmers, who had acquired land away from their home towns.

It was fortunate for the Akwapim farmers that the chiefs who had areas of uninhabited forests within their territories were willing to sell parcels of undeveloped land to strangers. They regarded the cash as a welcome windfall, and were even prepared to accept payment in instalments. This was a great advantage to the cocoa farmers, as it took some years before they could realize profits from their crops. Moreover the terms of the agreements meant that they enjoyed complete security of tenure, sustainable in the courts, provided that the traditional "guaha" ceremony had been performed. This made long term planning possible and gave them freedom to sell their land.

Konkonuru's position in the Akwapim State

Konkonuru was, as already mentioned, most probably established shortly after the Aburi war. As far as its people are concerned they have Akan origins and have always adhered to matrilineal patterns. Any deviations from strictly matrilineal observances are more likely to be due to outside contacts than to questions of origin. This is a boundary area between patrilineal and matrilineal societies and in addition there are the factors of foreign influence mentioned above As they trace their forebears to Nyanawase, and the ruling lineage is Abrade, it is probable that they originally came from Akwamu. Acknowledged descendants of the Akwamu do hold an important position in the Akwapim State, despite the defeat of their leaders. This is put down to the defection of

Ansa Sasriku's chief priest, Oppong Tin Tin, at the time of the Aburi war. He turned against his leader and went over to the opposing side, together with his messengers and some soldiers and as a result of this action became the first Adontenhene to the new Akwapim State and was given the Aburi stool.

As the Konkonuru royal lineage is it also Abrade, along with the other Abrade towns of Nsakyi and Agyamenti, plays an important role in the Aburi district, particularly in the election of the Adontenhene. The chief kingmaker in 1971 came from Konkonuru, but then lived at Amanfro. The Adontenhene in 1971, Nana Osae Djan, who died in 1974, came from Agyamenti, but because of his position he was buried at Nsakyi when he died. Nana Osae Djan was succeeded by Ntiful II. He abdicated in 1983 and was replaced by Nana Djan Kwasi II. Konkonuru is the biggest of these three Abrade towns and has grown in importance since its foundation, in recognition of which Addo Mensah II was made Gyasehene to the Aburi stool in the late 1960s. As such he was in constant touch with the Adontenhene, frequently travelling to Aburi to take part in meetings to discuss local affairs. No representative of Konkonuru has ever sat on the Akwapim State Council at Akropong, so its sphere of influence is very much confined to the Aburi district, and in conversations one rarely hears Akropong or the Omanhene mentioned. However, as a result of the recent developments, described above, Konkonuru now occupies an even more important position in the Adonten Division.

The *Odwira* (Yam Harvest) festival which takes place in September or October is the time when the people of the Aburi division really get together and when migrant citizens, at least in theory, return to their home towns. The ceremonies last for a week, each day being devoted to a special function, culminating in a procession through Aburi and a durbar outside the Ahenfie (house of the Adontenhene). Konkonuru has played an important part in these ceremonies. As the festival is still celebrated today it might seem more appropriate to deal with it in the next chapter. But the description given here, told to me in Konkonuru, was historical in so far as it was what traditionally was supposed to happen. By 1971 there had already been modifications in practice, and recent accounts given to me by my informants record even greater changes.

The description given to me in Konkonuru differs in certain respects from the account given by Opoku (1970) in *Festivals of Ghana*, but the main features are the same. Opoku's description is based on the capital at Akropong, and he says that other centres have their own versions. He describes Wednesday as a day of mourning, on which all keep a fast and mourn for the dead, particularly for those that have died during the previous year. It is the time to observe funeral rites for anyone whose death occurred during the ban on celebrations lasting 40 days before Odwira. He does not mention the preparation of food on this day as is found in the Konkonuru account where there is no reference to mourning on that day.

In Konkonuru, on the first day of the festival, a Monday, the Asafohene and his brothers carry firewood to the Adontenhene's house at Aburi. That evening, from about five o'clock onwards, all the villages in the District begin to fire guns in memory of their ancestors. During the day, members of the Abrade clan have been to the secret hiding place by the Nsakyi river where the Aburi stool is kept. This is within Konkonuru's boundaries. Libation is poured and sheep are slaughtered.

On the second day the women cry and sing traditional songs. Meanwhile the stool is being brought by men of the Abrade clan towards Aburi; on the way songs are sung, guns are fired, bells are rung and horns are blown. The chief horn is said to have been captured at the time of the Akwapim war with the Anums, and the man responsible for its capture, Kwame Wontumi, came from Konkonuru. As the procession approaches Konkonuru from Nsakyi it stops at the cemetery on the outskirts of the town for some minutes, while libation is poured and guns are fired. It then proceeds into Konkonuru to the house of the lineage head of the Abrade abusua (clan), which in 1971 was Obeng Kwaku, who lived near the Osofo shrine. There everybody rests for some hours. The Gyasehene and his executives come to take their share of the mashed yam and when they have finished eating the procession continues on its way to Aburi through bush paths, a distance of about three miles. Those who are carrying the stool arm themselves with a bronze sword. On leaving Konkonuru they stop at a special place in the forest to pour libation. It was at this spot a long time ago that members of the Abrade clan organized themselves into a union called *Nkabom* and the surrounding land is still known as Abom. From Abom they go straight to the Adontenhene's *ahenfie*, the chief's house at Aburi. All day long the Adontenhene has been unwilling to eat, waiting for the arrival of the stool and the mashed yam. He now eats it in company with his executives.

The third day of Odwira is spent in the domestic circle. Every household prepares food for itself. Goats, chickens and sheep are slaughtered to provide a special feast for the family the following day. It was on this day that Opoku mentioned mourning for the dead, but there was no reference to this in the Konkonuru account, although one would have expected that some such ceremony would form a part of this festival, particularly in the domestic circle where so much importance is given to these events.

The fourth day, Thursday, is a day of gaiety and feasting. Everyone puts on new clothes, friends are visited and there is much singing and dancing. This is a day thoroughly enjoyed by all.

On the fifth day the Adontenhene sits in state for his people to pay tribute to him. People come to Aburi from all the surrounding villages in the division and a grand durbar is held. The style this takes varies from year to year. In 1968, to celebrate the fortieth anniversary of Osae Djan's succession to the stool, it was a particularly grand occasion. All the chiefs rode in palanquins, followed by their retinues, many of which included bands of drummers, singers and dancers (Fig. 3). A special cloth was commissioned by the Adontenhene which was worn by all the women of his household and other members of his kinship network. But whatever the form, the intention is the same, to honour their leader, to listen to what he has to say to them, and to meet together to establish their solidarity. So the fifth day is the culmination of the traditional ceremonies.

Fig. 3: Nana Addo Mensah II sits in palanquin

The next day, Saturday, is spent in secular recreations, with sports and frequently a dance in Aburi. The town is crowded with people, everybody meets friends and relations, many of whom have returned especially for Odwira. It is a colourful, bustling scene, the streets thronged with chattering people.

On Sunday the Adontenhene and his people attend a church service to the Christian God for looking after them. It is not clear as to when this innovation was introduced. Osae Djan was a professed Christian, but this was only the case for a minority of chiefs in his division. Aburi, as the centre of missionary activities in this area, has been much more influenced by Christianity than the surrounding villages, even though geographically they are not far apart.

Adae butto is another important traditional ceremony when honour is paid to the ancestors. Proceedings start early in the day at the houses of the "original" individual clan abusua panin (clan heads). They continue by all the clans meeting at the house of the "original abusua panin of the Abrade, and this is a much more formal occasion, when all the priests are in attendance, although they do not take such an active part in the conduct of the ceremony at this stage as they do later. Long speeches are delivered, a sheep is ritually slaughtered, there is much drumming and pouring of libations to the ancestors. Later in the day another ceremony is performed at the chief priest's house, next to the Osofo shrine and this is followed by festivities in which all the people take part, the drumming and dancing continuing until the late afternoon, after which the elders retire to the Gyasehene's house.

Adae butto is a time for remembering the ancestors and is not normally an occasion for settling family disputes, as there is a special day set aside during the Odwira festival for this purpose, the one spent in the domestic circle. When I attended the ceremony in 1972 a heated argument arose in the middle of the proceedings at the Abrade abusua panin's house, but this is evidently unusual, and most of the elders were at pains to prevent the ceremony being used in this way.

There are also ceremonies held at the Osofo shrine for Obo Kofi, the name of the spring which is the main source of water. These are always held on a Friday, the name day of the spring and are conducted by the chief priest and his assistants.

Konkonuru has also been renowned for its traditional doctors, whose skills have been passed down from father to son, not in the matrilineal line of succession. The first remembered doctor was called Obuobi, not to be confused with the chief of the same name, he was succeeded by Kofi Yeboah, the father of the present doctor, and when he died one of his other sons, Kofi Ntow, took his place. When he died his brother, Kwasi Osae succeeded and he has practised until recently. He has now handed over his responsibilities to his son, Isaac Ohene Osae, who has recently been licensed as a herbal physician. Obuobi's fame was widespread and patients came to him from far afield, directed by a sign on the main Accra-Aburi road which pointed to the town. This was pulled down some years ago and has not been replaced. Kwasi Osae also had a high reputation in Konkonuru, but fewer of his patients came from outside the town, although many migrant citizens returned for treatment and testified to his success. He was helped by up to ten assistants and these were apparently young men who wanted to learn his skills and whom he was prepared to accept, without there necessarily being any kinship connection. This marked a departure from past practices.

Missionaries in Konkonuru

The Basel Mission never directly extended its influence to Konkonuru, but a Methodist Mission was set up in the 1890s, connected with the Methodist Training College at Aburi (Bartels 1965). This college was built on the south side of Aburi and was a rival to the Basel Mission built earlier on the north side. Students from the Training college used to visit surrounding villages to preach the gospel and to conduct services on Sundays, and once a congregation had been established, a catechist would be appointed from one of the village church members. So although in the 1890s a mission house was built in Konkonuru and later a chapel, there was never a resident missionary from outside the town. The first chapel was made of bamboo and palm fronds, but in about 1918 a swish building was constructed on a flat site near the top of the town and this was used until 1930 when it collapsed in a big storm. It has never been replaced and Sunday services are now held in the Primary School. The mission house, a small two-roomed swish building, later became the top form classroom and headmaster's room of the Middle School, but it is still used by the Methodist congregation for evening prayers and hymn singing.

The catechist at the time of the first household survey was E. K. Owusu who had succeeded his wofa (maternal uncle, or mother's brother), Moses Addo, a man, by all accounts, of outstanding personality, who did a great deal for the development of the town. It was in his time that the present Primary School building was built with the help of Community Development, and a Henderson Box was made to conserve the waters of the spring. E. K.Owusu attended the Primary School in the town, which had already been started by the Methodist Mission and is still denominational. He left school in 1918, a date he remembered well as it was the year of the great influenza epidemic which caused many deaths in the town. Later he attended Wesley College at Kumasi and on returning to Konkonuru he assisted his uncle, Moses Addo. E. K.Owusu died in 1983.

The church has a considerable following in Konkonuru, mostly of women and children. The traditional leaders in 1971, with one or two exceptions, were not Christians, although many of their wives were active members of the women's choir. At Christian festivals there was an attendance of between 200–

300 at services and on most evenings there were prayer meetings or choir practices. All the school teachers were Methodists and a good deal of emphasis was put on Christianity in the school curriculum. All children attending school were given "Christian" names which tended to be used for day to day purposes rather than their tribal names. Religion did not seem to be a cause of contention in the community, although some of the stauncher members of the church complained about what they regarded as "heathen practices", and were worried that the influence of the church on behaviour patterns was not greater. However, I never heard the traditional leaders complain about the influence of the church in eroding their customs, perhaps because most members continued to take part in traditional ceremonies.

As Appiah (1992: 218) says

> Most Africans now, whether converted to Islam or Christianity or not, still share the beliefs of their ancestors in an ortology of invisible beings. God can be addressed in different styles – Methodist, Catholic, Anglican, Moslem, Traditional and the ancestors can be addressed also.

Details about any theological issues are unimportant; that is a theoretical question, and theory is unimportant when the practical issue is getting God on your side. After all who needs a theory about who it is that you are talking to if you hear a voice speak? Appiah cites the case of his sister's wedding celebrations, when the celebrants included Methodist, Catholic, Anglican clergy and the Ashanti king's linguist poured the libation.

Cocoa in Konkonuru

The introduction of cocoa to Ghana has been well documented, as has the effect this had on Akwapim. Not only were the Akwapim farmers the first to plant cocoa, but the success of their enterprise led them to migrate in the search for lands on which to establish new farms (Hill 1963). In the early years the most adventurous of all Akwapim cocoa farmers were those of Aburi and its associate towns. Later, the advent of swollen shoot disease in the old plantations made this migration even more imperative. Cocoa was introduced into Konkonuru by "Nana" Toa, who first planted trees, on a site which is now part of the town, at the time of Tetteh Quarshie of Mampong, who is acknowledged as having introduced cocoa farming to Akwapim. At the time of Addo Mensah's (the chief in 1971) grandfather, which would be in the early twentieth century at the latest,the richer farmers of Konkonuru started to buy land for farms in other places, first at Asuboi, near Nsawam, from the chief of Kibi. These were family farms and are still worked as such, but nowadays more people, if they have money, tend to buy land for private farms so that they can transmit them to their own children. Chapter 6 looks at this subject in greater detail.

This outline gives some idea of the history of Konkonuru as seen by the people themselves, set in the wider context of the Akwapim State. The account given has been pieced together from informants in Konkonuru and Aburi, and in some cases there was a lack of consensus in the description of events; this was particularly true of the role allegedly played by different clans in the Aburi war, where, for example, the then abusua panin of the Agona clan in Aburi considered that his clan played a more crucial part than was conceded by the then head of the Asona clan, who was Mankrado to the Aburi stool. To the people of Konkonuru their history is an integral part of their pride in their home town, and affects relationships between members of the community. Allegiance to their traditional leaders and to the Adontenhene is still of importance to them, even though ultimate political power has, of course, passed to the Government of Ghana. It helps to explain the continued influence exercised by chiefs in rural areas, not only in ritual matters but in many other aspects of life. To what extent some of this influence is being eroded will be discussed more fully in subsequent chapters.

Chapter 4

KONKONURU TODAY

Although classified for census purposes as a village, the people of Konkonuru always refer to it as a town, and it will be so described from now on. *Kurom* is used in Twi for all except very small hamlets, and its translation as village is therefore not acceptable to the people. With a resident population of over 1,000 it is among the larger rural settlements in Ghana, even for the Eastern Region where the average size is greater than for the country as a whole (see Table 14)

Table 14

Structure of Rural Settlements

Population	Eastern Region	Whole of Ghana
	%	%
Under 100 population	60.7	67.9
100 – 500	30.1	23.6
500 – 1,000	4.5	5.0
1,000 – 2,000	3.0	2.6
2,000 – 5,000	1.7	0.9
	100.0	100

Source: "A Socio-Economic Survey". Eastern Region, Rural Planning Department, Accra. March 1970.

This information has not been updated since this survey, and as the rural population of Ghana as a whole has grown the proportion living in larger settlements has probably increased. The 1984 census (Republic of Ghana 1984) showed that not only had there been an absolute, but also a relative increase in the numbers living in settlements of less than 5,000 population. If these figures are accurate they have significant implications, which will be discussed later.

Approached along the dirt road from Jankama, which is on the main Accra-Aburi road, Konkonuru appears as a substantial settlement, lying on the slope of a hill, showing some orderliness in its layout. The town lies on the 1100 foot contour, but the five miles square, or so, of land belonging to the community ranges in altitude from just over 1300 feet to about 400 feet above sea level, the lowest part lying at the bottom of the scarp slope on the western border. The only motorable road within its boundaries leaves the main road at Jankama, at a height of about 1200 feet above sea level, winds steeply down into the little valley of the Ntare river, about 250 feet lower, and then climbs again some 150 feet to Konkonuru. Although somewhat improved since 1970 it is still only a dirt road and it is liable to become impassable for vehicles in the rainy season, with its slippery, rutted surface on the steep Jankama side and its wet, sandy stretch from the Ntare river to Konkonuru.

The hilly country is a beautiful place in which to live, with a far pleasanter climate than on the plains. In 1970 the area was well stocked with forest trees, some of them of great age where the land had not been cultivated. Since then there has been considerable deforestation, and by the accounts of the people themselves this may well be affecting the climate. Some of the deforestation was due to severe bush fires a few years ago, but another cause is the demand for firewood, not only for cooking but also to sell to charcoal burners who come from the Accra plains to buy supplies.

The land is fertile and until recently there has been adequate rainfall for farming all the year round, as the dry season is shorter than in Accra. Although some seasons in the 1990s have been disturbingly dry, since 1995 there has been better rainfall, so it is too early to say whether this is a permanent trend, contributed to by the factors mentioned above. The rainfall in Akwapim is still greater than in Accra, even though it is so close. Records in 1970 gave the average rainfall in Accra as 30 inches a year and between 45–50 inches in Aburi. Forty-five inches is considered to be the minimum for cocoa production, but the distribution of rain is also important. Although Akwapim shares the same dry season as on the plains it is rare for there to be absolutely no rainfall during these months.

The mean annual temperature at Aburi is 75.6 degrees Fahrenheit; in Accra it is 79.7°F. The difference seems small, and much of the greater pleasantness of the climate is probably due to lower humidity and fresher breezes. Certainly the early missionaries found it a healthier place in which to live.

Akwapim lies in the moist semi-deciduous forest area; this is similar to the rain forest, but differs in that some trees shed their leaves in the dry season. This type of forest is sometimes referred to as dry deciduous forest (Lawson and Enti 1972). The lower rainfall means that there is less leaching of the soil, so that more minerals and nutrients are preserved. Little of the original forest remains as this has for long been an active area for commercial farming and the population is relatively dense at 100–200, or now more, people a square mile.

There is a great deal of local variation in soils. The principal soils are forest ochrosols (meaning highly-coloured). They are similar to the forest oxysols of the rain forest, but because they are not as highly leached they are generally alkaline. On the steeper and often stony slopes the soils are shallower and belong to the lithosol group. This group of soils runs along the steep slopes of the Akwapim hills, and are therefore found on the western boundaries of Konkonuru land (Blay 1972).

The rocky, hilly nature of the terrain in Konkonuru means that very few farms are on flat ground and many of them are on extraordinarily steep slopes. Reaching them by bush path entails walking up and down and round and round the hills, so distances are far longer than they appear to be on the map. There is also the danger of erosion when land is cleared as the soil is quickly washed away by the heavy rains. So long as bush fallow cultivation is retained this problem is not serious as standing trees are left uncut and much of the rootwork of smaller bushes remains after burning.

The town of Konkonuru has suffered considerable erosion, and there is little vegetation left; many of the houses are being gradually undermined, some of the older ones having collapsed through lack of maintenance (Fig. 4). There

Fig. 4:   A badly eroded house showing the foundations of a building.

are no two-storey buildings and no modern conveniences such as piped water, electricity, sewage, telephone or GPO. But in its appearance it is far removed from what must have been its original state. Practically all the houses have iron or aluminium roofs and cement has been used for culverts and for terracing around buildings. The majority of houses are basically swish (mud construction), but concrete blockwork has been used for extensions and for such purposes as building verandahs and courtyard walls.

Most of the houses have some system of metal guttering to channel rainwater into collecting barrels or tins and this forms a useful supply during the rainy season. Only two compounds have concrete water tanks and even these are quickly exhausted after a short dry spell. For many years the spring, "obo kofi", referred to in the previous chapter was the main source of water supply, but sadly it no longer meets the needs of the community, and water has to be fetched from the Ntare river, or even further afield. The Ntare, although called a river is really only a stream, and the water gets very low in the dry season. Obo kofi never runs completely dry and the water is cool and pure, as the forests above the spring are untouched and reserved strictly for the water gods. In the 1950's a Henderson Box was built, with the help of the Department of Community Development, just below the spring, but by 1970 it had fallen into disrepair. The water container no longer had a lid to keep the water clean and the taps were broken. It was Moses Addo who initiated this, as well as other improvements, but since his time efforts to maintain them have been perfunctory.

It was in the 1950's that, with the active co-operation of Moses Addo, the Methodist catechist at that time, the Department of Social Welfare and Community Development obviously made a big effort to improve the town. It was then that the present Primary School was built, which has a large hall, divided during term-time to take the two lowest forms, and four other good sized classrooms. The school stands at the top of the town on a fine site facing east, with views of Aburi to the north; in front it has a playground with netball posts and an improvised volley-ball net made of palm fronds. The main street up the hill was also built in the 1950's, flanked by concrete gutters. By 1970 this was already badly eroded, and no repairs have been done since then; little of the rainwater now finds its way down the proper channels.

Although it is surrounded by forests and farm land there is not much vegetation in the town itself, as most of the soil has been washed away, except in the lower, flatter part where there are coconut palms and a few shade trees. In 1970 there was a fine shade tree near the entrance to the town, but this was cut down in 1971, as the trunk was rotten, and it has never been replaced, despite the fact that it was a popular meeting place to sit and gossip. The setting of the town is pleasant, but there is little attempt at what might be called "beautification" of the surroundings by the planting of trees, or the many flowering shrubs, such as hibiscus, which grow so well in this part of the world. My appreciation of flowers was always considered slightly eccentric and I was greeted with mirth when I returned from farming carrying bunches of ferns or flowers, collected in the bush, with which to decorate my room.

At the time of the Community Development activities a Women's Group was started, run by a visiting Community Development Assistant, but by 1970 this had been in abeyance for some years, and little evidence remained of its work. Kitchens are mainly open, or roughly enclosed with matting on some sides; none of them has a smokeless stove, which the Department of Community Development was trying to promote as a means of saving fuel. Some kitchens do have improvised shelving, mainly of bamboo, which may or may not reflect Community Development influence. Little food is stored by the majority of households, most families preferring to fetch it fresh from the farm at least two or three times a week. During the whole time I was working in the town in 1970–71. Community Development Officers only visited the town at my instigation for particular purposes, namely to see about the feeder road, to discuss repairing the Henderson Box, and to consider the possibility of restarting the Women's Group. The chief and his elders, at that time were keen to get assistance, but did not know how to set about it. After I left there was no follow up and the town was left once more to its own resources as far as Community Development was concerned.

A great many other Government officials do, however visit Konkonuru. The Rate Collector is a regular visitor, coming every two or three weeks for what in 1970 was still called a levy. In 1970 all adult males had to pay ¢2 a year and adult women ¢1; a cedi at that time was worth 50 pence, which may not seem a great sum, but was regarded as an excessive imposition by the people although the collector I met told me that he did not have so much difficulty in getting this levy from the people of Konkonuru, and did not experience so much hostility, as he did in some other areas. In 1970–1971 I also met the Education Inspector from the District office at Mampong, Public Health Officials from Aburi, a Leprosy Officer, members of the Red Cross, Health Service Personnel who came to give cholera injections and an Army unit which was carrying out a mapping exercise as part of its training programme. We also secured the services of the Veterinary Department to help us with a problem of disease with which the sheep and goats were afflicted.

At the time of our first household census in December 1970 there were 75 compounds, including three in outlying Ewe settlements, and two which were empty. All but the poorest of these compounds consisted of several buildings grouped around a central courtyard. The ideal is to have a courtyard enclosed on all sides by buildings, with the kitchens placed outside, but few attain this desired pattern. Although at first site living conditions seem fairly homogeneous there are, on closer examination, significant differences. This is as true now as it was in 1970; in fact in some ways the differences seem to have increased as a result of demographic and other changes that have occurred. The few compounds which, in 1970, had cement courtyards, rainwater tanks and a large number of rooms, such as those belonging to the Gyasehene, the Asafohene, the Asafosupi and E. K.Owusu, the Methodist catechist, were easily spotted; less apparent are differences in density of occupation and household goods, such as beds, cupboards, tables and chairs.

The overall density of occupation in 1970 was high, with an average for the whole town of four people to a room. In practice most male heads of households had a room to themselves, married women shared with their own young children, and many older children were left to sleep wherever they could find room. As they mainly slept on mats on the floor they could easily circulate between compounds of relatives or friends. In practice there was a high degree of flexibility in sleeping arrangements which was not generally regarded as a hardship. Some adults did consider that they were overcrowded, but little attempt had been made at that time to build additional rooms. A good deal of house building was carried out in the 1950's, most of it in swish construction, built by immigrants from Dahomey(now Benin). These craftsmen had already left the town by 1970 and few townsmen had any expertise in building in swish. In any case they considered it old-fashioned and preferred concrete block construction if they wished to improve their property. For most this was beyond their means, and any additions were made on a temporary basis, mainly of wattle and daub. Most of these additions were kitchens and bathrooms.

In our household survey of 1990 we did not go into as much detail about living conditions as in the previous survey. We did, however, record the number of compounds, and the number of households in each compound. There were 89 compounds in 1990, compared with 70 in 1970, an increase of 41 per cent. The number of households, however, remained constant at 266 in both years. Most of the new compounds were small and mainly lived in by the younger married generation with their children. But as the resident population had not increased to the same extent as the compounds it does suggest that densities are now somewhat lower. It was not a subject that raised much interest.

The majority of houses have cement floors on one or more rooms, and most of them have at least one wooden bedstead. The children mainly sleep on mats on the floor, as do many of the adults, but a raised bed is considered desirable if it can be afforded, as also are chairs, cupboards and tables, which are much in evidence in the richer households. Other modern consumption goods include plastic and metal buckets, bowls and kitchenware, plates and cutlery, soap and detergents, talcum powder, transistors and items of clothing. The extent of these items indicates that the town has a considerable cash income, although some of the inflow of consumer goods comes from visiting migrant citizens. In 1990 there was not much evidence of a great increase in such items, except in the case of transistors, which were more in evidence, although many of them were not functioning because their batteries had run out and replacements were too expensive.

A few compounds have private pit latrines, situated on the outskirts of the village, but most people rely on the public latrines, one for men and one for women, which were reconstructed by the Public Health authority in the late 1960's, or use the surrounding bush.

Food is mainly cooked on earth stoves, using wood as fuel; a few households also use coal pots fired by charcoal, although charcoal is not produced in Konkonuru and is relatively expensive. Methods of preparation are traditional and much use is made of earthenware pots both for cooking and serving. The town is self sufficient in the main staple foods, which are cassava, maize, cocoyam and plantain, as also in tomatoes, peppers, pineapples, citrus fruits and bananas. Most of the meat eaten is either hunted or trapped. The main meal is prepared in the evening after the women return from farming, and is eaten between 5–6 p.m (Fig.5). Breakfast for most people consists of a snack, and the only days when a substantial midday meal is taken are Fridays and Sundays, which are non-farming days. Fufu is made on these days as its preparation is a lengthy process. Some convenience foods such as sardines, other tinned fish and condensed milk are used, and there is a great liking for commercial preparations such as Bournvita and Milo. These are relatively expensive so are considered a luxury. The main food items bought are dried fish, salt, sugar and onions. These are brought to the town by women traders from Jankama, Kitase and as far away as Accra.

In 1970 there was a small shop selling matches, sweets and a few tinned foods. This was run by the wife of the Asafosupi, Kwamena Asamoah. She was an Ashanti woman, and made frequent trips to Kumasi. She had given up her shop by 1990, as both she and her husband were old and frail and have since died. But she was certainly a woman of means as she had sufficient capital to build a large compound in Kumasi for one of her daughters. I visited this compound in 1990, when I was working at the University, nearby. Her daughter ran a wine bar on the main road to Accra, not far from her compound,which was so extensive that most of the rooms were let to tenants. She, like her mother, had well developed entrepreneurial characteristics.

One woman used to cook rice and beans with sauce every morning except Sundays, which she sold from a bar outside her compound, and several women prepared kenkey for sale. In 1970 the Ewes, who lived in a clearing in the forest, about a mile from the town, prepared the fermented cassava, which is used for kenkey, but they left in 1971. Women traders come from time to time to sell cloth, sandals and trinkets; in 1971 a palm shelter was constructed to serve as a market place, but this soon fell into disrepair and has not since been replaced, so that transactions take place in the open air, and the location varies from time to time. There is an akpeteshie (local gin) bar mostly frequented by men.

There is no public transport to the town and no resident citizen after 1970 owned any form of motorized transport. In 1970 one man had an old truck, but it broke down about that time and was never replaced. Most of the marketing of produce is still done by headload to the main road at Jankama, one and a quarter miles away, where it is loaded on to vehicles to be taken to markets in Aburi or Accra. Lorries do visit the town, but getting a regular service for food produce has always been a problem. For example, after a discussion in 1971 arrangements were made for a truck to come two or three times a week, but by July 1972 these visits had been discontinued for the past three or four months, evidently because the truck had broken down and it had not been possible to secure a replacement service. The people keep saying that it is a problem and that they could market more of their surpluses if only they had transport, but no effective action has been taken on a long term basis. Firewood, on the other hand, is regularly collected by truck owners from Accra and Ayimensa, which is at the bottom of the Akwapim hills. A great deal of firewood is produced and is much sought after as fuel for cooking, charcoal burning and akpeteshie distilling (Fig. 6), and good prices are paid for it.

In the household census taken in December 1970 we collected data for all the resident and non-resident members of households in the compounds, the Gyasehene and the town committee being anxious to include this wider network as they were interested to know the total strength of Konkonuru citizens. This proved of great interest from the point of view of concepts of citizenship, not least by reason of whom was left out of the enumeration. The household was considered as the "eating group" and the average number of these groups at that time resident in a compound was 3.5. As well as more permanent migration, there is a good deal of seasonal migration, especially to cocoa farms in other parts of Ghana, as well as circulation to other towns for work or to seek work. We counted as "resident population" all those who had lived in Konkonuru for nine or more months during the previous year, and these numbered 1,085 out of a total enumerated population of 2,296.

Fig. 5:   Children helping in the kitchen

Fig. 6:   Akpeteshie distillery at Konkonuru

Figures of the age and sex distribution of the resident population showed that over 50 per cent were under 18 years of age and that 66 per cent of the over eighteens were women (see Tables 15 & 16). As can be seen from these tables, not only were there considerably more women in the older age groups but a marked scarcity of men from 18–56 years of age, only 12.7 per cent falling into this category. Eighteen years was used as the breakdown point for purposes of analysis rather than the more usual 15 years, as this was the time by which on average the four years of middle school had been completed. This, therefore was the time when young people, particularly boys sought work in the so-called modern sector of the economy. This was an indication of a demographic change which had far-reaching effects on rural communities, as was recorded for Zambia by Elliot in his study of the causes of rural poverty (Elliot 1980 and Kulick 1993). The shortage of adult men had resulted in

Table 15

Sex and Age Distribution of Resident Population Konkonuru, December 1970

Age in Years	Male		Female		Total	
	No.	%	No.	%	No.	%
Under 18	332	67.5	311	52.4	643	59.3
18–56	138	28.0*	222	37.4	360	33.2
57 and over	22	4.5	60	10.2	82	7.5
TOTAL	492	100.0	593	100.0	1085	100.0

*this equals 12.7% of the resident population, or just over one eighth.

Table16

Sex Ratio of Population by Age. Konkonuru, 1970

Age in years	Number of males per 100 females
Under 18	107
18-56	62
57 plus	37
TOTAL	83

the increased importance of women's role in agriculture, particularly in the growing of staple food crops. This is an obvious consequence which has often been noted. Moreover this part of Africa lies within the area designated by Boserup (1970) as one of "female farming". It has not necessarily led to a fall in family incomes because "external" sources from migrants supplement what is produced at home and also because the cash value of staple crops has risen.

In addition, as will be seen later, a lot of the migration of adult males is to other rural areas where they own cocoa farms, and this is an added source of income for those families involved.

The proportion of children in the population in 1970 had by all accounts greatly increased, not only as a result of migration, but also because more babies had survived. For many of them, however, their fathers, perhaps also their mothers, were not in town, so parental influence was likely to be less strong than in the past. Mothers and grandmothers were often left with the sole responsibility for children and had to work hard in their farms in order to feed them and to meet other expenses, as remittances tended not to cover the full costs. Inevitably children were left to their own devices for much of the time, although in the atmosphere of a place like Konkonuru everyone is each other's keeper (Kaye 1962).

More subtle effects of the demographic changes recorded in 1970 related to questions of leadership. Although there was much talk about improving the quality of life there were few adults who had the time or the resources to devote to the difficult business of making this a reality. Most of the men and women of an age to fulfil this role were not only busily engaged in earning a living, they also, on account of their lack of formal education, felt unable to cope with modern bureaucracy. Even for those that remained, quite apart from the factors already mentioned, their interests in improvement tended to lie elsewhere in their cocoa farms in other parts of Ghana, or in attempts to secure entry to the wage sector of the economy. These problems are discussed more fully later.

Returns from previous censuses did not prove very helpful in tracing demographic developments. The town was not separately mentioned in the 1891, 1901, or 1911 censuses and it is by no means certain that the "Konkonoo" of 1921 refers to Konkonuru. "Konkonoo" is enumerated in that census as having 17 houses, with a total population of 145. 69 were under 16 years of age, and the sex distribution was 69 males to 76 females. In 1931 Konkonuru is separately listed, but although 55 houses are mentioned the population is given as only 12 people, of which 10 are males under 15 and 2 are females between 15 and 45 years of age. The 1948 census is the first with any semblance of accuracy; the total population was recorded as 812, of which 384 were males and 428 were females. In the 1960 census the numbers dropped to 686, rising to 833 in the census of March 1970. K. Asare Opoku, who compiled the data for *The Akwapim Handbook* (Brokensha 1972) gave a figure for the total population of Konkonuru as 686 in 1968. The distribution by sex and age is similar to that in our 1970 census, although the proportion of children is lower; as Opoku does not specify ages this is probably due to his using the more conventional cut off point of 15 years, against ours of 18 years, but it could also be due to an under enumeration of children in the sources he used. In any case our own census figures for December 1970 are not strictly comparable with any of these as we included all those who had spent 9 months or more of the previous year in town, and some of these may have been away at the time. But we also obtained a de facto figure of 1085 of all those actually present at the time. It was a coincidence that the de facto and de jure figures were the same as they related in some cases to different individuals. It is probable, however, that there was some under enumeration in the official census, particularly of children.

In July 1972 we resurveyed a random sample of 25 compounds. During this time 22 citizens of Konkonuru had died and 16 had been born. One of my assistants had kept a register of births and deaths over this period, so this information is from this source and not from the resurvey. These numbers included non-resident citizens, so are not comparable, and in any case the register of deaths is likely to be more accurate than that of births as children born to migrants have probably not been fully recorded, whereas those who die are almost invariably brought home for burial. The overall impression gained from available information was that Konkonuru was not at that time an expanding community.

The 1990 household census was carried out by Isaac Ohene Osae, Jacob Ayesu and Stephen Asamoah, all of whom took part in the 1970 census. Although I was in Ghana I was not able to spend much time in Konkonuru as I was working in Kumasi. So I suggested that we should carry out a much simpler census, only recording those present and counting numbers, divided by sex and age, rather than enumerating everyone by name. But those carrying it out insisted on following, as far as possible, our earlier model. They collected information on all non-resident citizens, divided compounds into distinct households and asked for data on education and occupation. Their enthusiasm was tremendous, and their task was carried out without thought of reward. The results were very different from what we expected. I had been told that there had been a considerable increase in population. But our census did not bear this out. The increased number of compounds gave the impression of a larger community; it had, instead led to lower densities of occupation. On the other hand there had been significant changes in the sex and age distribution and this may well be reflected in other rural communities, as suggested by the census returns of 1981, which showed an overall increase, not only in numbers but also in the percentage of those living in rural areas. As a result of these changes men between the ages of 18 and 55 years were more strongly represented (see Tables 17 & 18), although they were still in a minority, and in the oldest age group the proportion of men also showed a marked increase.

The percentages in this oldest group had also increased, but still not at the expense of the large proportion of under eighteens. Many of the additional men were of the generation which had attended Primary and Middle School in Konkonuru and had subsequently migrated to Accra or other towns in search of work. They therefore had much more experience of living in the world outside their home town and were more conscious of the lack of facilities in rural areas.

They had been used to having electricity, piped water, paved roads and better access to medical services. They had mixed with other ethnic groups, including non-Ghanaians, and they had developed a more cosmopolitan outlook. No doubt if they had been more successful in the jobs they got, they would have remained in Accra or other towns. But the harsh economic climate of the seventies and eighties had not only led to loss of employment; it had also increased the cost of living, and wages did not keep pace with inflation. As a

Table 17

Sex and Age Distribution of Resident Population — Konkonuru, June 1990

| Age in Years | Male | | Female | | Total | |
	No.	%	No.	%	No.	%
Under18	278	54	280	47	558	50
18–56	192	37	249	42	441	40
57 and over	45	9	68	11	113	10
TOTAL	515	100	597	100	1112	100

Table 18

Sex Distribution of Population by Age — Konkonuru, June 1990

Age in Years	Number of Males per 100 females
Under 18	99
18–56	77
57 and over	66
TOTAL	86

result it was easier to maintain a reasonable standard by farming; not only did it meet subsistence needs, but the prices paid for any surpluses sold were good. As a result many young, or early middle-aged, men returned to their home towns; they had the energy and the ability to become effective farmers.

Isaac, Jacob and Stephen were examples of this trend and all of them seemed to be doing well. When I first met them on my return to Konkonuru, they were wearing fashionable bright orange boiler suits and sturdy boots, looking very like a trendy British farmer might look today. It was a striking contrast to my picture of a Konkonuru farmer in 1970.

Another new phenomenon was the leadership pattern. In 1970 the Gyasehene, Nana Kwadjo Bediako, was very much the traditional chief. He was adept in the affairs of the Akwapim State, but less able to follow the modern institutions of central and local government. He kept a tight control over his town, as is described later in this chapter. He had never attended school and spoke no English. The present chief, Nana Addo Mensah III, has formal education, speaks English and until recently worked as an accountant in the North Ridge Hotel in Accra. He now resides permanetly in Konkonuru. While working in Accra he used to come at weekends and was assisted in his duties by Deputy chiefs, one of whom worked at the airport in Accra. While in Konkonuru, or when dealing with Konkonuru affairs, he acted in a very chiefly fashion, insisting that all matters affecting his home town should be referred to him, such as the decision to carry out a follow up household survey. After he agreed that it would be desirable and he himself had previously made an attempt to assess numbers, it required some tact to get the work allocated to those I had in mind, in other words to those assistants who had helped in 1970. There seemed to be some concern about the abusua (clan) affiliations of those taking part, something I had not experienced under the old regime, and this seemed part of a greater undercurrent of feeling, if not actual conflict between different members of the community. This is consistent with what one might expect. Already in 1970 there were signs that the younger generation was rebelling against the elders, nothing very overt, but indicated by the chance remark or action. By 1990 so many of these younger people had mixed in a wider society, and were becoming more individualistic, more ready to be critical of the conduct of affairs in their home town. This may be a reflection of events after the 1979 and 1981 coups, when there was some encouragement of the young to be deviant to authority.

A positive result of these changes is that there is a new interest in planning for a better town environment. Konkonuru is fortunate in that the District Secretary, based at Nsawam comes from the town and lives just up the road in Aburi. He is a dynamic person and willing to give what help he can. A first priority of the people has been to get electricity, but as this area does not come under the rural electrification project a proportion of the cost has to be found by the people themselves. The main item they have to provide is the poles. As the distance from the point of connection is over a mile, this is a costly item.

However, by 1996 sufficient money had been found for the poles in the town, but they were still trying to get the Government to supply the necessary high tension poles, for which they were supposed to be included in the 1995–1996 schedule. Despite these delays it does seem now that electricity will be available in the near future, so it will be interesting to observe the effects this has on the life of the community.

The building of a new Middle School, now called a Junior Secondary School was completed in 1995 on the outskirts of the town. There had been a long delay in getting this project started as there was disagreement as to whether it should be sited in Konkonuru or Jankama. A new building and better facilities were certainly needed, as no improvements had been made since I was there in 1970. The Primary school is a more substantial building, but it suffered from lack of maintenance over the years and has only recently been renovated; its facilities also need upgrading and some progress is now being made, including the provision of a canteen (Osae 2000 pers com.).

In 1990, just after my visit, a Day Nursery was started, particularly aimed at providing child care for women when they were farming. It was called the Madam Hardiman Day Nursery in my honour. This has flourished and now has about 120 children, looked after by five voluntary attendants. It is housed in the old Mission House building which was previously used by the fourth form of the Middle School. It is hoped that eventually there will be a new purpose-built nursery constructed, and funds are being sought for this purpose.

Another project about which the Planning Committee is enthusiastic is the building of new "modern" houses. This is being planned in co-operation with Global 2000. I was shown the land that had been allocated for this project, was told that eventually everybody would be rehoused, and that the present site of the town would be cleared. It seemed a very ambitious project for a community of this sort and would need to be heavily subsidized by overseas aid; nor was it clear whether the so-called "modern" construction proposed would really meet the needs of the majority, or whether they had been consulted. To what extent, for example, would the compound model be retained, or was this considered old fashioned, not in line with current trends? So far no positive steps have been taken to start work, and it will be interesting to see what happens.

It might be expected that a better educated community which depends largely on farming would be keen to adopt innovations to improve output, but so far there has been little change in their practices. This will be discussed further in the next chapter.

The early introduction of Christianity to Konkonuru has already been mentioned. Of the 1085 resident population in 1970, 582 professed some Christian faith, the vast majority (554) being Methodists. Of the older generation it is mainly the women who belong to the church and attend services, the great majority of those recorded as Christian being school children. Membership of the church did not preclude attendance at traditional religious ceremonies or practices, and it was difficult to assess the influence it had on attitudes, as against the influence of education. For example, I was told that girls who went to school did not go through the traditional puberty rites; as most of the younger generation in 1970 had attended school this meant that these rites were rarely practised, and I met no instances of them during my time there. On the other hand very few marriages received a church blessing (there were only two cases amongst the resident population). The catechist in 1970 deplored the lack of Christian beliefs or practices, and said that most people were still very much influenced by superstition and the traditional priests. In fact most people had a fairly easy-going attitude to religion, enjoyed the ceremonial aspects and did not appear to see any inconsistencies between different creeds. One woman, for example was a member of the Methodist congregation, attended traditional ceremonies led by the priests, and was also a practising member of the Musama Disco Christo Church which met every Friday afternoon under the leadership of a man who came from Aburi. The Musama Disco gatherings were attended by about 20 men and women and were very jolly, with plenty of drumming and dancing.

Another instance of the flexible attitude to religion was the Children's Annual Festival at the end of the school year, which I attended in 1970. It was organized by the Methodist school teachers and was in two parts, which could roughly be described as "Sacred" (Part I) and "Secular" (Part II). The first was a conventional Methodist service concluding with a long sermon by a visiting Legon graduate who had at one time been a teacher at Konkonuru. Towards the beginning of the sermon the Chief, who was not a Christian, arrived and quite happily sat through the rest of it and the final prayers and hymns. He then took over as Chairman for Part II, and delivered his own address, followed by innumerable recitations from the Bible by all the Primary and Middle School forms in turn. This was followed by a play written by the Middle School Headmaster. The subject of this play was a court scene in which a man had been committed for the murder of his sister in the forest. Counsel was called for both parties, the culprit was found guilty and eventually the judge pronounced sentence of five years with hard labour. At this point the prisoner, who possessed very powerful "juju", bewitched the police warder, and dancing round the court gradually drew all the actors in his trail, demonstrating his traditional power over the modern paraphernalia of justice, or so the moral seemed to be, and subsequent discussions of the play confirmed this interpretation.

We were not able in 1990 to study the religious practices in the town. Those who attend school are all given "Christian names", prayers are said and religious instruction figures in the curriculum. But after school few of them, particularly the men, continue to practice Christianity in so far as attendance at services is concerned. My impression was that not much had changed in their general attitudes to religious beliefs. The influence of the traditional priests still seems strong, especially among the older generation, and the power of superstition is evident. Traditional religious beliefs emphasize the links between the ancestors and living people; reverence for the descent group ancestors helps to maintain the authority structure of the community, and is a part of the essential institutions and practices related to the kinship system. This system prescribes statuses and roles to people who are in a particular relationship. It determines, for example, the respective positions of men and women, mother and child, or husband and wife It determines the rules, duties and obligations of individuals and the groups with which they interact; for example, where a couple should live after marriage, how property is transmitted, who succeeds whom or who should worship at a particular shrine. As in other domaines, kinship is the key to the understanding of these societies. Certainly in Konkonuru today the importance of kinship and the lineage system is still apparent. Dr. Nukunya, of the University of Ghana, in his book on *Tradition and Change in Ghana* (Nukunya 1992), bears out the continuing role of kinship in Ghana. Modifications there must naturally have been as a result of economic and social change, and the extended kinship network is put under pressure as a result. This is particularly felt in matrilineal societies where the relationship between a husband and his wife's brother can cause problems. Where, for example, the mother's brother is a successful civil servant his sister may make what seem to be undue demands on behalf of her children. He, on the other hand, as a member of the new elite, is more concerned about his own children. A friend who belonged to a matrilineal group once remarked that if he met all his kinship obligations he would be permanently in debt. But custom dies hard, and people are reluctant to refuse help to their kin. After all they never know when they themselves may need help, and quite apart from these more material considerations it is the extended family that provides emotional and moral support in times of trouble.

So many traditional values and practices still predominate, though possibly not so strictly as in 1970. This is particularly the case concerning marriage and family affairs, such as the prevalence of customary marriage. The outdooring of newly born babies on the eighth day after birth is invariably carried out and it is still considered right that a Konkonuru woman should return to her home town for the birth of her children, although nowadays this custom is less likely to be observed by those who have migrated to Accra, Kumasi or any other of the larger towns where hospital facilities are available. Of the 1085 resident in Konkonuru in 1970, 1001 were born there and as the population included wives who had married into Konkonuru this means that virtually all those with Konkonuru mothers were born in the town, or were at least believed to have been born there. An interesting example of the latter was a friend of mine who was recorded as "born in Konkonuru". In fact his mother who was living at Asuboi was returning to Konkonuru for his birth, but he arrived before she reached her home town. Nevertheless she considered him to have been born in the proper place.

As with birth so with death it is considered imperative to be buried at home. Indeed this tradition will probably outlast the one concerning birth, as was powerfully demonstrated in the case of President Nkrumah, who was brought to Ghana for burial in his home town, after lying in State in Accra. Funerals occupy an important part of the life in Konkonuru, and a great deal of time, money and emotion are devoted to them. There are three traditional cemeteries on the outskirts of the town, two of them for the Abrade clan and one for general use, which is also used by Abrades; there is also a Christian cemetery on the approach road, but not all Christians are buried there as many prefer to join their ancestors in the traditional setting, and in all cases some traditional rites will be performed.

In 1970 there was a strong preference for marriage to another Konkonuru citizen rather than to an outsider; this is still said to be the case, although it is inevitably breaking down as far as the younger generation is concerned, and has in any case been difficult for some time if the rules of clan exogamy are to be observed. In the household survey of 1970 it was interesting to find that the only cases of clan endogamy were amongst Abrade. As Abrades formed 60 per cent of the resident population this was perhaps not surprising given the preference for inter-Konkonuru marriage arrangements. Various explanations were given to account for the bending of this rule, the main one being that marriage could take place between a pure, or "special", Abrade and an "ordinary" Abrade. As the ruling class is Abrade any strangers accepted into the community, such as slaves, would become Abrade, but they would not belong to the pure lineage. Nor would it be considered wrong for a person from another tribe, such as an Ashanti, who was Abrade (Aduana in Ashanti) to marry an Akwapim Abrade, but they would not belong to the pure lineage. When examined in detail this appears to be something of a rationalization, as it was impossible in individual cases to distinguish between pure and ordinary. Asked what the child of a pure Abrade father and an ordinary Abrade mother became, it was laughingly said that of course the child could be counted as special. So that by a logical process all children are likely to be special except those of two ordinary parents, and we were unable to trace any of these.

On the other hand there is a marked change in the practices and attitudes to the traditional practice of parents arranging marriages. The younger generation consider that they should choose their own partners and this is generally agreed by their fathers and mothers. Cross-cousin marriage is still considered as desirable, but it is not pressed if it is against the wishes of the child. I found, in 1970, two cases of parallel cousin marriages in the older generation (father's brother's child). The age of marriage for girls has probably, on average, risen as a result of education, but evidence on this is conflicting. Because so many children start school after the age of six years and frequently miss a year, it is quite usual for them to be 18 years of age by the time that they leave Middle School. Most of them, both girls and boys, then try to find employment away from Konkonuru, and even if they do not succeed it is some time before they settle down. Men in this society have always married at a later age, so this may mean that the discrepancy between the ages of husbands and wives at first marriage is being reduced, but there is not much statistical evidence on this subject, partly because there are no statistics for the past and because changes are probably taking place relatively quickly. The indications can only be induced from the fact that there are a number of single women in their twenties, and from the opinions expressed by informants.

It is the younger members of the community who make up the majority of the literate group and who have learnt to speak English. The changes that have taken place in the past twenty years in this respect are looked at in detail in the chapter on Education. Community Development Assistants did, in the 1950s, run an Adult Education Literacy Class in the town and a few of the older generation have retained the ability to read and write, but as these classes were in Twi and there is little published literature in the vernacular there was not much incentive to learn. Very few of the older generation, in 1970, spoke more than a few words of English. As mentioned earlier, there are now more people with a working knowledge of English, although not many of these read either books or newspapers, and books can still only be found in a small number of houses.

In 1970 leadership of the community was strongly vested in those with no formal education and it was therefore natural that they should feel more at home when dealing with town politics and family affairs than with development projects, especially where this involved dealing with modern bureaucracy. The change in leadership patterns has already been mentioned, and clearly there is more concern now with trying to improve living conditions; recently some progress has been made in building housing of a better standard (Osae 2000 pers com.). The people of Konkonuru have, for many years, been aware of the facilities available in urban areas and there were earlier attempts to effect development, as at the time of Moses Addo in the 1950s.

During the time of the Nkrumah regime all communities were statutorily obliged to set up town development committees; the designation of these was changed under the Busia regime (1969-1972) to town committees. Such a committee was set up in Konkonuru under the chairmanship of the Asafohene, with 14 members, including 3 women. We met this committee on several occasions from October 1970 to March 1971 in connection with the community development work which students from Legon were doing in the town. When I returned to Konkonuru in August 1972 I was told that the committee had not met since then, and was now generally regarded as having been disbanded, some said because since the coup there was no obligation to have such an institution. Gyasehene Bediako was never a member of the committee although he was always free to attend meetings. In 1990 there was once again a town development committee headed by the new Chief, and it was said to hold regular meetings.

In 1970 town affairs were, in practice, mainly decided by the Gyasehene and his elders, and different groups met together for different purposes, and this still seems to be the case. Family disputes were in the first place dealt with by the heads of clans, and only brought before the Gyasehene when a settlement could not be reached. Likewise, town disputes were dealt with by the Gyasehene and only referred to the Adontenhene or the civil power if agreement was impossible, which seldom happened. I only found one case of a land dispute, concerning the inheritance of a cocoa farm in another part of Ghana, which was taken to the civil court, but there may well have been others. There is a fierce pride in settling affairs within the community and a corresponding reluctance to admit taking them elsewhere. There was one instance, in 1971, of the Gyasehene referring a case to the police at Aburi; this was when some Ewe residents failed to turn out for communal labour on a Friday and subsequently refused to report to the Gyasehene or to pay a fine. The police did take action and ordered the offenders to report to the Aburi police station every day for a week. This particular Ewe community, which lived in a hamlet on Konkonuru land about a mile from the town, returned to Togoland in 1972. They had lived on Konkonuru land for 40 years, many of their children had been born there, but they never became fully integrated members of the community, although they acknowledged allegiance to the Gyasehene.

Communal labour takes place every Friday, the non-farming day, organized on the traditional pattern by the Captain of the Asafo Company. The Asafo system is of Fanti origin but has been practised in a modified form in this part of Akwapim for as long as people can remember, and according to District Commissioners' reports, in Colonial times, formed a strong pressure group. Both men and women turn out to carry out allotted tasks, such as clearing bush paths, weeding the town surrounds, maintaining the dirt road, constructing a market place or a temporary structure for ceremonial purposes. The Asafo Captain gets very angry with those who fail to turn up and a fine is imposed on them; in 1970–1971 this was 50 pesewas (about 25 pence).

Farming is still the main occupation for those resident in Konkonuru, although there are now more pursuing other occupations than there were in 1970, (see Table 19), and the values attached to land and the production of staples predominate. Land tenure systems and methods of production are traditional, although the question of how land is acquired for use by individuals is complicated, and will be dealt with more fully in the chapter on farming. A great deal of the migration away from Konkonuru and the seasonal circulation to and from the town is to cocoa farms in other parts of Ghana. In 1970 thirty-one of the normally resident population claimed to have interests in farms away from Konkonuru; the figure was 227 for the whole population (in the household survey "normally resident" was defined as those who had spent nine months or more in Konkonuru in the past year).

In 1970 84 per cent of the men and 88 per cent of the women of 18 years and over gave farming as their main occupation. In 1990 the percentages were somewhat less, particularly amongst the women, where more described themselves as traders. But the difference is more a question of the proportion of time allocated to these different activities, as those stating trading as their main occupation said that they also farmed, and visa versa. For example, in 1970, 57 men and 162 women traded as a secondary occupation. Trading is mainly in farm products, and women do most of the actual marketing, so that where men said that they traded the transactions were often carried out by their womenfolk. Farm produce is normally sold to traders on the main road or in the Aburi market, a town about three miles from Konkonuru, which had a population of around 6,000 in 1970, rather than direct to the consumer. The people are aware of the fact that they could obtain more for their produce if they sold direct, but there are various constraints to this. Their nearest point on the main road is Jankama, and they would not be permitted to sell there by that community. Of greater relevance is the time taken in retailing, which can be spent more profitably in farming activities.

Many of the trading activities in Konkonuru are carried out by outsiders. Market women regularly come with fish from Accra, petty traders bring ground-

Table 19

Occupational Distribution of Resident Population of Konkonuru — Main Occupation only: 1970 and 1990

Occupation	Men 1970 No.	Men 1970 %	Men 1990 No.	Men 1990 %	Women 18 years and over 1970 No.	Women 1970 %	Women 1990 No.	Women 1990 %	Total 1970 No.	Total 1970 %	Total 1990 No.	Total 1990 %
Farmer	135	84.4	156	65.8	249	88.3	233	73.5	384	86.9	389	70.2
Trader	—	—	5	2.1	6	2.1	43	13.6	6	1.4	48	8.7
Teacher	5*	3.1	2	0.8	—	—	7	2.2	5	1.1	9	1.6
Fitter	—	—	—	.8	—	—	—	—	—	—	8	1.4
Driver	—	—	5	2.1	—	—	—	—	—	—	5	0.9
Clerical	—	—	3	1.3	—	—	—	—	—	—	3	0.5
Tailor	3	1.9	—	—	—	—	1	0.3	3	0.7	—	—
Seamstress	—	—	—	—	2	0.7	1	.5	2	.5	1	0.2
Food Processor	—	—	—	—	—	—	—	—	—	—	—	—
Goldsmith	1	0.6	—	—	—	—	—	—	1	—	—	0.2
Labourer	2	1.3	2	0.8	—	—	—	—	2	0.5	2	—
Priest#	—	—	—	—	1	0.4	—	—	1	0.2	2	0.4
Shoemaker	1	0.6	—	—	—	—	—	—	1	0.2	—	—
Housewife	—	—	—	—	6	2.5	2.8	.8	—	.8	1.8	—
Parks/Garden-	—	—	—	—	—	—	—	—	—	—	—	—
Contractor	—	—	—	—	.4	—	—	—	—	—	1	0.2
Mason	—	—	—	—	.4	—	1	—	—	—	1	0.2
Domestic Work	—	—	—	—	—	—	1	—	—	—	1	0.2
Nurse	—	—	—	—	—	—	—	—	—	—	1	0.2
District Sec.	—	—	1	0.4	—	—	—	—	—	—	1	0.2
Still in Edn.	—	—	13	5.5	—	—	12	3.8	—	—	25	4.5
None	13	8.1	10	4.2	11	3.9	18	5.7	24	5.5	28	5.0
No Reply	—	—	23	9.8	—	—	1	0.3	—	—	24	4.3
TOTAL	160	100	237	99.5	282	100	317	100	442	100	554	99.7

nuts, sandals, cheap jewellery, cloth and other consumer goods and do a brisk trade, particularly on non-farming days. The only serious trader in the town in 1970, as mentioned above, was an Ashanti woman, married to the Asafosupi, who ran the small shop adjoining their house, and frequently went on buying expeditions to replenish her stocks.

Sixty per cent of the resident population in December 1970 was under 18 years of age, but very few of them farmed as a full-time occupation, only 12 boys and 20 girls. There was a six form primary school and a four form middle school in the town and most children attended at some time, even though they might not stay the whole course. Great importance was attached to sending children to school with a view to equipping them to enter the modern sector of employment. Education was not seen as relevant to producing better farmers or to improving the life of the community, but as an escape from the rural scene. Peppy Roberts (1972), in an Unpublished Cambridge thesis, refers to this phenomenon. Of the few recent Middle School leavers who were still in Konkonuru in 1970, the boys, without exception were looking for jobs outside. This applied to the girls to only a slightly lesser extent, although in their case they were by then of age to marry.

In 1990 it was not possible to go in so much detail into how many of the recent school leavers had already left the town, or were still there but seeking jobs outside. As mentioned before, the proportion of men over 18 years of age had increased since 1970, but this increase was mainly in the 35 to 50 age group, so no doubt the young still have aspirations to join the wage earning sector of the economy when they leave school.

The overall picture of Konkonuru today is of a community that has been in process of change for many years, and in which change is likely to accelerate in the future. It is not an isolated community and it shares many aspirations and values with the "modern" sector of Ghanaian society. It retains much of the traditional social structure as far as household patterns, family values and town leadership are concerned, but people are in many ways becoming more individualistic, and this in time, if it has not already done so, will affect social relationships, particularly inheritance patterns. People still have a strong sense of identity with their "home town", however independently they may behave when they are away. They pay allegiance to their chief and are aware of their kinship obligations. In their minds they seem to retain a distinction between traditional institutional patterns and values which they consider to have existed "from time immemorial" and what goes on in the undoubtedly in many ways attract modern sector of Ghana. In this Konkonuru is probably typical of many rural communities today.

Chapter 5

FOOD CROP FARMING

Farming is the basis of Konkonuru's economy; the primacy of agriculture makes land the most important source of capital (Nukunya 1990). In 1970 there were still a few cocoa farms within the boundaries of the town, but by 1990 these had all disappeared. They were already in a poor condition in 1970 with swollen shoot disease; the trees were old and for many years little had been done to replace them. The growing of cocoa still makes an important contribution to incomes, but this now comes entirely from farms in other parts of Ghana, where the bulk of cocoa production has been for many years. This will be discussed in Chapter 6.

The development of farming is a major topic of discussion in Ghana today. Land is one of the chief economic resources of the country and about 60 per cent of the labour force still consists of farmers. Cocoa is the main export, and despite the fall in prices on the international market is a vital source of foreign currency.

Discussions about agriculture centre around two aspects; on the one hand the improvement of agricultural technology, and on the other the question of land ownership. These two aspects cannot be neatly separated, particularly when considering proposals for the development of the agricultural sector of the economy (Feder 1991). Certain groups are proposing courses of action which suit their sectional interests, without questioning what kind of development will ensue, or who will benefit from it. Traditional systems of land tenure have been attacked as a constraint on increased productivity, as a discouragement to investment in farm improvements, and generally as a brake on the change from subsistence to commercial agriculture. (See, for example. La Anyane, S. "Issues in Agricultural Policy" in Background to Agricultural Policy in Ghana, Proceedings of a Seminar organized by the Faculty of Agriculture, University of Ghana, Legon 1969). These critics argue that a move towards contractual systems would lead to better land utilization, and the emergence of more able managers and entrepreneurs. As contract replaced customary tenure systems, so ability would replace status, and the progressive producer would be able to expand his holdings to the limit of his competence and financial resources.

A different opinion is expressed by those who see the problem from the point of view of the masses of existing farmers, for whom a contractual system might not be in their long term interests. Land is becoming a scarce commodity and the urban elite is increasingly interested in exploiting the possibilities of acquiring land and earning farm profits, often as absentee landlords. In the short run local communities or individual families are tempted by the offer to buy or lease, and may consider that they have more than sufficient land for their own use. But in the longer run there is a prospect that the development of large scale commercial farms will lead to the creation of a rural proletariat. It is argued by those who take the opposing view that what is needed by the majority of existing farmers is not so much a change in tenurial systems as assistance in improving their agricultural practices, and in marketing their products. Most agricultural research has concentrated on methods that depend on the use of modern technology, such as tractors, irrigation and artificial fertilizers; the introduction of swamp rice cultivation in the Volta region is an example of such a development. The introduction of new strains of cocoa trees has benefitted cocoa farmers, but as far as staple food crops are concerned there has been little research into ways of improving strains in order to enhance their quality and yield. Recently there are encouraging signs that more attention is now being paid to the possibilities of improving production in the traditional sector; for example, a Canadian funded project started in 1990 to experiment with improved varieties of maize and other cereals.

Behind these arguments there are ideological differences, for example between those who talk mainly of the gross agricultural product and how it can be increased, and those who concentrate more on the question of the distribution of farm incomes. Benneh (1976) expresses a preference for the Gandhian "production by the masses, rather than mass production" and points to the disadvantages of capital intensive methods. He considers that the task of a tenure system is "to put people to work rather than out of work" — or even "working as wage labourers for others". He does not agree that traditional systems of tenure are a necessary constraint on greater productivity, provided that suitable services and infrastructure are created.

The debate is complicated and goes far beyond the issue of land alone, affecting as it does the whole fabric of rural society (Robertson 1987). It is also connected with wider issues of the direction of economic development, and the provision of employment opportunities outside the agricultural sector in rural as well as in urban areas (Bentsi-Enchill 1964).

Ghana in any case is a good example of how traditional systems have adapted themselves to new economic opportunities, as the history of cocoa farming demonstrates (Hill 1963). But new forces have now entered the situation, which if left to work themselves out on the free market may well produce much more radical changes in land ownership than have occured in the past. It is perhaps no longer possible or profitable to adopt a "laissez faire" policy. The question is "In whose interests will Government introduce land legislation?". And in the decision making process "How will the views of the majority be ascertained?". Already the role of the chief as the representative of the people may not afford sufficient protection for the masses. In many cases chiefs are already involved in land and administration as capitalists, landlords and developers, rather than as defenders of the traditional sector. This is more true of the bigger chiefs than of village odikro, and more prevalent in some parts of Ghana than in others. Nukunya (1990) comments that "the notion that land is a communal property and should not be alienated is still mentioned, but it is now a rule which is obeyed more in the breach than in the observance" This is not yet the case in Konkonuru, and the Adontenhene at Aburi came down heavily, some time ago, on the chief of Jankama, who had "sold" land to an outsider. Akan communities are perhaps more conservative in this respect than other ethnic groups in Ghana.

Food farming is still the main occupation of the people in Konkonuru, as was seen in Table 19 in Chapter 4, and daily life centres round the land and the values attached to it. This chapter looks at food crop farming in a rural community which still follows traditional systems of agriculture and land tenure. It is an illustration of the situation in many rural communities in Ghana today, mainly those under bush fallow cultivation, although it makes no claim to being typical. It is interesting to note that this community is only 25 miles from Accra, in Akwapim, a region of Ghana that has for many years been influenced by forces of economic and social change.

Pride is taken in a well kept farm and fine crops and these are frequent topics of conversation. Often in the course of a discussion a person was referred to as "a good farmer", or alternatively as "someone who neglects his farms". My own interest in farming and my desire to learn about methods of cultivation proved to be one of the most fruitful entries into the life of the community. They were always eager to know what was grown in England, what methods of cultivation were used, whether families could feed themselves. One day, while farming, a woman, referring to the fact that I only had two children, said sympathetically. Well, I suppose it is difficult for you to grow your own food in London; but here we can feed all the children we have, so it is no problem. The existence of other bottlenecks in the child rearing process, such as the difficulty of educating them, or finding cash employment, occured to her as a rather novel way of considering family size. Food was the important determinant and the more children produced the more help was available on the farm.

Children start to help their parents to farm at an early age, even if they are attending school. An estimate, made at the time of the 1960 census, was that a child could produce the equivalent of his or her food needs by the age of 11 years. As soon as they can walk they accompany their mothers on farming expeditions, learn to carry headloads, how to plant crops, to weed and other farming skills (Fig. 7). Later the boys help their fathers and other male relatives to clear the bush for new farms. They learn about the soils that are suitable for different crops, and they acquire knowledge of who farms where and the extent of the lineage lands. Most young people these days do not think of farming as a sufficient career, but most of them expect to return to it in later life. Perhaps when rural conditions improve, with better water supplies, electrification and the provision of more adequate health and education services, attitudes may change, especially if farming becomes more profitable. So far there have not been substantial changes in these directions in Konkonuru, as in many other parts of Ghana, but more attention is now being paid to these matters.

Fig. 7:   Farmers returnig from farm

Sixty-five per cent of the adult farmers in Konkonuru at the time of the household census in 1970 were women, a reflection of the demographic situation as a whole. In 1990, although there were then more men in the over eighteen age group (43 per cent in 1990 against 36 per cent in 1970) women still accounted for 60 per cent of the adult farmers. The norm is for a married woman either to help her husband with his farm, or to be given a farm of her own on his land. The tendency is for a wife to help on her husband's farm when she is first married and later to be given her own farm. A more detailed study in 1970 of 28 of the 70 compounds in the town shows that out of 35 married women living in the same households as their husbands, 22 (63 per cent) did not have a farm of their own. The average age of this group without farms was 36 years, and those with farms 46 years. Widows or divorcees, or those with husbands in other parts of Ghana, were much more likely to have farms of their own.

The predominance of women farmers in the community indicates the importance of their economic role, and this is particularly true in the production of food crops. Akwapim is in an area described by Boserup (1970) as one of "female farming" They are, however, dependent largely on men for clearing the bush and this can act as a limitation on the amount of land cultivated. Because of the shortage of adult men, not now quite as great as in 1970, but still substantial, there is an increasing trend to use wage labour for clearing and the sums paid out are considerable. In 1970 Ewe labourers living within Konkonuru's boundaries and Grusi labourers from nearby Jankama were used, as well as boys from the town who were hired for this purpose and worked either on contract or for a daily rate of 70–80 pesewas (worth about 30–40 pence at current values of the currencies). The Ewe families left Konkonuru soon after 1970. The time taken to prepare a given acreage of land for cultivation varies according to the terrain and the extent of growth. If land has been left fallow for a long time the work is harder, but the rewards on terms of soil fertility and firewood for sale and fuel are greater; so those who have sufficient land prefer to leave it fallow for eight years or more.

Methods of farming are traditional, not only in terms of adherence to the practice of bush fallow cultivation, but also as far as implements and crops are concerned. The cutlass, the hoe and the axe are the only tools used. The cutlass is a versatile implement which is used not only for cutting the bush, but also for weeding, preparing cassava for planting and in the preparation of food crops for market. Farmers take a lot of trouble to buy what they consider to be the best cutlasses and to keep them in prime condition by honing; imported cutlasses, although much more expensive, are preferred and generally used, as they are sharper and retain their cutting edge longer. An imported cutlass cost two cedis in 1970 (about one pound sterling) and an axe three cedis, whereas a local cutlass could be bought for as little as 40 pesewas (40 pence). Most farmers bought cutlasses at Nsawam and purchased two or more a year.

The main staples grown are not indigenous to Ghana, but were introduced many centuries ago by the Portuguese and other traders; they have been cultivated for as long as Konkonuru has been in existence. Cassava, maize and cocoyam are grown by all farmers, and many of them grow some plantains, oil palms, pineapples, tomatoes, peppers and citrus fruits. Oil palm was at one time an important agricultural crop in Akwapim, and palm oil and palm kernel were exported to European markets (Brokensha 1972). In course of time the quality of oil could not compete in world markets, so the palm oil industry was no longer a paying proposition, and palm trees were neglected. In any case the introduction of cocoa superceded it as a more profitable cash crop (Szereseweski 1965). However, by 1970 there were few cocoa farms in Konkonuru and by 1990 there were none. Palm trees were only grown on a small scale, mostly for home consumption. There was no recollection of there ever having been a trade in palm tree products from the town. A few farmers grow yams, but they are not an important crop here as they are in Ashanti. They are knowledgeable about different varieties and ready to try new ones if given to them, but they never consider buying seeds or tubers, always relying on their own crops for propagation purposes. Nor do they ever use fertilisers; they know about them but do not think them necessary or even desirable with their methods of culti-vation.

The land is well suited to the crops grown, rainfall for the most part has been adequate, and not many problems of disease to crops are experienced. As intercropping is used it is rare for a farm to be a complete failure. In 1972 there was a lack of rainfall for the first planting of maize and on the drier, hillier farms there was a poor crop, but these same farms produced plenty of cassava and cocoyam. There is, however, now more concern than in 1970 about rainfall levels, as there have recently been a number of years when they have been so low that crop yields have suffered severely. One man commented, when we were discussing this, that he thought it was due to less tree coverage. Certainly the difference in the Akwapim hills between 1970 and 1990 was striking. Some of the deforestation was attributed to forest fires during an exceptionally dry season a few years ago, but this could not account for the general reduction in forest densities over a wide area. As in other parts of Ghana cutting trees to use as fuel for cooking or for sale to urban areas has taken its toll. It is one of the consequences of the rapid increase in population, which has more or less doubled in the past twenty years.

However, since 1995 there has been, in most years, an improvement in rainfall, and recent reports from Konkonuru indicate that crop yields have been good. As a result there has been an increase in surpluses for sale, and market prices for foodstuffs have been satisfactory, according to information received from Isaac Ohene Osae, who keeps me briefed on this as on other matters.

Clearing of the bush starts just after Christmas, during the dry season, and this is a very busy time. First the undergrowth is cut; the trees to be used for firewood are then cut and collected together for head loading back to the town and the rest is then burnt on site. This kills the weeds and leaves the ground friable for the first planting, which is usually maize, except on the dry ground where it is considered advisable to plant later (Fig. 8). Cassava cuttings are then interspersed with the maize, sometimes with the addition of tomato

Fig. 8: Author cutting cassava sticks for planting

seedlings and peppers. Some farmers plant yams in specially prepared mounds, but these are not an important crop in Konkonuru. Cocoyam grows by itself, as the tubers remain in the ground while it is fallow and start to grow soon after the bush is cleared. To one unaccustomed to this type of cultivation the whole process seems extraordinarily haphazard, but the farmers themselves know what they are doing and are discerning about the best use of a particular piece of land; they know, for example the best site for a pineapple farm, or where tomatoes will flourish. They appreciate that dry stony ground on a steep hillside has to be treated differently from low-lying ground by a stream. Benneh (1973) drew attention to the expertise of farmers in appreciating different soil types and considered that their methods of classification were often superior to those of agronomists. Government initiated farm improvement projects too often fail to take account of the knowledge of local farmers.

The first maize ripens in May and is the occasion for the annual ceremony of "watoburow". The decision as to when this should be held is taken by the chief, the head priest and the elders and no maize can be cut until the ceremony has been completed. They meet at the osofo shrine, pour libation and slaughter a goat, after which there is great rejoicing as people go to their farms to gather the first cobs, which are brought back, boiled and eaten. These first fruits are always regarded as particularly delicious, as indeed they are. Although there are two crops of maize a year there is only one ceremony and no ceremonies for cassava or any other crop except yams at the annual Odwira festival. Cassava takes a minimum of six months before the roots can be dug, and it is often left in the ground for much longer until it is required, as this proves the best method of storage.

Although the main clearing of the bush is from January to March there is a second minor clearing in August, after the main rainy season, for the planting of the "adom" crop in order to supplement supply in what would otherwise be a hungry season of the year. It provides a second crop of maize just before Christmas and means that cassava is continuously available throughout the year. Cleared land is only cultivated for one year, but some of the standing crop of cassava are left until well after the new farms have been made. When a farmer speaks about his farm he is referring to the piece of land prepared for cultivation; he will therefore say, "I have three farms this year", or whatever the number may be, and this is quite distinct from the total extent of land over which he holds usufructory rights.

The economics of farming under a system of bush fallow cultivation is a difficult subject for study as far as assessing the return of labour is involved, and very little accurate data is available. One of the problems is the variety of labour used on any one holding; it may, for example, be worked by one woman, but she will have been helped in clearing the bush by her husband or her brother, and her children will accompany her from time to time to weed, plant or collect produce. The amount of time spent in walking to and from the farm, in head loading produce to market, in preparing foodstuffs for sale, all have to be taken into account, and unless a day-to-day check is made over a period of a whole year it is only possible to give rough estimates of man/woman hours employed. It would also be necessary to weigh all the produce.

A survey that was carried out of 28 farmers during the 1971, 1972 and 1973 seasons did not attempt to get information of this order. The main purpose of the survey was to study methods and patterns of work, division of labour between the sexes and age groups, ways in which usufructory rights were acquired, and decisions about how much land to farm and what crops to grow in any one season. It was possible, however, to measure the amount of land cultivated, the cash expenditure on hired labour, and very approximately the value of crops sold after family needs had been met, taking into account the size of the eating group. Table 20 gives the estimated acreage of food farms for the sample in 1971, 1972 and 1973. As farms are of an irregular shape these figures can only be regarded as approximate. Where the information was available the number of years which the land had lain fallow is given and where hired labour was employed the amount in wages. Although there are more women farming than men there are fewer women in the sample, due to the fact that only those farming on their own account were selected, and not those who were helping spouses or other relatives. Of the eleven women farmers seven were widows, two were divorcees and only two were still married.

These acreages apply to land cleared in the current year, so that farmers would also still be gathering food crops from some of last years farms. These were recorded but are not given in Table 20 as measurements taken were less accurate, it frequently proving impossible to penetrate the growth and difficult to estimate just how much cassava remained to be collected unless the particular farmer happened to be present. Seven additional farmers were studied in 1972, partly to make up for those who had dropped out of the survey, but they have not been included in Table 20. These additions did not extend the range of acres cultivated, and from general observation of the farming community as a whole the survey seems to represent variations from the largest to the smallest acreages cultivated by any one farmer. The sample happens to include four of the biggest men farmers, Kwaku Donkor, Kwamena Asamoah, Osae Kwasi and E.B. Osae and three of the biggest and certainly most industrious women farmers, Yaa Adjei, Kate Asare and Abena Ntowbea. Seven of the men and two of the women farmers also owned cocoa farms, in most cases in other areas of Ghana, and these occupied some of their time and provided additional income.

Table 20

Farms and Acreages of sample farmers in Konkonuru, 1971, 1972 and 1973

Farmers	*1971*		*1972*		*1973*	
	No. of Farms	*Acreage*	*No. of Farms*	*Acreage*	*No. of Farms*	*Acreage*
Men*	23	44.02	27	43.98	30	44.94
Women#	15	14.91	15	17.17	11	7.81
TOTAL	38	58.93	42	61.16	41	52.75

* 17 men farmers were surveyed in 1971 and 15 in 1972 and 1973
The average age of men farmers in the sample was 54 years in 1971
11 women farmers were surveyed in 1971 and 10 in 1972 and 1973
The average age of women farmers in the sample was 58 years in 1971

The Chief was not drawn in the sample, nor the Asafohene and they were both large landholders. The Chief was an active farmer, but he also had cocoa interests at Cape Coast and spent at least three months of the year there, not all at one time but intermittently. In 1972, in response to "Operation Feed Yourself", which was mounted by the National Redemption Council which seemed to have seized the imagination of the people, he had a greater area cleared, but most of the additional acreage was given for use to others and he did not appear to be farming appreciably more himself. It would in any case require more than a period of three seasons to establish reliable patterns for individual farmers and even then changing circumstances would have to be taken into account. However, of the original 25 still farming in 1972, 14 had cleared roughly the same acreage; in six cases the variations were only moderately great and in only five cases were there significant differences. The general opinion in the town was that 1972 was a good season and that a particular effort had been made to bring more land into production; this to some extent brought out in the sample, but the differences are not great, as is shown in Table 20.

If those farmers who dropped out of the survey in 1972 because of death or old age were credited with their performance in 1971, the 1972 totals would be brought up to 46.37 acres (30 farms) for the men and 18.81 acres (16 farms) for the women, a total increase of 4.03 acres, or 6.6 per cent. The two women who had considerably increased the size of their farms had deliberately invested more in wage labour for this purpose, and they fully expected a good return in the form of increased crops for sale. Only one woman, Yaa Sakyibea was farming appreciably less land and the position was complicated in her case by the fact that she was also helping her husband on his farm and a sister living in the same compound was farming with her in 1972 on the same land, so that she was only credited with a half share of the acreage. Kwamena Asamoah controlled a lot of family land, and the decrease in acreage farmed directly by himself did not reflect an overall decrease for his family as a whole. In 1973, whereas the men farmers in the sample continued to increase their acreage there was a sharp fall in the performance of the women farmers. As I only calculated these acreages after leaving Ghana I was not able to find the reason in all cases. Apart from sickness and old age, Isaac Osae's only comment, in correspondence, was that "in some years they clear a large farm and in other years a small farm".

Although there is a wide range of variation the average acreage farmed by the men in the sample was nearly twice as much as the one by the women, 2.6 acres per male farmer in 1971 and 2.9 acres in 1972; women farmed on average 1.4 acres in 1971 and 1.7 acres in 1972. This was to be expected as most of the women had less call on adult helpers than the men. They were assisted by their children, but when it came to clearing the bush they were handicapped. It must also be remembered that women had considerable household duties in addition to their farming activities. Abena Ntowbea, a very industrious farmer, was the only woman in the sample who was helped by her husband; others were helped by relations, but 7 out of 10 of the women in 1972 spent money on clearing, as against only 6 out of 15 of the men.

The amount of produce is not only dependent on the acreage but on the nature of the terrain and the quality of husbandry. It has already been mentioned that there is a strong belief in the advantage of using land that has lain fallow for a long time, not only because of increased fertility and the lower incidence of crop diseases, but also because of the greater return on firewood. This is an important source of cash income and is readily marketable. It was estimated by one farmer in 1971 that the gross return on two and a half acres of land that had been fallow for ten years was 200 cedis (£100 at that time, which was a considerable sum of money in comparison with the GNP per capita for Ghana of US$ 390). If he had left it for only five years he would probably have got about one quarter of that sum. He employed labour to collect and bundle the wood and altogether paid out about 100 cedis for this, but it still represented a useful cash sum. This was well above the average; for example, in 1972 the average firewood sold by farmers in the sample fetched 35 cedis. Fuel is in great demand, even more so in the 1990's than in the 1970's, and there is no problem in disposing of it as trucks come regularly to collect it from Accra, Aburi and surrounding towns. Unlike foodstuffs, for which there is still no regular collection, it only has to be headloaded to Konkonuru and not from there to Jankama or beyond. In 1972 the average number of years in which the land had remained fallow, where this information was available, was 8.3 years for men farmers, and 5.5 years for women.

Marketing of surplus food products is more laborious and attempts to get a regular lorry service to collect them have not been very successful. The services of a contractor were secured in 1971, but by July 1972 he had not visited the town for over three months, it was presumed because his lorry had broken down. The dirt road from Jankama was, at that time, badly eroded and impassable for most vehicles in the rainy season. From the mid-seventies until the end of the eighties there was, in addition the difficulty of obtaining petrol, as well as the shortage of spare parts to keep vehicles on the road. Since then petrol and spare parts are more readily available and efforts have been made to improve the road; however Isaac has written that the road surface has again deteriorated and that it is difficult for lorries to get through, particularly in rainy weather.

There seemed to be a certain inertia in tackling this problem, perhaps because those most able to make arrangements were not too concerned about it, and because most of the hard labour involved in marketing was performed by women, who in any case enjoyed their trips to Jankama or beyond despite the heavy work involved. The richer farmers rely greatly on cocoa for cash income. By 1990 all cocoa production in Konkonuru had ceased, and in the other parts of Ghana where people had their farms the crop was marketed through the Cocoa Board. Some of the richer men in the community also had interests in the akpeteshie distillery, which was run by a partnership, called by them a co-operative, of eleven members. In 1972 production of akpeteshie was at a standstill because of a shortage of molasses and this may have been an additional reason for an increased interest in farming in that year. This was suggested as a reason, but could only have affected a minority, although perhaps the absence of cheap liquor had a more generally sobering effect on the male population as a whole.

Despite difficulties of marketing, considerable quantities of food crops are sold. In the 1971 to 1973 surveys only three of the farmers said that they sold virtually nothing. In all these cases they provided for large numbers in their eating groups, from 18 to 24 people, and in one case the wife of a farmer used any surplus of maize for making kenkey, much of which she then sold. A much more detailed check on food eaten and amounts marketed would be needed in order to assess farm incomes accurately, but the indications, during the years of the surveys was that on average farmers sold as much as they consumed. That this was the case is borne out by a household budget survey carried out in 1969 by the Institute of Social and Economic Research at the University of Ghana (Dutta Roy 1969). It was estimated that the sale of farm produce by farmers in this survey was greater in value than the consumption of their own produce. An average of sales for a farm family was given as 17.86 cedis, as against 11.38 cedis for the value of food consumed over a period of 30 days. It was pointed out that this was above an urban counterpart's income at that time.

Few methods are available which accurately measure rural living conditions. As Appiah (1992: 148) comments, "...the generally subsistence nature of economies in the developing world makes application of techniques developed in wage-earning societies less effective in rural areas. Further, the in-depth approach needed to collect such data is hampered by inadequate village access roads ...".

Dickson and Benneh (1969) refer to this area as being one in which a large percentage of production is intended for sale. Commercial agriculture has been established here for longer than in many other regions in Ghana. It is therefore not correct to describe farming here as subsistence agriculture. Farmers expect to meet their own needs, but they deliberately plan to do more than this, as food crops are considered as a source of cash income.

In the 1972 survey of farmers in Konkonuru estimates were made for the value of food crops eaten by the households. This value was calculated at prevailing prices for produce sold and would have been considerably more if reckoned at retail prices. Information was collected about the amount of produce sold; as with the case of food consumed, prices used were those obtained by the farmer. Table 21 gives the results. The exchange rate in 1972 was 2 cedis to the pound, and total incomes have to be considered in relation to the prevailing GNP. The Table only gives the value of staple foods and does not include additional sources for consumption or sale of plantain, oranges, poultry, goats, game and other minor products. It can be seen that most farmers sold at least as much as they consumed, and estimated cash incomes compared

favourably with average incomes of the majority of urban workers. It is interesting to note that one woman farmer had a higher total income than any of the
men in the sample.

It was not possible from our survey to calculate return to labour, but a
very rough estimate based on the time taken to cultivate a one acre farm, and
including time spent in headloading produce home and to the market, worked
out at a return to labour of about 60 pesewas a day in 1972 for an adult
spending 6 to 9 hours on each of five days a week. This has no claim to
accuracy but was in line with the 70 to 80 pesewas a day paid to wage labour
for clearing the bush. This confirms what has been stated above that overall
farm incomes, including the value of food consumed, represent a standard of
living well above subsistence level and higher than that enjoyed by the majority of unskilled workers in the modern sector of the economy, especially when
the value of cash crops, housing fuel and livestock are taken into account. It
bears out the impression that Konkonuru is a relatively prosperous farming
community. As well as the survey reported by Dutta Roy (1969) this is borne
out by "A Socio- Economic Survey, Eastern Region" undertaken by the Rural
Planning Department in 1970 (Repulic of Ghana 1970).

Table 21

Farm Incomes from Staple Crops — Konkonuru   1972

Sex of Farmer	Value of Food Eaten Cedis		Income from Sale of Staples Cedis		Total Income Cedis	
	Average	Range	Average	Range	Average	Range
Male	306.8	156.0–748.8	394.6	0.0–662.0	701.4	396.0–1005.2
Female	271.4	31.2–530.4	324.5	100.0–865.0	595.9	249.6-1145.8
Total	294.2	31.2–748.8	369.6	0.0–865.0	663.8	249.6–1145.8

Livestock has been mentioned as an additional source of income, although only in a small way. In June 1971 an Animal Health Survey was made.
At that time 41 compounds had some livestock, but in some cases this only
consisted of one or two hens. A total count was made of 107 sheep, of which
42 were lambs, 242 goats, of which 72 were kids, and 78 cocks and hens, not

including chicks. Livestock is mainly used for ritual occasions and not as a regular part of the diet or for sale. Animals roam freely, which necessitates fencing farm perimeters near the town, although in 1972 an order was made that they should be restricted to the compounds until after midday. There still seemed to be goats wandering around, but not so many sheep. The standard of husbandry is not high, and only one or two farmers seem really interested in stock raising. Particulars of a livestock census carried out in May 1971 are given in Appendix 1:4.

Cash crops are not an additional source of income for all families and it is in this respect that the greatest differentials can be observed. The best built houses and those displaying the greatest number of consumption goods are all owned by those with cocoa farms. In our household census in 1970, 227 people had interests in cocoa farms in other parts of Ghana; of these only 31 were resident in Konkonuru for more than three months of the year. Of the 28 farmers in our sample survey 10 of the men and one of the women had cocoa farms elsewhere. This subject is dealt with in greater detail in the next chapter. It is these families that are better able to finance the further education of their children, and in turn probably receive more assistance from their migrant members. For the others, although their cash incomes from farming may compare favourably with the wages of unskilled workers, these incomes are certainly not excessive in relation to the numbers with whom they are shared, particularly now that the cost of consumer goods is so high. Although self sufficient in staples, all families have to buy salt, sugar, onions and fish, cooking utensils and cloth. School children require uniform and registration fees have to be paid. For those without much produce to sell life is indeed hard and although there is no starvation in the town there is certainly a degree of deprivation for a minority.

The discussion so far has confined itself to the number of farms culti-vated by individual farmers, but it is also relevant to look at the total number of farms made in a year by all the members of a compound, as food distribu-tion from a farm is not always confined to a particular eating group. The question of who provides the food for the cooking pot is complicated. Accord-ing to Akan tradition a wife is expected to make provision for herself and her children from her own economic activities. Her husband may supply the land, or the initial capital for trading, but having done this he expects her to meet her own needs. My own observations did not altogether bear this out. Produce was brought back from the farm to the compound and a proportion of it was allo-cated for sale, either before or after processing. All members of the eating group were expected to contribute to the cooking pot and this included sons who were farming on their own account. Several informants told me that a husband was expected to provide food for his family. Food crops were, in any case, marketed mainly by women and they were the ones who handled the cash. They were, therefore, able to exercise considerable control over the family budget. Men sometimes remarked, rather wryly, that their womenfolk gave them back just as much as they decided, and kept the rest for themselves, but I never witnessed these transactions giving rise to major disputes or complaints. Men in Konkonuru as well as women are industrious farmers, a point which is important to make in view of many statements suggesting that men in these areas leave all the hard work of farming to women.

Distribution of food also cuts across compound divisions, for example where a man has two wives living in different compounds, or is supporting a widowed mother. But if the farm sample is taken as a whole it gives a better idea of total numbers fed in relation to resources, although the "other farms" enumerated were not surveyed, so acreage cannot be given. Table 22 gives the number of farms being cultivated by all farmers in the 28 compounds from which the sample was taken.

Table 22

Distribution of farms of all members in sample compounds — Konkonuru, 1971

Sex of Compound Head	No. of Food Farms worked by Cpd. Mems,		No. of People in Compound		No. of farms worked per capita	
	Average	Range	Average	Range	Average	Range
Male (21)	6.3	2–15	20.7	8–36	0.31	0.14–0.69
Female (7)	4.0	2–7	11.0	6–18	0.36	0.29–0.50
Total (28)	5.8	2–15	18.3	6–36	0.32	0.14–0.69

In our household census we had not asked about number of farms, as without probing into the question at length there would inevitably have been double counting, so this sort of question is not appropriate when a complete population count is being made. If, however, the sample survey is used as a basis it would mean that a total of approximately 450 acres was cleared in a year, the average size of farms cleared being 1.5 acres; men's farms averaged 1.8 acres and women's farms 1.1 acres. All the land is intensively cultivated and gives a high yield of food crops, a higher gross return per acre than oil palms or cocoa land in Konkonuru. Yields from cocoa on farms in other areas, such as Akim Abuakwa, are higher as the trees are younger, more hybrid trees have been planted and the standard of husbandry is better. As mentioned earlier there are now no cocoa farms in Konkonuru.

The 28 compounds in the sample represent two-fifths of the 70 compounds in Konkonuru in 1971, excluding the Ewe compounds in outlying hamlets, whose members worked as labourers. If the other compounds had on average the same number of farms this would mean that altogether 302 farms were made in 1971. The average number of people in the 70 compounds is lower than for the sample, 15 against 18.3. In any case it can only be regarded as a rough estimate, although it corresponds to estimates given by informants. In fact, most informants regarded 300 farms as a conservative estimate, some saying that 400-500 new farms were made every year.

Rourke (1971) gives estimates of internal rates of return for different crops in the Eastern Region, which suggests that plantain mixed with cocoyam would be a more profitable crop than cassava or maize. These calculations include a high cost for marketing in relation to prices paid to the producer. Although plantain was grown in Konkonuru the farmers did not consider switching to a greater concentration of it. Cassava is their staple food and they set value on being self-sufficient in it; it is also a low risk crop, less likely to fail. This is now even more important than twenty years ago, as the rainfall has become less reliable. There are few families which feel that they have sufficient land to devote more of it to crops other than those providing their staple diet, preferring, if they have the money, to acquire land elsewhere for this purpose. In view of the finding of our survey that considerable quantities of staple crops were surplus to the requirement of feeding the family this may appear contradictory. It was, nevertheless, given as an explanation by the farmers themselves.

This discussion leads to the question of land use, land tenure and to what extent there are surpluses or shortages of potential farm land, a notoriously complicated subject. The first settlers in Konkonuru moved into empty forest land, which they were given the use of by the Adontenhene of the Akwapim State. They were of the Abrade abusua and, therefore, all the land originally belonged to Abrade, and it was divided between matrilineages as the settlement developed. The land was originally acquired through hunting expeditions, and not by conquest or as a reward for bravery in wars, as was the custom with some new settlements. But abusuas other than Abrade now hold usufructory rights; the explanation given for this was that the land could be acquired through marriage and through the personal wishes of the deceased if these had been expressed in his lifetime and had been agreed by the lineage head and the Chief. If no wish has been expressed and agreed then land is inherited according to matrilineal rules; that is, it passes to the next eldest brother or sister of the deceased and then to the next generation in the matrilineal line.

Land could also be given for use to strangers with the consent of the lineage head and the Chief, but this land could not subsequently be disposed of by strangers if this meant permanent alienation of land from Konkonuru. There is no stool land, as such, as there is in some other Akan communities, although in conversation people would talk of stool land having been given to a person for use. This really meant that the Chief had given usufructory rights to the person concerned. The Chief holds land belonging to his matrilineage, over which he has rights, and it was said that no land has ever been sold, only given for use or rented. Despite this assertion I found one possible exception to this rule, a Ga, Atta Kwasi, now an old man, was said to have "bought" land. Later information revealed that it was probably Atta Kwasi's father who had acquired the land before Atta Kwasi was born, although on exactly what basis was not clear. He lived in a clearing in the bush about a mile from Konkonuru and had been there for many years. As he had married a woman from the town he was probably considered an integrated member of the community, although he continued to live somewhat apart. He was a good farmer and had introduced the favourite variety of cassava which was known after him as Atta Kwasi.

There is no free land within the territory of Konkonuru; all land is considered as belonging to somebody, even though it may never have been cultivated. They know that other towns have sold land to strangers but they do not think that this is a desirable practice and do not believe that it is necessary for them to sacrifice their heritage in this way. In Jankama, the nearest township, the Chief sold land to an American and this has led to endless disputes which to the citizens of Konkonuru seem to be a most disruptive element in community solidarity. This whole question is highly relevant to the debate about the most effective way to improve agricultural productivity, which was referred to above. To what extent are traditional land tenure systems detrimental to development? Some believe that they are, because they stifle individual enterprise and land cannot be used as a colateral for loans under present financial arrangements. Others affirm that they at least safeguard the interests of rural people, safeguarding them from exploitation by rich outsiders, eager to acquire their land. These people would prefer to see development coming through, for example, a change in the rules about borrowing, more research into the ways of improving traditional agricultural practices, and better extension services.

Acquiring the use of land for farming therefore depends on one's connections by kinship and marriage. It was found in the sample survey that the ways in which the farms had been acquired were diverse, and often seemed to cut across strictly matrilineal patterns. This is certainly so in the short run, but the people themselves do not see it as permanent isolation from the traditional holders of usufructory rights, that is the lineage, although there were contradictory elements in statements made by informants.

Table 23 gives details of the sources from which farms were acquired by the sample of compounds surveyed in 1971, 1972 and 1973. It must be stressed that this Table gives a picture of usage at that time, not of ultimate ownership. The expression "given" implies that it is for the recipient's use, and not acquired by inheritance. But the distinction was not always clearly made by respondent's, and certainly the "gift for use" was rarely considered as short term. Questions of terminology are a perennial problem when translating terms and concepts into a different language and culture. Roberts (1972) notes that the word "sale" was often used when legally it should have been "rental", and   that the difference is not immediately perceptible to a man desiring land which has been rented "in perpetuity". It was frequently stated that a son could go on farming his father's land after the father's death if he had expressed the wish during his lifetime. This could even extend to the next generation, that is, the son's son. If, however, the son stopped using the land it would revert to the matrilineage, and cases were cited of this happening. The fluidity of the situation is no doubt due to there not yet being any shortage of land in this community.

It is significant that, despite the value attached to the matrilineage never permanently alienating land, so many men had been given the use of land by their fathers or other patrilineal kin. This reflects the tendency for a father to wish to transmit his house property and his privately acquired cocoa farms to his own sons rather than to his sister's sons. Uchendu (1969) found that in his sample of cocoa farmers in Akim Abuakwa, 14 per cent of his respondents said that they had been given cocoa farms by their fathers. It is interesting that a number of women in the Konkonuru sample had been given the use of farms by their fathers, although Table 23 conceals differences between women of different marital status. It was mainly widows and divorcees who were farming on their fathers' land. Table 24 gives a more detailed picture of the 82 women farmers in survey compounds, in 1971 only as the information is more complete for that year.

The renting of land by six women farmers, shown in Table 24 covered a variety of arrangements. Most frequently a cash payment was made, averaging 10 cedis (£5 in 1971) for the once-only use of a farm, and most of the land acquired in this way was in the territory of surrounding townships. An alternative system was for land to be given as a pledge in exchange for a loan. In this case the land was held until the loan had been repaid.

Table 23

Sources of Farms of Farmers in Survey Compounds — Konkonuru, 1971, 1972, 1973

Source	Men		Women		Total	
	No. of farms	%	No. of farms	%	No. of farms	%
Patrilateral line						
Father	35	27.1	14	17.3	49	23.3
Other patri.	17	13.1	5	6.1	22	10.5
Total patri.	52	40.2	19	23.4	71	33.8
Matrilineal						
Mother's brother	25	19.4	10	12.3	35	16.7
Mother	9	7.0	10	12.3	19	9.0
Lineage (unspec.)	13	10.1	2	2.6	15	7.1
Other matri.	6	4.7	6	7.4	12	5.8
Total matri.	53	41.2	28	34.6	81	38.6
Affines						
Husband or ex-husband	—	—	24	29.6	24	11.4
Other affines	10	7.7	1	1.3	11	5.3
Total affines	10	7.7	25	30.9	35	16.7
Rented	13	10.1	8	9.9	21	10.0
Lent (No Relation)	1	0.8	1	1.2	2	0.9
Grand Total	129	100.0	81	100.0	210	100.0

* This Table only includes those farms for which information was available. Details were obtained from all the 28 farmers in the intensive sample, but it was not always possible to get accurate information for all the other farmers in the 28 compounds.

Table 24 illustrates the norm referred to earlier that a married woman relies on her husband for land. For those still married who were not living in the same households as their husbands the numbers are too small to draw any conclusions; for those whose husbands were not in town it was not possible to get details of their activities from eight of them because they were away at the time, probably visiting their husbands. Although the sample of widows is small it shows their dependence on the matrilineage; if those not giving details are excluded 73 per cent of them had acquired the use of land from this source.

Table 24

Sources of Land worked by Women Farmers in Sample Compounds — Konkonuru, 1971

Women farming on their own / How farms acquired	With husband in household	With husband in other household in town	With husband away	Widow	Divorced	Total
Given by husband for use	18	2	—	—	—	20
Given by former husband for use	—	—	—	—	3	3
Given by father for use	1	—	—	3	2	6
Given by full brother for use	—	—	—	2	1	3
Given by patri-brother for use	—	—	—	1	—	1
Inherited from mother's brother	—	1	—	5	1	7
Inherited from mother	—	—	1	3	—	4
Inherited from mother's mother	—	1	—	—	—	1
Family land (unspecified)	1	—	—	5	1	7
Rented	2	—	1	3	—	6
No details	—	—	3	4	2	9
Total Farms on own*	22	4	5	26	10	67
Total Women	13	3	5	17	7	45
Farming on husband's farm	22	—	—	—	—	22
On son's or sister's	—	—	1	1	—	2
Farming (no details)	—	—	8	1	4	13
Total Women	35	3	14	19	11	82

* These figures refer to the number of farms made in 1971; for example, the 22 farms in column 1. were made by the 13 women farmers who still had husbands living in the same household, an average of 1.7 farms per woman.

Of the few divorcees in the sample, three of·them were still farming on land given them for use by their ex-husbands; three had land from their matrilineage and one had been given land to farm by her father.

The extension of farming activities into surrounding territory might suggest that there is a shortage of land in Konkonuru. This has to be looked at from an individual as well as a territorial point of view. Informants said that there was no great difficulty in obtaining the use of land for anyone who wished to farm, but the question was "what sort of land and where?". Some families had easier access than others to better land, both in terms of distance from town, soil fertility and topography. Some of the land was on a steep scarp slope, and much of it was hilly and rocky. In such cases a person might prefer to rent land rather than to use land given to him or her three or more miles from home. There was a reserve of virgin forest land in outlying hilly and inaccessible parts of Konkonuru territory which is at present used solely for hunting. It takes over an hour to reach this land, so it is not at present considered an economic proposition for food farms. It is in any case not free land, but belongs to one or other matrilineage group. Although great stress was placed on the undesirability of permanently alienating any land some outlying tracts were "sold" some time ago to some Ga people from Peduase, in addition to the alleged "sale" to the Ga mentioned previously. This has given rise to boundary disputes and was not a subject about which the Chief was anxious to talk. The people of Konkonuru today are ready to buy land in other parts of Ghana for cocoa farming, but they are still, at least in theory, jealous of their own territory. It might be expected that over the course of more than twenty years since this study started there would have been marked changes in attitudes and practices. But as far as land was concerned this did not seem to be so.

The amount farmed on one year is therefore dependent on a number of factors. There is, firstly, the availability of land and its location; a farmer does not want to have all his farms a very long distance from town, nor does he, for preference, want it all to be in the drier, hillier areas. He may not overtly estimate that the returns to labour from these locations are lower, but this is in fact the case. Secondly there is the availability of labour to clear land to consider. A farmer who has plenty of family workers to call on is more likely to clear a larger area. As clearing is confined to certain periods of the year, chance factors such as sickness, funerals or travelling on family business enter into this. Thirdly there is the availability of cash to pay wage labourers in cases where family workers are insufficient. There is also the individual farmer's own industry and allocation of time in relation to other activities. If a farmer has cocoa farms, is a member of the akpeteshie distillery co-operative, or does a lot of hunting, these activities will be balanced against food farming.

When questioning informants it was difficult to arrive at clear ideas as to how decisions were made and to what extent these different factors were determinants. A better understanding was often gained on visits to farms, when reasons were given spontaneously for a particular course of action, such as, "My husband started to clear my farm, but after a week he had to travel to his uncle's funeral. He was away for three weeks and when he came back he had still not cleared his own farm. I got some boys to complete the work and paid them 12 cedis," or "I was sick in January and February, so it was March before I could start clearing my farm that is why this year I have only a small farm, but I hope to make an *adom* farm in August", or "My son was home on leave from the Army for four weeks in February, so I was able to make a bigger farm this year". The desire for cash incomes to raise standards of living is clearly expressed, and although these farmers may not make their calculations on a precise cost-return basis they do bear these considerations in mind, and in this sense can be said to represent "economic man".

On the other hand farming is mixed up with traditional beliefs and value systems which can only indirectly, if at all, be looked upon as "economic". For example, one day a week is devoted to the land gods and the soil must never be disturbed on that day. Friday is the non-farming day in Konkonuru, as this was the day that Nana Takyi Aprokyewa discovered the spring, "obo kofi", and this is still strictly observed. It is permissible to visit the farms on that day to collect food or fuel, but no planting or weeding may be done. I never found any instance of this rule being broken. Some of the older members of the community also observe their "birth" day as a non-farming day. All Akans are given a "birth" name according to the day of the week on which they were born and this has tremendous significance for them. My landlord was named Kwamena, which meant that he was born on a Tuesday, and he never went to farm on that day. This practice however, is dying and very few instances of it could be found, even in 1971. Christians do not go to farm on Sundays, and this in practice is also observed as a non-farming day by many non-Christians, which brings the average number of farming days a week to five, although activities connected with farming are carried out on other days. Friday is used for communal tasks and this often involves the clearing of bush paths, a very necessary task if farmers are to have easy access to their land. Women take produce to market on Fridays and spend time in preparing food crops for sale, and men go on hunting expeditions. It is therefore unlikely that traditional beliefs about the land curtail farming activities to any large extent. A worker must have some rest from his labours and farming is hard work.

The value attached to growing all one's own staple food supplies, rather than concentrating on cash crops, may cut across economic considerations, as has been found in other studies, such as those of Swift (1965) in Malaysia. It might in the long run be more profitable for a farmer to devote all his land to tree crops and to buy his food supplies, yet no farmer considers this as a serious proposition, and only uses land for tree crops that is surplus to his food crop needs, including a margin to provide for a poor year's harvest. There are economic factors as well as traditional values to be taken into account. Tree crops take a long time to mature and in the meantime a farmer must eat. The risk of failure or low market prices means that his livelihood may be permanently endangered. It is even doubtful whether the return on tree crops at current market prices is better than the return on food crops; more research needs to be undertaken on this subject before farmers are persuaded to change their existing practices. The farmers themselves are sceptical; they value cocoa, citrus and other tree crops as an additional source of cash income but would not be prepared to rely on them entirely. It is interesting to note that in some countries where a switch has been made in favour of cash crops this has had a deleterious effect on the health of the people, particularly of children. The Chief Medical Officer in Swaziland (Hardiman & Nott 1976b) was seriously concerned about the switch to cotton in parts of the Ngwavumu valley, as he had perceived an increase in malnutrition amongst the under-fives. The farms in this area appeared more prosperous than in other parts of the valley, with more consumer goods in the household and often a tractor or truck in the farmyard, but it was doubtful whether the men who controlled the budget were spending enough of it on food to compensate for what had previously been grown on the homestead.

Farming is a way of life and is valued as such. The work may be hard, but it gives satisfaction and is carried out in a social atmosphere. I was once again struck with this when I returned to the town in 1990. My arrival on a Saturday was unannounced and the town was practically empty, except for a few old people and children. Immediately one of the children was told to take me to find some of my old friends on their farms, and this they did with great glee. First we came across Isaac and Jacob looking very smart in their bright orange boiler suits, a gift from a Canadian. They were keen to show me the farms they had made that year and to talk about the progress of their crops. And together we sought out Kate Asare, my town sister, now well into her 70's. She was busy on her farm, which as always seemed to be of above average size for a woman farmer, and it was being kept in good order. A farmer, even when working alone is not isolated; as she walks to her farm a woman will meet others, stop to pass the time of day and discuss their crops; at midday when she breaks for lunch, perhaps some roasted cocoyams cooked on the farm, others will join her. Always the bush seems alive with people and the greetings *"Ayekoo* and *Yaayee"* can be heard. Children may join parents for their midday meal and take back a headload when they return to school. Fruit is plentiful and tastes particularly good when picked fresh and eaten in the open air. There is no overseer breathing down one's neck to goad one on, so if the work is exhausting a rest can always be taken. The sun is hot, but the air is fresh and there are shade trees under which to sit. There is the excitement of watching crops grow and the satisfaction of harvesting. This may sound sentimental and these pleasures certainly have to be balanced against the days when it pours with rain and one returns soaking wet and cold, or when one drags oneself to farm suffering from a raging headache or aching limbs. But the impression I gained, after walking many miles through the bush, visiting farms and sharing in the work, was that this satisfaction was real and a fitting reward for toil. Women of an advanced age still go to their farms. They may not be able to perform many of the tasks themselves, but they like to see what is going on.

What then is the future of traditional farming in the face of agricultural modernization? Great efforts have been made in Ghana for many years to increase food production and schemes have been put forward to mechanize large tracts of land and apply modern methods of cultivation. So far most of these developments have been in the north and in the Volta River basin, south of the Akasombo Dam. But little has been done, or even proposed in areas that are not well suited to the use of large-scale mechanical equipment. Methods of improving existing systems of bush fallow cultivation at an intermediate level have not so far been devised. Some experts, such as La-Anyane (1963) believe that little progress can be made until land tenure systems are rationalized, but little has been said, until recently, about the technological improvements that might be possible. However, there are now some encouraging signs that the importance of this sector is becoming better recognized. A Canadian project is experimenting with improved varieties of maize suitable for bush fallow cultivation, and the Ministry of Agriculture has set up demonstration plots to show the potential of alley farming. Alley farming uses leucaena, a shrub which is planted in alleys to form divides between which crops are grown (National Research Council 1984, Kang and Reynolds 1989). *Leucaena* is a potent source of nitrogen, so it acts as a fertiliser, which means that a plot of land when cleared can be used for several years, hence eliminating the hard task of clearing the bush annually. It has additional uses as fodder for livestock and as a source of fuel. So far few farmers have adopted this innovation, and it is too early to assess its long term benefits.

For many years most of Ghana's food will be produced by traditional farmers, so it is still relevant to study their methods and the possibilities of expansion within the existing socio-economic structure of this sector (Gubbels 1993). Already their achievement in increasing output is considerable, given the fact that population has nearly doubled in the past twenty years. The opening up of rural areas by the building of better feeder roads and the improvement of transport facilities would in the short run probably do more to increase supplies than the wholesale conversion to modern methods. It would certainly be acclaimed by the farmers themselves who could then concentrate more on production, freed from some of the burden of distribution. The question of marketing has already been mentioned, and was often discussed. At one time there was a food market in Konkonuru and a sign on the main road directing passers by to it. But when the condition of the road deteriorated people were unwilling to come, and the sign was removed; even although the road has now been improved the town market has not been revived. Farmers are aware of the fact that they could receive more for their produce if they sold it direct to the consumer and they resent the fact that traders at Aburi and Jankama to whom they sell get the profits. But there is a time factor involved (Becker1965). The longer they spend away from their farms the less they can produce, and they regard themselves primarily as farmers. A parallel situation was found in a village in the Volta Region where women set off at 5 am in the morning to sell their produce to market women at Ho, 3 or 4 miles away, and returned immediately to work on their farms. They realized that by sitting in the market themselves they could get greater cash returns, and they also resented the fact that profits accrued to traders whom they described as "just sitting about doing nothing". But they never seriously considered changing their way of life because it would lead to the neglect of their land. One could, of course, attempt to assess the net returns on alternative courses of action, imputing an hourly rate earned. Obviously this calculation would not be made overtly by the women concerned, but some such concept no doubt lay in the backs of their minds.

The importance of marketing has been stressed by different Governments over the past twenty or more years, but progress in implementing plans has been slow. The depressed economic position of the country in the 1970's and 1980's was accompanied by an acute shortage of transport and little fuel to run even what existed. As the situation has improved there are now greater possibilities of introducing more effective schemes. Better arrangements for marketing would encourage not only an increase in the production of staples, but a greater diversification. For example, vegetable and salad crops could be grown in areas where at present they are impossible to market. Commercial poultry farming, which has already made great strides near the cities, could be introduced in more remote rural areas, and livestock rearing could become an additional source of income if practices of husbandry could be improved. A great deal of research and agricultural extension work is needed to exploit these possibilities; at the moment farmers do not readily call on the services of experts, perhaps because in the existing circumstances they do not find their advice very helpful. My own efforts to elicit the assistance of the Faculty of Agriculture at Legon never resulted in any useful advice. This was not due to unwillingness but an inability to understand the particular limitations and possibilities of bush fallow cultivation. For example it was suggested that it would be beneficial to use fertiliser to improve crop yields. The result of this when applied to cassava was that growth was more rapid; but when the roots were dug many of them had rotted in the ground, possibly because the rapidity of growth had led to the development of softer tubers. So, although recent signs are more encouraging there is still much to be done, and unless higher priority is given to this sector progress will continue to be slow. In any case, unless there is co-ordination between innovations in agricultural practice and facilities for marketing little progress will be made in raising farm incomes.

How relevant is the question of land reform to communities like Konkonuru? If asked this question directly the people are puzzled, even disturbed. They see no reason for it, considering that the existing system is sufficiently flexible to meet their needs. They are not against technical innovations if they think that they can help to increase farm incomes, but they see no necessary connection between these and tenurial systems.

This is their present stance. The position may well change if land becomes scarcer due to pressure of population or to external demand (Harris 1982). If permanent cultivation were introduced the consolidation of holdings would become a more rational solution, but this is another issue. The demographic changes that have taken place in Konkonuru over the past twenty years means that there are more men farmers in the 18–65 years age group. Although no systematic count of the amount of land being cultivated was made in the 1990 household survey, the views expressed indicated that there had been an increase in the number and size of farms being made, with a consequent fall in the number of years that land was left fallow. But there was no feeling that available land had yet become insufficient to meet the needs of the community. Much will depend on the extent to which the new younger generation take up farming, and whether, if they are able to do this on a commercial scale, this way of life will compete with the rewards of employment in the wage sector of the economy. The average age of farmers is lower now than in 1970, but it is still relatively high, and there is as yet little evidence that farming is the preferred choice of the school leaver, whether or not the incomes from farming compare favourably with unskilled and semi-skilled labour. If the position changes, and more young people stay in rural areas, this is likely to lead to significant changes, not only in the structure of these communities but in their attitudes to, and acceptance of, traditional practices.

In this chapter it has been demonstrated that women hold a key position in the economy of the community. The role of women in bush fallow cultivation is well known in Akan society. It leads to questions about how this economic role relates to women's position as a whole (Hardiman 1974a). To what extent does it contribute to their economic independence, and in what ways does their position compare with that of men? An Akan wife is expected to support herself and her children in staple crops. The "meat money" customarily given to a wife by her husband is intended mainly for his own food, although no real distinction can be made in cases where a wife is working on her husband's farm. And in Konkonuru, as has been seen, responsibility for feeding the family is shared by men.

As far as food crops are concerned a woman exercises a great deal of control through the marketing of produce. She is the one who receives the cash and has a large say in how it should be spent. Men frequently asserted that because of this a woman controlled the purse strings. Even an unmarried son, farming on his own account, would get his produce sold by his mother or other female relatives. She did not necessarily give back to him the whole of the proceeds from the sale, keeping a little as a return for her entrepreneurial services.

For tree crops the position is different. Women can and do own cocoa farms, but their holdings are smaller than those of men. They are not so likely to be given or to inherit farms, and they have less cash to invest or access to labour. A man frequently has another wife living on his cocoa farms in other parts of Ghana, and the option of a second husband to look after her property is not open to a woman. So their incomes from this source is less than for men.

Access to land for women depends heavily on men, either their husbands or their matrikin. A woman is never the abusua panin, that is the head, of a lineage, so decisions about allocation are in the last resort out of her hands, even though she may influence those decisions. The importance attached to the role of the Queen Mother in Akan society is well documented. As far as the royal lineage is concerned she plays a significant part in the deliberations of her abusua, and there are women in other abusuas who form part of the inner circle. But, in Konkonuru, although there was nominally a Queen Mother, she did not seem to wield the same power as her Ashanti sisters.

Migration has resulted in a predominance of women in many rural areas. Also a higher proportion of women than men are widowed, divorced, or living apart from their husbands. This emphasizes their economic responsibility, a responsibility which they have always borne, but has, as far as food farming is concerned, increased as a result of economic and social change. Changes in this respect, as in others, have not so far benefitted women to the same extent as men, as they have been less likely to move into cash crops or into the modern sector of the economy.

Chapter 6

MIGRANT CITIZENS OF KONKONURU

Migration is a familiar feature of countries in Africa, and light has been thrown on the position in Ghana by the work of Caldwell (1969). From a sociological point of view a particularly interesting feature of his survey is its use of the technique of "family reconstitution", that is the enumeration of members of households who were absent at the time but had been born there, as was the case in the 1970 and 1990 household censuses of Konkonuru. As a background to the Konkonuru material it is relevant to look at some of the findings of Caldwell regarding the types of migration and the characteristics of the migrants, Caldwell's survey was about rural-urban migration whereas this study was equally interested in migration to other rural areas. Caldwell did not regard this latter type as an antithesis of the other as he considered that both involved moves from less developed to more developed areas, from more traditional to less traditional ways of life, and from subsistence to cash economies. Although this contention is to some extent born out by the Konkonuru study there were significant differences between the two types, which were not explored in his study.

Migration is not a new phenomenon in Africa, but it has greatly increased in scale and pace in this century, and large towns have experienced very rapid growth rates. In Ghana the estimate of the 1960 census was 10 per cent per annum. Gil & Omaboe's survey (1966) based on the 1960 census, found that in Accra 85 per cent of the 15–24 age group and 69 per cent of the 25–54 age group were composed of immigrants, and that their main occupations were labourers, service workers, transport workers, and "white collar" jobs, few of them being engaged in trading. This survey emphasized the importance of migrant labour in the Ghanaian economy, not only for urban occupations but also for the production of cash crops, particularly cocoa. Different patterns and directions were found for different regions; in the Eastern Region, Accra was the most important single destination. There was also found to be some immigration to the Eastern Region, but this was mainly to towns, such as Koforidua, rather than to rural areas.

Since these surveys were made there have not been any comparable studies of migration, as research has been inhibited by the economic situation unless it has been funded from overseas. The 1984 census did indicate that the pace of increase in urban areas had slowed down and that a higher proportion of the population was living in rural areas than at the time of the two previous censuses. But as the economy improves this may well change again.

Caldwell (1969: 52) found that 72 per cent of his rural sample, broken down into 68 per cent of the males, and 77 per cent of the females, had never migrated to towns,a figure swollen by the inclusion of children. Of these a considerable number had frequently visited towns and were therefore not altogether insulated from urban life, or unaffected by the new ideas generated there. Looking at the determining factors he found that the greatest flow was from the larger and less distant rural areas, and he commented that "the short distance migration from such socially and economically advanced areas as the Akwapim Ridge into Accra is very different from the movement from the near subsistence villages of the Savannah". The young and educated are more likely to migrate than the old and illiterate, and more males than females leave the rural areas, as is illustrated by the Konkonuru surveys, although for the younger generation Caldwell found that the differences in the sex ratio of migrants were decreasing and were in any case less than in many parts of Africa. Marriage was not considered an obstacle; for men the decision to migrate was normally taken before marriage and wives and children seemed to be remarkably mobile, although they could become an embarrassment in town because of the expense of family accommodation and food. The eldest children were less likely to migrate, particularly the eldest sons and the eldest daughter, and most likely to return if they did.

In discussing the urban pulls and pushes Caldwell considered the overriding forces to be economic and attributed the net flow to be a consequence of the differential in favour of urban job opportunities and incomes (Fei and Ranis 1961). On the other hand there were strong counter forces of a non-economic sort, most important being the reluctance to break close ties with one's family and one's home town. His survey brought out the strong sentiments attached to one's place of origin, and the continuing links that were maintained; 75 per cent of his urban sample returned annually to their home towns, 80 per cent of them had already built, were building or hoped to build a house in their town, and nearly all of those who came on visits claimed that they brought presents or money for their relatives. Over 30 per cent of both his urban and rural samples thought that village families would be very poor without these remittances, and Caldwell thought that the high water mark of rural dependence on towns might still lie ahead. This again is something that may have changed since the time of his survey as a result of the high rate of unemployment and underemployment in urban areas and the low level of wages in relation to the cost of living. Of Caldwell's urban sample 92 per cent said that they intended ultimately to return, and of the rural sample 79 per cent of those over 65 who had migrated had already come back.

Of particular interest to the Akwapim situation, in view of Caldwell's remarks about this area, were the trends he predicted for the future. He considered that migrants were increasingly likely to take their families with them and to pay more frequent but shorter return visits. They would, he thought, be less likely in future to take presents, remit money or build a house in their town, and when they did send money, it was more likely to be through the Post Office.

For as long as anyone in the town can remember people have been migrating from Konkonuru to other parts of Ghana, and even further afield. The main reason, as found by Caldwell, is economic, but there is also the attraction, particularly for the younger generation, of getting to know the world outside, experiencing the excitement of living in a big town and enjoying the independence of an individual pay packet. Most families have contacts outside, some relative who lives in a town, and this acts as a stepping stone for establishing a more permanent base. Many citizens have made good in the outside world and this provides an example to emulate for those remaining. One of them is a lawyer practising in London, another a doctor in England, and there are others in the USA and Germany, not to mention successful contractors operating in Accra, Tema and elsewhere in Ghana. Education has been the key to their success and for most of them their further education has been paid for out of the profits of cocoa farming (Siddle and Swindell 1990).

But for most, migration is more spasmodic and they see it as a stage in their life, rather than as a permanent condition. They regard Konkonuru as their home town and expect to return to it after a period away. This view is still held, at least in theory, but the 1990 survey recorded such a great increase in absent citizens that it is probable that in fact many of them will make their permanent homes elsewhere. Whereas migration at first was mainly to cocoa farms in other parts of Ghana the present younger generation is less interested in going to live in another rural area prefering to seek wage employment in a big town, preferably Accra.

The Konkonuru household census of December 1970 afforded some information about migrants, including educational levels (see Appendix 3), but certain personal details relating to them could not be as accurate as those for the resident population; for example, it is not possible to make a valid comparison between the composition of rural and urban households for those away from Konkonuru as those not considered to be citizens, even if they were spouses, tended not to be included. A follow-up sample survey of 25 compounds (one third of the original total of compounds) was carried out in July 1972 and additional questions were asked about time spent away from town. More information was collected informally through conversations, and particularly in connection with farm land away from Konkonuru. There was constant discussion with the younger adults of the community about employment opportunities in Accra and elsewhere, and a great deal of talk about those who had successfully found jobs. When these young people returned home on visits there was much curiosity about their experiences, and questioning about likely prospects for others to follow in their footsteps.

The number of Konkonuru citizens living away from the town is high, and the figures for 1990 were more than double those for 1970, 2428 against 1211. Table 25 shows the distribution of resident and non-resident citizens, by age group in 1990.

Table 25

Distribution of Resident and Non-Resident Citizens by Age Group — 1990

Age Group	Resident						Non-Resident					
	Male		Female		Total		Male		Female		Total	
	No.	%	No.	%	No.	%	No.	%	No.	%	No.	%
Under 18	278	54	280	47	558	50	467	40	460	37	927	38
18–56	192	37	249	42	441	40	640	55	712	56	1352	56
Over 56	45	9	68	1	113	10	64	5	85	7	149	6
TOTALS	515	100	597	100	1112	100	1171	100	1257	100	2428	100

The 1970 census collected data on the location of migrants, but this was not repeated in 1990. The numbers in Accra, although considerable, were not as great as would be supposed from casual conversations, and by no means reflected the close contacts that the town had with the city. It perhaps demonstrated just how much circulation takes place on a short term basis, young people, particularly, making frequent visits to relatives living in Accra, often with the hope of finding employment there, but in the meanwhile returning to spend most of their time in Konkonuru. Table 26 shows the location of Konkonuru citizens in 1970.

Table 26

Distribution by Place of Residence and Location in December 1970

Residence	Konkonuru	Other E.R.	Accra	Other Ghana	Abroad	Not Stated	Total
			Location at time of Survey				
In Konkonuru for 9 months or more in previous year	1048	20	4	8	—	5	1085
In Konkonuru for less than 9 months in previous year	37	686	267	201	11	9	1211
TOTAL	1085	706	271	209	11	14	2296

Apart from Accra, 50 of the non-resident citizens at the time of the 1970 survey were located in towns with populations over 5,000; this left a large majority of migrants (74 per cent) in rural areas. Table 27 and the map showing the distribution of farm lands acquired in other places show the nature and extent of this movement. The occupational distribution of those that had moved away, shown in Table 28 shows that 60 per cent of the working population of migrants were still farmers. The 1990 census was not able to go into the same detail as 1970, partly because the families interviewed were less certain of the location of those of their members who had migrated. There were a much greater number of migrants recorded in this census, and the general impression was that a higher proportion had moved into larger towns rather than into rural areas. There is however some contradiction, if this is so, as it is not consistent with the fact that the poor economic situation, leading to greater unemployment in urban areas, seemed to have encouraged those in the working age group to return home to look after their farms, or to decide not to seek jobs elsewhere for the time being.

The characteristics of migrants from Konkonuru conform to Caldwell's model in terms of age and education, though not to the same extent in terms of sex, but this may be due to an under-enumeration of male migrants. There were many more adult women than men resident in the town in 1970, (66 per cent of the over 18 years population were women) and my first assumption that this was largely the result of migration was no doubt correct. I found

Table 27

Distribution of Population by Farm Land in other parts of Ghana

Residence Status in Konkonuru in 1970	E.R.	Volta	Ashanti	Brong-Ahafo	C.R.	W.R.	All Cocoa Farms elsewhere	No other Farms elsewhere	Total Population
9 months or more									
Male	20				3	2	25	467	492
Female	4				2		6	587	593
Sub-Total	24				5	2	31	1054	1085
3 months or less									
Male	93	2	4	5	9		113	505	618
Female	72	2	3		6		83	510	593
Sub-Total	165	4	7	5	15		196	1015	1211
Grand Total	189	4	7	5	20	2	227	2069	2296

several cases of men, by then middle-aged, who were successful contractors or business men who were not included in our 1970 census, and of whom I heard subsequently when I was constructing family genealogies. They had cut themselves off from their home town almost completely, not having visited it for many years, in some cases because of family disputes which had led to a feeling of bitterness against those left at home, so they no longer had close ties with the community. In 1970 this seemed to be unusual, but no doubt it is now more prevalent as life becomes more individualistic, and oriented towards the nuclear family. Those responsible for the 1990 household census took great pains to record non-resident citizens, but the lack of detailed knowledge about many of them does indicate that ties had to some extent slackened. It seemed that many of them rarely returned to their home town, often only if there was a funeral of a close relative to attend.

The striking feature of migration from Konkonuru is the movement to other rural areas, and here the characteristics of migrants are no different from the resident population as far as age, sex and education are concerned, as the

Table 28

Distribution of 1972 Sample, by Residence and Occupation — 18 years and over

Occupation	In Konkonuru 9 mths, or more July '71- July '72		Other rural areas		Accra		Other towns		Not known		Total		
	M	F	M	F	M	F	M	F	M	F	M	F	All
Farming	49	96	60	64							109	160	269
Trading		2	2	4	5	16	1	4			8	26	34
Skilled Manual			7		2						9		9
Driving	1		3		1						5		5
Labourer			3		1						4		4
Clerical					1					1	1	1	2
Seamstress		1				1						2	2
Nursing								1				1	1
Teaching					1	1	1				2	1	3
Domestic work							1	1				2	2
Armed Forces					1						1		1
Police								1	1		1		
Still in Education	8	5	3	2		2	2	5			13	14	27
Retired or NA	2	4	1		2	1	1	2	1		7	7	14
Total	60	108	66	70	23	21	8	13	3	2	159	215	374

determining factors lie elsewhere, being closely related to lineage membership. As stated by Okali (1983) the establishment of cocoa farms without assistance from kin is a difficult proposition. Many of the points made by Hill (1963) are borne out for migrants from Konkonuru. The lands acquired at the time of the first migration by the matrilineal Akwapim are held as "family lands"; in the case of land acquired later the tendency for individuals to acquire lands privately and to transmit them to their sons and their daughters, as well as matrikin, is apparent. Hill found it impossible to derive any satisfactory procedure for estimating the number of lands in which the informant had a potential interest and found that "the only practicable procedure was to ask informants to list those 'abusua lands' in which they had a personal stake, either as inheritors or by usufructuary rights" (*op cit:* 196). She did not include in the total lands acquired by fathers, as she was not able to ascertain the extent of the son's benefit.

The first Konkonuru farmer to acquire cocoa lands elsewhere was Kwadjo Densu. One day, in about 1910, he set off with his wife, carrying with them all their possessions. On the first day they reached Nsawam, a distance of about 12 miles, along forest paths. There they spent the night, and on the next day they walked to Asuboi, another 8–10 miles, where they negotiated with the Chief, who agreed to "sell" them land. The term "sell" was used by informants. It ignores legal terminology regarding the distinction between freehold and leasehold rights. In the Twi language it is not possible to make the same distinction as would be made in Britain as there is no concept equivalent to freehold in Akan society.

Kwadjo Densu and his wife cleared the land they had acquired and planted cocoa trees, later being joined by other members of their family. This land was, and still is, regarded as "family land" and members of the matrilineage are the inheritors. About twenty years later Kwadjo Densu decided to move to fresh fields and travelled to Asabidie in Akim Abuakwa. By then it was possible to go by lorry from Accra to Oda, but beyond there the last thirty miles had to be travelled on foot through the forest. At night they camped out wherever they reached by nightfall and slept in the barks of trees. The land he acquired came under the Chief of Oda, and Kwadjo Densu secured a portion roughly one square mile in area for a payment of 9 (old) pounds. The present users of the land still pay annual tribute to the Chief, but for all intentive purposes it is regarded as theirs, and there is no question of its return.

Kwadjo Densu acquired this land for himself and did not consider it as "family land" in the same way as that at Asuboi. He therefore felt free to give it to whomsoever he chose, and the resulting pattern of inheritance is an interesting mixture of matrilineal and patrilineal. Both Kwadjo Densu and his wife died in 1946 and the present users of the land are related to them in the ways indicated in (Fig. 9). In cases where a holder of land died without "willing" who should succeed him, the land was inherited by a member of the matriclan, as was the case when Yaw Oppong and Kwame Sekyi died, although Yaw Oppong had already given a portion of his land to his son, Kwadjo Densu II.

When Yaw Oppong died there was a dispute over the inheritance of that part of his land that he had not given to his son. Kwame Afram, an older brother of his, was then working in Nigeria, where he had spent 35 years, and there is always reluctance to hand over land to an absentee member of the family. It proved impossible to reach an acceptable settlement within the family and the case was eventually taken to the court at Akropong, where an award was made dividing the land between Kwame Afram and Kwadjo Densu II. This was the only case I heard of a dispute over land being taken to court, but there may well have been others; people are reluctant to admit resorting to a form of legislation which they still feel is alien to them, and he who takes such a step is looked upon with disfavour. It was remarked, a propos of this

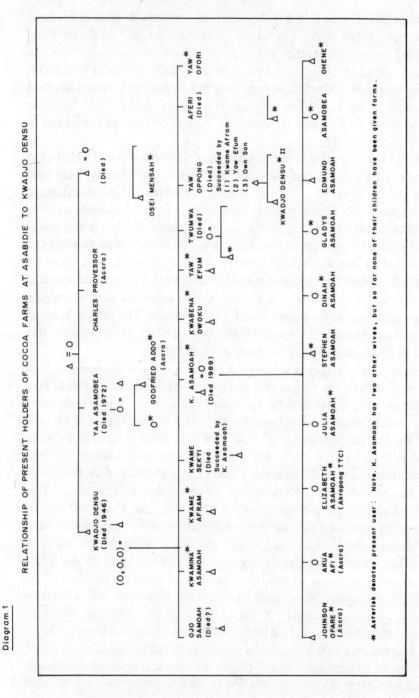

Fig. 9: Relationship of present holders of cocoa farms at Asabidie to Kwadjo Densu.

Diagram 1

RELATIONSHIP OF PRESENT HOLDERS OF COCOA FARMS AT ASABIDIE TO KWADJO DENSU

* Asterisk denotes present user: Note: K. Asamoah has two other wives, but so far none of their children have been given farms.

case, that "You can only do that sort of thing if you are rich". A dispute over stool land in Konkonuru, at the time of the destoolment of Obeng Kwaku, was, so it was said, taken to the Adontenhene at Aburi, but this was a subject about which people were not very willing to talk.

Kwadjo Densu himself was inherited by two brothers and a sister, as well as by his sons and one of his daughters. He had many wives, and even more numerous children, most of them not included in the diagram as they were not inheritors of land. He made his own decision before he died as to who should inherit, and as he regarded land at Asabidie as privately acquired the inheritance pattern cannot be considered in the same light as customary matrilineal inheritance. It does however, illustrate the flexibility and variations in inheritance practices in this matrilineal society, which has no doubt been influenced by trends in Akwapim as a whole where matrilineal and patrilineal societies live in close proximity. In Aburi, as a consequence of this, the rules of inheritance were changed some years ago to allow more property to pass to a man's own children.

The way in which the matrilineal pattern of inheritance works is also complicated, and depends on individual preferences and decisions. For example, Kwadjo Densu's sister's son, Godfried Addo, acquired land direct from Kwadjo Densu before his mother's death. The land which his mother acquired from her brother did not pass to her son when she died. At his mother's funeral there was disagreement as to who should inherit the land, some thinking that it should go to her sister from whom she had been alienated for many years, others thinking that it should go to her daughter. At the time of writing this dispute had not been finally resolved.

Godfried Addo remembers that the land had been given to him when he was a boy, still attending Primary School. In 1939 when he entered Achimota College his fees were paid out of profits from the cocoa harvest, one example of a frequent use to which such profits were put and which in this case undoubtedly proved an excellent investment, both for the individual, for the family and for the wider society to which he contributed his skills. As a result of his education he was able to enter the Civil Service and rose to a senior position in the Ministry of Social Welfare and Community Development. He regularly visited his mother in his home town and always brought gifts in cash and in kind. In return his mother looked after his children when they were very young.

As can be seen from the diagram there has been considerable fragmentation of land since Kwajo Densu first acquired it in the 1930s. In 1970 the major user was K. Asamoah, who was the most active cocoa farmer in the area, and Treasurer to the local branch of the Cocoa Marketing Board. The absentee landowners worked their farms on the *abusa* system, with Ewe or Fanti managers, who were generally regarded by the resident of Konkonuru farmers as being less efficient. K. Asamoah spent most of the year at Asabidie, and his wife from Konkonuru visited him there about six times a year. He also had a second wife, who was a Fanti, living there. His son, Stephen Asamoah, helped him and he and his brothers and sisters were handed over farms in his father's lifetime, thus avoiding this portion of land going to the matriclan. In 1970 this farm was run on the *abusa* system by a manager, and Stephen worked on his father's farm when he was in the area, and more importantly assisted him as Treasurer of the CMB. Stephen has for many years run his father's farms, as K. Asamoah became very old and frail, and spent more of his time at Asabidie; he has since died. As virtually all his farms had already been handed over to his sons and daughters during his lifetime they have remained in the patrilateral line.

Hill made the point that migrant communities had lost none of their attachment to their home towns, and that although involved in the exchange economy to a far greater extent than hitherto had not extricated themselves from the traditional system. She considered rather that the migratory process derived much of its strength and impetus from the fact that it was based on traditional organization, in which the lineage structure provided mutual insurance for the whole group, at the same time ensuring sufficient flexibility in economic affairs to permit individual enterprise and private profit. As far as acquisitions of land after 1930 are concerned there is in Akwapim some variation in the lineage basis of inheritance and the trend is towards a more patrilateral pattern, as can be seen in the case of K. Asamoah's farms. But as far as the structure and organization of the settlements is concerned tradition is surprisingly strongly maintained, albeit in a watered down form, with some variations from the home town norms. This can be illustrated by the settlement founded by Kwadjo Densu.

The Konkonuru migrants built a village in the forest about one and a half miles from the nearest Akim town of Asabidie. This is known as "Konkonuru" and in 1972, when I visited it, consisted of five "Konkonuru" compounds and four houses of Ewe labourers' from Togoland; this in itself was a departure from the norm as in the home town the Ewe settlements were isolated, at a distance of nearly a mile away. However, despite the presence of some Ewe compounds in the hamlet, most of the migrant labourers live in their own distinct settlements, of which there were at least six in 1972, four of them occupied by Fanti families and two by Ewes. The total population of the village was slightly over one hundred. The largest Compound belonged to K. Asamoah. It was mainly of swish construction, with wattle and daub additions and concrete verandahs. Housing in the hamlet as a whole was simple, but generally well maintained, and one found the same sort of consumer goods as in Konkonuru in Akwapim. It was bizarre, after walking miles through virgin forest, to be greeted by the blast of a transistor, even before the settlement had come into view.

In March 1973 Stephen Asamoah carried out a household census, the results of which are given in Tables 29, 30 and 31. At the time there were 10 compounds in the settlement, all of them headed by men. K. Asamoah acted as head of the settlement and owned the best built, largest compound. Of the total numbers enumerated 60 out of 134 had been away for three months or more in the previous 12 months, of whom 20 had spent 6–7 months in the settlement; others had been away for longer periods. In the Tables residents are counted as those who spent at least 9 months in "Konkonuru" during the previous year.

As can be seen from these Tables, the population is fairly mobile, with constant coming and going from the home town. In the early 1970s a lorry came from Aburi daily, leaving at 7 a.m., arriving at Asabidie at about 2 p.m. and returning to Aburi in the afternoon. The fare in 1972 was 1.50 cedis single. Another lorry used to leave Aburi twice a week for a nearby settlement founded by farmers from Jankama, and known locally as "Jankama". This settlement is about two and a half miles by forest path from "Konkonuru", but had the advantage of a dirt road, negotiable by lorries, from a junction of the Akim-Oda-Ayiribi-Asabidie road. Konkonuru could at that time only be reached by forest path, so everything had to be headloaded to the settlement from Asabidie.

Table 29

Population by Age, Sex and Residence — 1973

Age	Resident 9 months or more		Resident less than 9 months		Total	
	Male	*Female*	*Male*	*Female*	*Male*	*Female*
0–5	12	11	4	4	16	15
6–12	10	2	6	2	16	4
13–17	7	4	5	4	12	8
18–35	6	8	11	15	17	23
36–56	2	5	1	6	3	11
over 56	6	1	2	—	8	1
Totals	43	31	29	31	72	62

Table 30

Resident Status of "Konkonuru" population by Ethnic Group — 1973

Ethnic Group	Resident	Non-Resident	Total
Akwapim	25	46	71
Fante	9	4	13
Togolese	40	10	50
Totals	74	60	134

K. Asamoah, as leader of the settlement at that time fulfilled the role of Odikro in relation to traditional duties. The day before our visit in 1972 they had been celebrating "Adae Butto", the festival of the ancestors, which precedes the Odwira festival by 40 days. This coincided with the celebration in their home town and was evidently carried out in the same fashion, although naturally on a much smaller scale. At the time of the Odwira they said that as many of them as possible return "home", leaving the very old and the children behind.

The settler communities remain apart from the local population. They seem to have a good relationship with them, and there is some intermarriage, but on the whole they prefer to remain distinct. K. Asamoah, in addition to his Konkonuru wife and an Ewe wife, now divorced, had a Fanti wife who lived permanently in the settlement. These wives were local, but not Akim, as they came from a group of migrants who had moved into the area as wage labourers or managers. He had not at that time given the use of any of his land to the four offspring of these wives, but they were still very young at that time. However, it seems unlikely that it would be considered desirable to alienate land from Konkonuru citizens. This feeling of separateness leads to generalizations, such as "The Akims don't go in for much cocoa farming because they are lazy. They just leave the forest to grow by itself and then sell the timber to contractors", the implication being that they could do far better for themselves if only they were more enterprising and industrious. The Akwapims are always eager to extend their empire by acquiring more land. As we passed through one area of virgin forest I was told "This is the land we haven't yet managed to buy, but we shall some day".

Table 31

Distribution by Ethnic Group and Compound — 1973

No. of Compound	Ethnic Group of Head	No. of Members Resident	Non-Resident	Total
1	Togolese	8	7	15
2	Togolese	8	3	11
3	Akwapim	11	2	13
4	Akwapim	13	11	24
5	Akwapim	7	—	7
6	Akwapim	—	15	15
7	Akwapim	—	20	20
8	Togolese	15	2	17
9	Togolese	6	—	6
10	Togolese	6	—	6
Totals		74	60	134

This separateness and allegiance to the home community is bound from time to time to cause some friction. For example, in 1932 the Chief of Akim Abuakwa, Nana Sir Ofori Atta, complained that the Omanhene of Akwapim had sent his cocoa inspectors into his territory without permission and that they had gone so far as to fine Akim Abuakwa farmers for selling below standard beans (National Archives ADM 32/1/6). In an exchange of letters between these two, and to the District Commissioners in Kibi and Koforidua, it was claimed that the inspectors did not have the necessary certificates from the Agricultural Department, and that they were accompanied by two of the Omanhene of Akwapim's Tribunal police in uniform. In forwarding the complaint to the DC at Kibi, Sir Ofori Atta wrote on the back, "I have just received this report. I thought the Omanhene of Akwapim has been told not to irritate us in this manner?"

A counter letter, dated 8 November 1932, was sent from the Omanhene of Akwapim to the DC at Mampong, defending his action and accusing the Odikro of Asuboi of malpractices. It said, "We all have lands at and near Asuboi and Suhum and we claim the right to inform, by beating gong-gong, our subjects and relatives what we consider best for their general welfare.

When the Omanhene of Akim Abuakwa collected the produce of the Akims in 1930 he did not consider himself qualified to collect Akwapim owned cocoa, in which he certainly has no interest... I assure you that whatever I have done hitherto was done in my anxiety to improve the quality of Akwapim owned cocoa, which was becoming grossly neglected as a result of the low prices, and I crave your pardon... I wish Osei Bonsu (Odikro of Asuboi) every good luck in his attempts to obtain all his ends at my expense... signed, Ofori Kuma II". Ofori Atta also complained that the Omanhene had extended his interference to the control of licences to sell palm wine. This dispute was referred to the Commissioner of the Eastern Provinces at Koforidua.

Both men and women work extremely hard on their cocoa farms, and they also cultivate food crops for subsistence. The villages are almost deserted from early morning until mid-afternoon, as all the able-bodied are away on their farms. Although men are the main inheritors of cocoa farms, and much of their effort goes into these rather than into the cultivation of food crops, there are as many women farmers as men working in areas away from their home town, as is shown in Table 28, which was constructed from data collected in the 1972 Sample Survey. The organization of production and marketing shows a high degree of enterprise, and the use of profits to build up capital, which can be used to create greater efficiency. For example, at Asabidie, the nearest point to "Konkonuru" on the lorry road, substantial concrete sheds have been built to store the cocoa. They are kept in good repair and are well equipped with weighing machines, and concrete aprons for lorries.

The area in the north of Akim Oda, of which Asabidie is a part, has the greatest concentration of cocoa farms belonging to citizens of Konkonuru, but the picture is repeated in other parts of Ghana, as is shown in the map showing the distribution of farms (Fig. 10). It serves to demonstrate the extent of Konkonuru's "imperial" interests. Moreover, it reflects and makes more understandable differences in wealth and status within the home community. A great deal of time, money, interest and energy is put into land in these areas. Some of it is brought back to improve standards of living at home, mainly in the form of consumer goods and expenditure on education, rather than investment in farming on Konkonuru soil, although it may be reflected in a greater use of hired labour to clear land for food farms.

The acquisition of cocoa farms in other areas has important implications for inheritance patterns, as was observed by Hill (1963) and more recently by Adamako Safo (1971) and Okali (1983). Adamako Safo found that cocoa farmers from matrilineal communities who had purchased land outside their home areas and established farms in co-operation with wives and offspring, were attempting to preserve their interests against those of the customary prop-

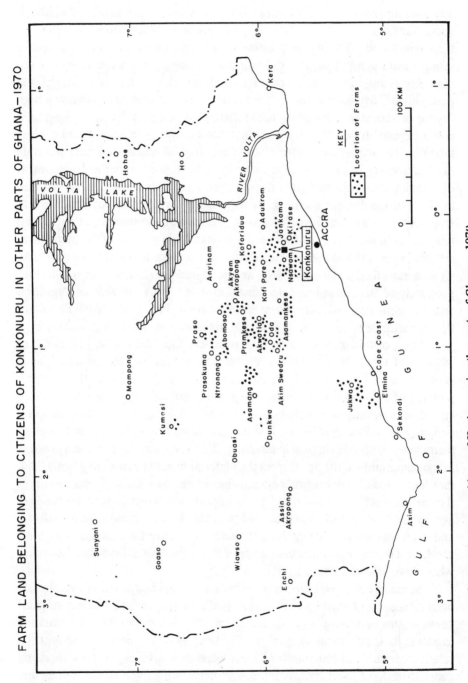

Fig. 10: Farmlands belonging to citizens of Konkonuru in other parts of Ghana – 1970.

erty holding group, the matrilineage. Okali, however, considered that although cocoa farmers might be "expressing a desire to establish property rights on their wives and offspring, opposition on the part of the customary property group would seem to suggest the continued strength of descent groups rather than any change towards acceptance of claims due to ties of marriage and parenthood". My impression in Konkonuru was that there was already a high degree of acceptance for patrilineal inheritance of cocoa farms, so long as it could be established that the land had been privately acquired and a clear intention was expressed before death. This, after all has always been possible in Akan society, but it did not assume such importance before the development of standing tree crops and other forms of property. It does mean, however, that the hold of the descent group is correspondingly weakened. An Ewe Student from Legon, who visited Konkonuru, was struck by the strength of patrilineal ties, and believed that there had been a considerable erosion of the matrilineal system in general and not only in relation to cocoa farming. It is, in any case, an area described by Goody (1969) as one of interpenetration, due to the close proximity of matrilineal and patrilineal systems. This, as well as migration and the acquisition of cocoa farms in other areas, has probably led to a more flexible attitude to inheritance than that prevailing in other Akan societies.

Most of this discussion on migration has focussed on the movement to other rural areas. It was this aspect that was studied in greatest detail, as it was not only of interest in itself but in its implications for the structure and patterns of behaviour in the home town. Rural-urban migration is, of course, equally important, and perhaps even more influential in affecting people's perceptions and value systems. It is the ambition of every family that some of their members should succeed in their migration to the city. It gives them prestige in the community, quite apart from the material benefits that it may bring. The fact that some of Konkonuru's citizens have been outstandingly successful in the outside world bears testimony to the importance of members of the younger generation seeking outlets in these fields. It also bears testimony to the efforts, and often sacrifices, that have been made to secure the education of their children. The unfortunate consequence of this is the disillusionment that occurs when these efforts seem to have been in vain.

Some of the consequences of migration for the home town have already been discussed, at least by implication, and they are familiar features of rural communities in developing countries today. To what extent then is it possible to assess their effects on the quality of life and value systems in what is still a relatively traditional community? This is a complex question, because for many years there have been outside influences penetrating such communities, and these are inextricably mixed with migration patterns. After all Konkonuru was founded in the first place, and not so very long ago, by migrants who, although bringing their traditions with them, created a new community for themselves. Ever since its foundation it has had links with other communities, and individuals have been eager to exploit opportunities to sell their products for cash. Over the years this has led to inequalities of wealth, which have intensified as a result of education and the opening up of new employment opportunities, particularly since the metalled road to Accra was opened in 1927. It is easy to conclude that this has eroded much of the traditional solidarity of the home town, but it has also enriched it and led to many advantages, not all of them material. There is a great interest in the outside world, a great excitement when members return and recount their experiences. It may lead to greater dissatisfaction with their lot and a certain inertia in improving their home community, particularly amongst the young, and in this respect these contacts are a less fortunate consequence. But this dissatisfaction is accompanied by a very real sense of attachment to the home town, a real feeling that it is the place where one belongs. In discussions with young people this was brought up time and time again. They wanted to get away, to earn cash incomes and experience the excitement of city life, but they expected and even looked forward to retirement in Konkonuru. We were talking one day in 1972 about what would happen if all the young, educated people left to work in towns. What would happen to the farms if there were no able- bodied men and women to work them after the present generation died. "We shall come back" was the reply. "Everybody should learn to farm when they are young. Then they will always have security in their old age. But farming alone, for a lifetime, no longer spells success for the younger generation". It was some of these young people, recent school leavers in 1972, who had by 1990 returned to farm in their home town. So their prophecy has been fulfilled. They are still only early middle aged, and their return, as mentioned earlier, has been precipitated by the economic climate of the seventies and eighties. To what extent this trend will continue will depend on the recovery of the economy as a whole,as well as on the way in which the rural areas are developed. There is the question not only of returns to farmers, but also of the improvement of living conditions, which would bring standards of services in line with those in urban areas.

For many years successive governments have attempted to change this attitude to farming, both in order to improve agricultural production and to stem the tide of migration. For example, in 1972 the government of Acheampong mounted a "Feed Yourself" campaign, and as was mentioned in the Chapter on Farming, it did seem to have drawn some response from the people. But this and subsequent attempts to persuade farmers to increase production have not been sufficiently supported by other measures such as marketing or the better provision of services. Rural electrification is a high priority in the minds of rural people, and this has been recognized by governments. The building of the hydro-electric works at Akosombo raised the hopes of rural people that electricity would soon be available at reasonable rates. But villagers, although they could see the power lines passing overhead, were soon disabused of the belief that they would benefit from these new developments. In 1970 the Busia administration initiated a policy to make rural areas more attractive, and communities were to be assisted to use diesel generators. This programme was not at all realistic, either in terms of cost or of the ability of rural communities to maintain such sophisticated equipment without special training. The Acheampong regime, in 1972, asked the Electricity Generating Board to pre-finance rural electrical projects and to submit the costs for reimbursement to the government. But it soon became clear, as the economic situation deteriorated, that the government could not foot the bills, and so the programme died. In 1980 another initiative was taken, the policy this time being to assist settlements situated near grid lines to be connected, provided that they were willing to shoulder most of the cost. Not much was achieved under this plan, and it was not until 1985 that the Director of Fuel and Power called for a national policy. A five year development plan was formulated to extend the national grid to every region. There was to be a reactivation of national rural electricity projects, and a continuous development of identified hydro- electric power sites at suitable locations. In 1987 provision was made for the establishment of a Technical Committee of the Energy Board to supervise and co-ordinate work on the formulation of policy, to decide on priorities, and to set up annual targets. This Committee was also charged with the responsibility of mobilizing both local and foreign resources. It was agreed that financial assistance should be made available to rural communities which initiated electricity projects on a self help basis. But progress was slow, and it was eventually realized that far more input into the infrastructure would be needed than could be found by most rural communities. So, in 1990, foreign aid was mobilized in order to provide services to villages in the poorer parts of the country, such as Brong-Ahafo, and other regions in the north. But in other areas, including Akwapim, villages wanting electricity have to make a substantial contribution to the cost of installation, a contribution far beyond the capacities of most communities.

It might have been thought that Konkonuru, with its wealth of migrant citizens, would be able to find the necessary means. There is a Konkonuru Society in Accra, and the present Chief and his assistants work in the City, but still sufficient funds are not available. Even in 1972 the average attendance at the Society's meetings in Accra were not more than forty, out of the approximately 270 Konkonuru citizens living there. And although the Society was concerned about improving conditions in the home town, when it came to cash contributions there was great reluctance to part with money for the good of the community in general. Most members felt that they had sufficient commitments of their own to their families. It seems that the position has not changed greatly since that time. There is today more talk about potential improvements to the town, but although in 1990 there were projects that were said to be in hand, such as the building of new houses on a site adjacent to the town, eight years later little progress has been made.

This chapter has presented a picture that in some respects appears contradictory. The results of the 1990 household census established that there had been a significant shift in the age distribution of the resident population and this suggested that more young adults had either remained at home or had returned from urban areas. On the other hand the numbers of citizens recorded as living in other parts of Ghana had greatly increased. A high proportion of these were children, and the much greater numbers than in the 1970 census may to some extent be due to the enthusiasm of the enumerators. The general opinion in the town was that the home population had increased, but this was not borne out by the census. The view of the people themselves may have been due to the fact that there were indeed more adults in the community and that this had been accompanied by an increase in the number of houses.

Migration will continue to be a powerful influence in rural communities. This in itself is not necessarily detrimental to the life of the community, if migration does not drain it of its vigour or its ability to provide a satisfactory life for its citizens. The much greater attention now being paid to the importance of improving living conditions in rural areas is a sign that this problem is being taken more seriously, although the urban bias in planning, policy making and budgetting, described many years ago by Lipton (1977) still exists. Until greater priority is given to these matters the young will continue to seek employment away from home.

Chapter 7

THE EDUCATION OF THE YOUNGER GENERATION

Education is a lifelong process and much of it takes place outside the confines of formal educational institutions. In any society before a child goes to school it has already learnt important skills. It has learnt how to walk, to talk, to manipulate objects and to relate to other people. The fundamental bases of a child's socialization into society have been laid, and the way in which this has been done will influence his or her subsequent educational experience (Firth 1966).

Before the introduction of formal schooling, education was undertaken by all adults in the community, mainly by the parents of the child. Everybody thus became a teacher at one stage in their lives and passed on to the younger generation the technical and social skills required. There was no professional group of specialist teachers to whom a child could be handed over, and so parents and other adults bore the entire responsibility. The dichotomy between parents and teachers did not exist. There was no mystique about the process of teaching. Specialist skills, such as those of the traditional doctor or priest were usually passed on within the family, although in some cases young people from other families might be taken on as apprentices (Kaye 1962).

In a place such as Konkonuru the basic skills required for life in the community are still imparted by parents. It is they who teach their children to farm, as has been described in Chapter 5. Children are also instructed in domestic chores; at an early age they learn how to sweep out the courtyard, fetch water by headload from the spring, prepare crops for cooking, light fires, cook, wash clothes and all the other necessary household tasks. Both boys and girls share in these activities and before they reach school age they have already developed a fair degree of competence. They have learnt to regard themselves as participant members in the work of the household group, and in so doing they have begun to understand the moral codes that regulate social relationships.

The life of children in Konkonuru appears to be carefree. They roam around the town as they choose, they are welcomed by all as they stray in and out of anybody's compound. They can play as they like, make as much noise as they please, without the constant nagging of adults. Sometimes they get bustled out of a house, told to keep quiet, stop quarrelling, and so on. But the whole atmosphere is one in which children are greatly desired and loved, and a good deal of indulgence is shown. On the other hand they quickly learn what is expected of them, and parents can be hard taskmasters. The demands on a child's time may not be great but he is not allowed to neglect his duties; he must obey the orders of his elders, whether they be his parents, other adults or even older members of his own generation. While still young children are given responsibility for their younger brothers and sisters. A girl is taught how to carry a baby on her back, how to bathe, feed him or her, and satisfy a baby's other needs. She is brought up to look on the bearing and rearing of children as an important role. Just as boys, as they take part in hunting expeditions with their fathers, learn what it means to be a "man" in this society. In such ways are ideas about the division of labour between the sexes perpetuated.

These non-formal methods of education are well-tried and effective. Inevitably their application is not uniform; some parents make a much more conscious effort to instruct their children and to instill in them a sense of discipline. And much depends on whether or not a child is in close contact with a father as well as a mother; after weaning a child may not, in practice, be in close contact with either, as both parents may have left the town and handed over their child to a grandparent or other relative. Fostering of this sort is very common in African societies and is done for a variety of reasons. Sometimes it is just a case of convenience, as when the parents have gone to work in Accra, or a child may be given to a widowed grandparent in order to keep her company, to help her in the house, and give her an interest. It may be considered better for a child to be brought up in his home town, and access to schooling is easier here than in the cities. It is believed too that a child benefits, especially in adolescence, from being reared by someone who is less personally involved with him or her. It is a tradition in Akan society that the mother's brother (wofa) is admirably suited to fill this role. He has his own special relationship with the child, but it is less emotional than that of the mother or father. He is of the same matrilineage from which the child will inherit and is concerned that he should be a worthy custodian of the family property.

Formal schooling, however, has for many years in Akwapim supplemented the efforts of parents and other adults. It may in the first instance have been forced upon them by external well-wishers, and is strongly connected with the presence of the Basel Mission, and later the arrival of Methodist missionaries, in the 19th century. But it became, in the course of time, a greatly desired commodity, a means of entry into the world outside. It is not only newly independent governments that have regarded it as a "key to development", an agent for modernization. This belief in the importance of education is reflected in the aspirations of rural people, who know that it is a major factor in occupational mobility. It is an investment which they hope will yield returns in higher incomes and a different way of life, even though it may only be a small minority of individuals who reach the higher echelons of the "new elite". But this is an attractive prospect despite its only being achieved by the few.

Developing countries, looking at the high rates of literacy and educational attainment in industrialized nations, have given high priority to expenditure on education. The proportion of national income spent on it has, in many cases, reached levels far in excess of that in more economically developed countries. There is now a good deal of skepticism about the automatic relationship between education and economic growth, and a sense of disillusionment, not only amongst academics, but amongst those who see the the educational levels they have strived to attain becoming devalued in terms of job opportunities. As a result a more critical approach is developing towards the provision of educational institutions, and more attention is being paid to their appropriateness in particular contexts. But education is a consumer good as well as a national investment, and the demands of individuals may be very different from what the rulers or the experts consider to be the best for the country. It may be advisable to limit educational expenditure in favour of investment in agriculture, factories or the health service; what the individual parent is concerned about, however, is whether his child can go to school and to what extent his schooling will equip him to enter the modern sector of the economy. To be told that there are no places in Primary Form I, or that having passed Common Entrance there are no Secondary School vacancies, are heartbreaking experiences for parents, and lead to a situation where the competition for places accentuates the disadvantages of the underprivileged.

In this Chapter we look at the role of the school in one rural community as an illustration of the problems encountered by teachers, parents and children. Some of the wider effects of education have already been mentioned in other chapters, such as its relation to rural- urban migration, its erosion of customary rites surrounding puberty and its contribution to more flexible attitudes to traditional marriage rules. Here we shall look more closely at individual viewpoints as seen from the rural community itself.

Ghana was in the forefront, in sub-Saharan Africa, of the development of formal educational institutions and since Independence there has been a rapid growth of provision at all levels. One of the early pronouncements of the Nkrumah regime was that there should be universal compulsory free primary education, and although this has never become a reality a high proportion of the age group attend school, at least for some years. The Ministry of Education is responsible for the public system and there is a highly structured organization at Regional and District levels. Until the 1970s the majority of primary and middle schools in the public system were managed by church educational units, a legacy of earlier missionary activities, although in the Northern and Upper

Regions the Central Government assumed this responsibility, as missionary schools were not so numerous in these places. Local Authorities in the South were responsible for the buildings and equipment and the payment of teachers, so that the main expenses were no longer borne by the missionary societies. The Government has now taken on full responsibility for all these institutions and since the 1970s there have been changes in the structure of the educational system, particularly affecting post-primary education. At the time that this study was first made, primary education was of six years duration, beginning at the age of six, and this was followed by a four year course in the Middle School, leading to the Middle School Leaving Certificate. Candidates for the Common Entrance Examination to Secondary Schools could present themselves at the second or third year of Middle School, and, if successful, they then proceeded to a five year course leading to the West African School Certificate Examination, the equivalent of what at that time was the English GCE O level. The Sixth Form course took another two years and in 1970 only 40 out of 125 Secondary Schools had Sixth Form Departments, with a total enrollment of 2,969 pupils, compared with altogether 49,182 Secondary School pupils. In that year there were 7,239 Primary schools with a total enrollment of 975,629 children, and 3,422 Middle Schools with 424,430 pupils enrolled. These figures illustrate the shape of the educational pyramid at that time. In terms of the proportion of the age group attending school at different levels only broad indications can be given, as children not only entered schools at very different ages, but frequently missed years before completion of a particular level. For example, in Konkonuru at this time the ages of those who had just left Middle School ranged from 16 years to 21 or more. So figures produced by the Ministry of Education have to be viewed with caution, not only for this reason, but also because the numbers registered may not reflect the actual numbers attending school on a regular basis. There are also wide variations between different parts of the country, with proportionately fewer of the age group attending school in the North. Akwapim has always been amongst those parts of the country with the highest attendance figures.

Until recently it took about 13 years of schooling for a child to reach the level of School Certificate. In order to reduce this period the system has now been reorganized, so that pupils can be selected for Secondary School at the end of the Primary School course. The Middle Schools are being replaced by Three-Year Continuation Schools in which the courses offered are in science and arts subjects. A few Three-Year Schools were opened in the 1970s but the whole system is still not entirely organized along these lines. In 1990 Konkonuru still had its old Middle School, renamed as a Junior Secondary School, but after much controversy with Jankama, whose children would share the school, over the question of siting, a new school was to be built on the approaches to the town. The new school was eventually built in 1995, with the help of Global 2000, which contributed 1.1million cedis to the project.

The introduction of this new system was on the one hand an attempt to stem the rising cost of education, and on the other to relate it more closely to the needs of the country. Although conceived a long time ago it has taken many years to get around to implementing it, due to the political and economic situation, and during this time there have been modifications both to the policies themselves and into the structure of administration. The structural changes are significant as they have devolved considerable powers for decision making and implementation to District level. To what extent these changes will improve the opportunities of children in rural areas will depend on the quality of education that can be provided, particularly at primary level, where standards at present make it difficult for children to compete in gaining entry to Secondary Schools or other further education institutions. It is still too early to assess whether the new type of Junior School, when it comes into operation, will give those children who do not go on to Secondary Schools a more worthwhile education. This matter has become increasingly important in view of the developments described below.

Since Independence, social mobility through education has in many ways become more difficult, as access to Secondary Schools, especially those with a high reputation, has increasingly been biased in favour of the more privileged. Realizing the crucial importance of the Common Entrance examination, which is still taken in English, parents who can afford the fees send their children to private schools, such as the International Schools in Accra. This has led to a growth of fee-paying schools at the Primary level. The Headmistress of the Aburi Girls School, who retired in 1970, said that the most significant change that she had observed in the past twenty years was that, whereas previously many of her girls came from illiterate farm families, this was no longer so. Practically all of them by 1970 had parents who were civil servants, doctors, lawyers, academics or businessmen, and who worked in Accra, or one of the other larger towns in Ghana. So long as Common Entrance puts such a premium on knowledge of English the opportunities of those in village schools are bound to decline.

Akwapim has a long history of missionary activity in the educational field. Some sort of school was started in Konkonuru by the Methodist Mission before 1900, although no records are available giving details of enrollment or the numbers and qualifications of teachers. The proportion of the older generation without any formal education is nevertheless still high. Table 32 shows the position in 1970, and also illustrates the relationship between

Table 32

A Comparison of Resident and Non-Resident Population. By Age, Sex, and Education in 1970

Percentages : 18 years and over only

Educational Level	MALES						FEMALES ALL						ALL	
	18–35		36–56		57+		18–35		36–56		57+		Resident Males & Female	Non-Resident
	R	NR	R	NR	R	NR	R	NR	R	NR	R	NR		
None	24	21	80	53	59	76	65	52	92	69	97	83	68	47
At School	13	4	—	—	—	—	4	4	—	—	—	—	4	3
Primary	11	3	6	3	—	5	9	6	3	2	3	17	7	4
Middle	46	65	5	27	18	19	21	28	1	10	—	—	17	36
Secondary or Higher	4*	3	2	8	4	—	—	1	—	—	—	—	1	3
Adult	2	2	7	9	14	—	—	3	4	4	—	—	3	4
Vocational	—	2	—	—	5	—	—	1	—	—	—	—	1	1
No Information	—	—	—	—	—	—	—	5	15	—	—	Trace	—	2
Total	All add up to 100%													
Number =	83	178	55	104	22	37	143	242	79	48	60	24	442	633

*All these were teachers at the Primary School who lived in the town

education and migration and between men and women. Practically none of the older women in Konkonuru at that time had any formal schooling, and only a slightly larger percentage of those who had migrated. For the men in the 57 years and over group a higher proportion of residents than migrants had some formal education, if adult education is counted. This could be due to the efforts of Moses Addo in the 1950s. But the numbers in this age group are small and the five men with middle or higher level schooling had all spent some time away as teachers or in offices. Most of the older migrants were in rural areas on their cocoa farms.

The differences between residents and migrants in the 18–56 age groups have already been discussed in Chapter 6. It was not possible to collect data on the education of migrants in the 1990 household census, but changes during this period were probably in line with those of the resident population, which are shown in Table33. For the reasons relating to social mobility and the economic situation, outlined above, it is unlikely that there have been significant shifts in the balance between these two groups.

Table 33

A Comparison of Educational Levels of the Resident Population

Educational Level	1970 and 1990 Male				18 years and over. Female				All			
	1970		1990		1970		1990		1970		1990	
	No.	%	No.	%	No.	%	No.	%	No.	%	No.	%
None	76	48	62	26	222	79	152	48	298	68	216	39
At School	11	7	—	—	6	2	—	—	17	4	—	—
Primary	11	7	24	10	17	6	38	12	28	7	61	11
Middle	45	28	123	52	31	11	111	35	76	17	233	42
Secondary/Higher	5	3	7	3	—	—	—	—	5	1	5	1
Adult	10	6	—	—	6	2	—	—	16	3	—	—
Vocational/Tech.	21	5	2	—	—	3	1	2	trace	11	2	
No Information	—	—	16	7	—	—	13	4	—	—	28	5
Totals	160	100	237	100	282	100	317	100	442	100	554	100

This comparison shows that there are now fewer with no education, and over twice the proportion have reached Middle School. But the percentage with Secondary or Higher Education has not changed, and still only a small minority have been to vocational or technical institutions. So in what ways has education contributed to the development of Konkonuru? More of its citizens now are literate and speak English. Many of the middle generation, as a result, have worked in cities and have developed a more cosmopolitan outlook. They should be more capable of dealing with modern bureaucracy, and therefore able to secure for their home town the benefits to which it is entitled. But as far as social mobility into more elite occupations is concerned little has changed; if anything, fewer achieve these heights than in the past.

In 1970 most parents in Konkonuru expressed the view that both boys and girls should have the opportunity of formal education, and it was repeatedly asserted by both parents and teachers that nearly all the children in town attended school for at least some years; they might start late, miss out a few years, drop out early, but it was taken for granted that they should be enrolled. However, the 1970 household census did not bear out this claim for the present school age groups, so it either expressed future intention or indicated the difference between normative and actual behaviour.

Table 34 shows the situation for the 6–17 year age group. The degree of late entry, or missed years, would have to be great to account for this discrepancy. This Table shows that over a third of this age group had not yet attended school. A further breakdown by age group showed that over 40 per cent of the 6–11 year olds had not yet entered school, and that girls were marginally more likely to have been kept away than boys. In the 12–17 year age group 15 per cent of the boys and 24 per cent of the girls had never attended, an overall proportion of nearly one in five. So Primary schooling was by no means universal and this is reflected in the figures recorded 20 years later, where still the proportion of those never attending school, especially amongst the women, is high. The statistical analysis hides the incidence of non-attendance, which was concentrated in certain compounds. So it could be inferred that it was only a small minority of parents who were reacting against sending their children to school. "Reaction against" may even be too strong a term, no doubt they just never got around to the small amount of organization and financial sacrifice required rather than that they were positively anti formal education.

Some time after our 1970 census the teachers had a big drive to persuade parents to send their children to school as soon as possible after their sixth birthday, and by July 1972 there were 51 pupils enrolled in Form I of the Primary School. Forty was supposed to be the maximum number in one form, but it was expected that there would be a sharp fall in the Autumn Term as

Table 34

**Percentage Distribution of the 6–17 year Age Group, by Educational Level
Resident Population only   December 1970**

Educational Level	Boys %	Girls %	All %
None	30	36	33
Still at School	63	55	59
Completed Primary	4	4	4
Completed Middle	2	4	3
No Information	1	1	1
Total Percentage	100	100	100
N =	213	199	412

some moved up to Form II. Table 35 gives the picture of attendance in July 1972, which is very different from the situation in December 1970. These enrollment figures are not strictly comparable with those in Table 34 not only because of the different date and unusually large numbers in Form I, but also because enrollment figures include children from surrounding villages, although the numbers of these are not great, and are probably matched by children from Konkonuru who attend school elsewhere.

The Akwapim Handbook gave school attendance figures for Konkonuru, based on 1968 data, as 243. This is comparable with our 1970 total of 248, but the proportion of girls, at 38 per cent, against our 44 per cent, is less.

In June 1990 data were collected of the numbers in different Forms, shown in Table 36. This is more comparable with the 1972 data as it is based on enrollment figures and the size of the 5–17 age groups are broadly the same for these two dates. The most striking difference is in P1, the reason for which has been explained. In 1990 a Kindergarten was opened, so this will have increased the age range, but it also may have had the effect of delaying entry to P1. Another change that had taken place was that the Junior Secondary School had replaced the Middle School, and had three forms instead of four. There

Table 35

Pupils at School in July 1972, by Form and Sex

Form	Boys	Girls	Total
P 1	30	21	51*
P 2	18	10	28
P 3	17	10	27
P 4	17	3	20
P 5	14	6	20
P 6	18	9	27
Total Primary	114	59	173
M 1	12	10	22
M 2	11	6	17
M 3	13	9	22
M 4	7	7	14
Total Middle	43	32	75
Grand Total	157	91	248

* Only 34 of these were on the Register; the others had been admitted in the Summer term in preparation for full enrollment in September.

was, in practice little difference in the education offered, as the same buildings and teachers were being used. In both years there were, in 1990, fewer girls than boys in school, and in terms of the proportion of the age group attending girls seem to be more disadvantaged in 1990 than they were in 1970, although it is not possible from the data to make more than a broad comparison, as in 1990 no information was collected of those in the age group who were not currently attending, but might already have completed Primary, Middle or Junior Secondary levels. The numbers of these in 1970 were small. Table 37 groups Primary and Junior Secondary together, and also includes those in the Kindergarten. If the latter were excluded the picture would look rather different, that is, the proportion in the age group attending school would appear less. But as is discussed below, it is usually misleading to give much importance to comparisons based on chronological age.

Table 36

Pupils in School in June 1990, by Form and Sex

Form	Boys	Girls	Total
P 1	16	6	22
P 2	14	18	32
P 3	17	12	29
P 4	16	10	26
P 5	13	17	30
P 6	12	5	17
Total Primary	88	68	156
JSS 1	18	16	34
JSS 2	12	10	22
JSS 3	11	2	13
Total JSS	41	28	69
Total Primary & JSS	129	96	225
Kindergarten	11	7	18
Nursery	11	14	25
Total KG & Nursery	22	21	43
Grand Total	151	117	268

Table 37

Percentage Distribution of the 5-17 years age group, by Sex and Education June 1990

Education	Boys %	Girls %	Total %
None*	24	44	34
At School	65	46	55
KG & Nursery	11	10	11
Total %	100	100	100

*This figure may include some who have completed Primary or JSS.

These figures indicate that although attending school is considered to be the norm progress through school is erratic, especially for girls. Another way of illustrating this is to consider the age range in different forms, details of which were collected in 1972. For example, as shown in Table 38 the oldest pupil in P 6 was 19, the same age as the oldest pupil in M 4, but two years younger than the oldest pupil in M 3.

Table 38

Average Ages and Age Range of Pupils in Different Forms

| | *Primary School* | | | *Middle School* | |
Form	*Mean Years*	*Range*	*Form*	*Mean Years*	*Range*
P 1	8.0	5–12	M 1	14.8	13–17
P 2	10.0	8–12	M 2	14.6	13–16
P 3	10.8	9–14	M 3	16.4	13–21
P 4	12.0	10–18	M 4	16.5	15–19
P 5	13.0	10–15			
P 6	14.0	11–19			

Before discussing the role of the school in the community, a brief description will be given of the programmes and teachers in the Primary and Middle schools. This is based on the situation in the early 1970s. Since then the Middle School has become a three form Junior Secondary School, but as mentioned earlier this had not by 1990 made any appreciable difference to the education offered.

From 1970 to 1972 both schools had a full complement of teachers, one for each form. So, apart from Primary Class I, the teacher-pupil ratio was favourable, more so than in Ghana as a whole and much more so than in urban areas. The schools were Methodist and all the teachers were of this denomination. On leaving Training College they could opt for a particular category of school, although they might not always be successful. Three of the teachers in 1972 were pupil-teachers and hoped later to enter a Teacher Training College. With the exception of one of the pupil-teachers, they all lived in Aburi and commuted daily. In December 1970 five teachers had been living in town. This was a point of contention in the town and will be discussed later. It certainly led to late arrivals in the morning and a good deal of absenteeism, so on many days a teacher had to take responsibility for an additional form. The Ministry of Education had ruled that the headmaster of a Primary School should teach the First Form, which, as it was usually the largest and in many ways the most difficult, was a heavy burden on top of administration. The headmaster was not only responsible for keeping records, assigning duties, and so forth, but also had to visit the Circuit Office at Aburi and the District Office at Mampong, as well as Local Government Offices at Nsawam. When problems arose, such as an occasion when there was a shortage of desks and chairs for the new entry, these visits could be very time consuming and frustrating.

The Primary School day started at 8 a.m., broke for lunch at 11.30 a.m., resumed at 1.45 p.m. and closed at 3.30 p.m. The long lunch break was given because most children either had to cook their own food or seek out their mothers or grandmothers on their farms to eat with them there. The Middle School kept slightly longer hours, not finishing until 4 p.m. There were many days, however, when hours were shorter, particularly during the rainy season. The Primary School roof was reasonably waterproof, but as the classrooms were open to the verandah from three feet upwards, and as the school was on an exposed site, driving rain swept in. During the rainy season the temperature drops and the teachers and children feel the cold, so the work becomes "impossible". The first three forms of the Middle School were in a temporary wattle and daub building, with no protective verandahs, and it only needed a little rain to make it uninhabitable. There were also fairly frequent occasions when lessons stopped early, some of them not altogether unconnected with school activities, such as a football match with a neighbouring village, which all the pupils had to attend. The "National Education Week" was an occasion when teachers get together at a central place in the afternoon, and this was another reason for closing the school.

The school day started with an assembly, taken by each of the teachers in turn. A hymn was sung in Twi, a prayer was said by the children, a psalm was sung in the metrical version, followed by the Ghanaian national anthem and finishing with the benediction, after which there was a marching song as they filed back into their classrooms. By the time that they had congregated and gone through this ceremony it was usually at least 8.30 a.m. Lessons then proceeded until 11.30 a.m., each form having a break at some time when they could go out into the playground in front of the school. In the first form all instruction has always been in Twi, and by 1972 this was being extended throughout the Primary School, having by that time reached Form 3. The teaching of English was started in the first form as a "foreign language" and the amount of instruction gradually increased throughout the school. In practice, even in the Middle School, a lot of explanation was given in Twi, and it was used for dealing with most administrative questions. When we were conducting the school survey on eating and sleeping practices we automatically used Twi in the Primary School, and even in the Middle School it was necessary to use it to make points clear.

The language problem was very real in a community where few adults spoke English and where out of school activities were entirely conducted in the vernacular. It made the pace of learning slow, and contributed to a situation where it was difficult for children to compete with those who had English speaking parents and attended schools in areas where there was a more linguistically mixed population. Although many more of the adult population now speak English than in 1970 it is still not used as the primary means of communication, and as more of the curriculum is now taught in Twi, the children of the younger generation are still disadvantaged when it comes to access to Secondary and higher education. In 1972 there were four children resident in Konkonuru who were attending Secondary School at Aburi. Two of these, a brother and sister, boarded, during the week, with their mother's sister, who was the wife of the headmaster at the Adonten Secondary School. They came from a family which had a considerable number of educated members, and lived in one of the few houses where there were books. Their father had not been to school, but he had attended Adult Literacy classes, could write and read English, and had taken every opportunity to further his own education. Literacy classes were held in Konkonuru in the early 1960s and it was interesting to follow the progress of those who attended, through the 1970 household census. One marked effect seemed to be their greater determination to send their own children to school and at an earlier age.

In 1972 no children took the Common Entrance Examination for Secondary School Entrance. This was partly an administrative error, due to a change of Middle School headmasters, but the chance of any of them obtaining a place was probably slim. It bears out the remark, quoted above, made by the late headmistress of the Aburi Girls School, when she retired in 1970, after 16 years in office, and since that time opportunities for children to continue their education beyond Konkonuru have not significantly increased, although in 1990 four pupils were attending Secondary School in Aburi.

A great many extra-classroom activities centred round the school. Netball, volleyball, physical training, ping-pong and football were organized by the teachers and were keenly participated in by the children. A football team was a great source of pride and in 1972 Konkonuru won the competition for all the Aburi village schools. Much effort also went into such occasions as the School Harvest Festival, which was run by the teachers and involved preparing children to recite, sing and perform plays. Rehearsals often took place during the lunch break or after school hours; teachers appeared only too willing to give extra time for this and to come to the village on Sundays to attend ceremonies. The school garden and the school farm were looked after in working hours and again teachers supervised these activities. All in all a great deal of versatility is required of a teacher, and on the whole in Konkonuru they seemed to carry out their duties conscientiously and with a commendable degree of enthusiasm.

The education given was perhaps necessarily stereotyped, with a great deal of repetition and not much opportunity for creativity. The pace was inevitably slow, but encouragement is given and achievement is commended. There seemed to be a real effort to improve standards and great attention was paid to yearly promotion examinations. At the time of the survey on sleeping and eating practices, in 1972, the end of session examinations were taking place and there was practically no absenteeism. Parents were anxious that their children should not be made to repeat a year, whatever their record had been with regard to previous attendance or level of achievement.

A consideration of the role of the school in the community and the relationships between parents and teachers is well illustrated by a meeting which took place in 1972. The history of this meeting is in itself instructive, as it was the culmination of many months of effort on the part of the Primary School headmaster. When I first went to Konkonuru in the autumn of 1970 I was told that there was a Parent-Teacher Association and that it was supposed to meet twice a month. It seemed, however, that it was difficult to arrange meetings because parents were out farming during the daytime and in the evening nearly all the teachers had left the town. Some urgent problems had been discussed with the Town Committee, such as the distance of the public latrine from the school building, leading to a latrine being constructed in the school garden for the use of the children. On another occasion, the Gyasehene had beat gong-gong to assemble the town to talk about the teachers' complaints of absenteeism, and he considered that this had remedied the situation. But it appeared impossible to get the parents and teachers together for a general discussion of problems. In March 1971 a meeting was eventually arranged for a Friday, which is a non-farming day, but it did not come off as planned and the teachers only met the Town Committee. At this meeting the teachers complained of lack of discipline amongst the children, symptoms of which were irregularity of attendance and failure to complete the homework set for them. The Town Committee considered that there would be an improvement in these matters if only more of the teachers lived in town, to which the teachers replied that there was no suitable accommodation. Some members of the Committee offered rooms in their compounds, but married teachers in particular did not consider this adequate as they wanted to live on their own. At that time three single teachers were resident in Konkonuru, one of whom lived in the

Gyasehene's house, so that despite promises on both sides to remedy the situation there had in fact been a further deterioration, as some time previously there were five teachers living in town, or 50 per cent of the full complement. What did not come into the open at this meeting was that some of the teachers were unwilling to live in the town, whatever accommodation was offered. They found life in Aburi more interesting, they could meet friends more congenial to them and they considered Konkonuru a conservative, traditional sort of place. One teacher remarked, privately, that he would not like to bring his wife to live there because the people were so full of superstition and still maintained traditional practices, such as the menstrual taboo on women. He seemed concerned about the hold of the shrine priests over the community, and considered that shrine practices were much stronger in Akwapim than where he came from in Ashanti. His evidence for this came from what school children had told him, and he said that they believed implicitly what they had been taught. He maintained that there were many shrine priests in Konkonuru, probably nearly one in every compound. Myself, I could only trace six priests and priestesses and as they all took part in traditional ceremonies, and therefore were easily identifiable, he had either exaggerated their numbers, or had included herbalists and their trainee assistants, who were more numerous, and whose leaders performed rituals which might have been confused with those of the priests. These views do, however, indicate the attitude of an educated man, who had adopted the Christian faith in his daily life, to the person who still adheres to traditional practices. He maintained that even those who called themselves Christians sought the help of shrine priests in time of trouble. He found this distressing, especially as far as the younger generation was concerned. He was, however referring to a phenomenon that is widespread. Western type education and Christianity have by no means put shrine priests out of business. If anything the new stresses of modern life have increased the need to resort to help of this kind as was demonstrated by Field (1960) in "Search for Security".

This then was the background to the Parent Teacher Meeting which eventually took place at the Primary School in June 1972. There was a full attendance of parents, including the Gyasehene, and the meeting lasted for three hours. A great many people contributed to the discussion.

The meeting opened with points being put by the teachers, and these are dealt with alongside the comments made by parents:

(1) Parents should cultivate in their children the habit of learning at home. It was the practice to let children take school books back to the house and to set them homework, but it was found that most of them did not complete the work set. This immediately gave rise to the complaint the teachers

should live in the town. They would then be able to supervise the children in the evening, or could at least see how they were spending their time, and their presence would have a good influence. The same arguments were gone over as with the Town Committee, the teachers saying that there was a lack of suitable accommodation, the parents maintaining that rooms were available. Nothing was resolved. No comment was made about the teachers complaint that many children were not given lights to read by after dark.

(2)   Pupils should be fed before coming to school in the morning. Parents offered no comment on this point. Nobody eats much breakfast in Konkonuru.

(3)   Essential materials asked for by the teachers for the purposes of instruction should be supplied by parents without delay. Parents said that they would like to be given more detail about what was needed, whether it involved payments and to what purposes the materials were to be put. The teachers agreed to do this in future.

(4)   An appeal was made to parents to help further the education of their wards by encouraging them to go on for vocational training after leaving school. Parents said that they found this a difficult problem as they had so little knowledge about what was available. Teachers only gave information about Common Entrance and Teacher Training; other openings had to be gleaned from advertisements in the press and on the radio. As most parents were illiterate they had to rely on their older literate and English-speaking children in order to discover this sort of information. There were certainly strong grounds for the provision of more and better vocational information, a need which was not being met by the Ministry of Education. It was hoped that when the structure of the education system was reformed and two-year continuation schools were set up that the situation would improve.

(5)   Teachers complained about the habit of parents and guardians taking pupils away from classes, and about absenteeism generally, particularly on Mondays and Fridays. On Mondays children must appear in clean uniforms, so those who only have one uniform, and have failed to wash it over the weekend, stay away. Friday is a non-farming day and a great deal of washing of clothes is done, a task with which the children help. Grandparents often send for children if they are sick and need food

collected from the farm. They also like them to help on the farm and think that it does not matter much if a child does not return to school after the midday break. The townspeople did not have much to say about this. People agree in principle that it is wrong to take children out of school, but feel that there are extenuating circumstances when it is justifiable for higher priority to be given to household and farm tasks. They felt that there were other reasons for absenteeism and these came up later in points raised by the town.

(6)   Teachers said that parents should be tolerant when children came home and told stories about what had been going on at school or what a teacher had done. They should keep an open mind and always feel free to approach teachers to talk about everything that was worrying them. There was no particular reaction to this, but it was referred to later under general comments about teachers.

(7)   Teachers complained that some townsfolk were taking away school equipment, particularly chairs, to use in their houses. This behaviour should stop forthwith. The Gyasehene was very shocked by this news and immediately said that he would beat gong-gong to warn people that any offenders would be brought before him and fined.

(8)   Parents should not talk about teachers in the presence of pupils. No immediate comment was forthcoming on this point.

(9)   Action should be taken on the building of a new Middle School, as the present one was totally inadequate. This was a complicated issue, which had been the subject of much argument for some years. Konkonuru, soon after the building of the Primary School, started collecting money for a Middle School, which was to be built at the lower end of the town, next to the playing field. They had raised 200–300 cedis and some concrete blocks were bought and brought to the site. They were still there in 1972 and rapidly deteriorating. The District Education Officer had said that his Department was unwilling to support separate Middle Schools for Konkonuru and Jankama, which are barely one and a half miles apart. He insisted that they should jointly decide on a suitable site, but so far the two towns had not been able to reach agreement, as both of them wanted the school as near as possible to their own town. The teachers wanted the matter to be decided by the District Headquarters at Akropong, but the townspeople were anxious about the possible outcome of such a

decision. The numbers in the Middle School hardly justified separate schools for the two communities, but the people of Konkonuru felt that it belonged to them and that they did not want to share it with another town.

(10) The head teacher explained that the policy of the Government was to place more emphasis on gardening and farming in the school curriculum, as part of the drive to improve agriculture in the country. This, as mentioned in the Chapter on Food Farming was the year of the "Feed Yourself" campaign. It was not at all clear how schools could help in this respect, as it was a rather pious hope that it would make more school leavers want to stay on the land. And as far as teaching improved agricultural practices was concerned it was doubtful whether the average teacher was equipped to do this. So long as the present system of bush fallow cultivation continues the farmers probably know more about the best methods for their own land than the policy makers in the Ministry of Education. The parents were certainly not interested in this aspect of the school programme, as their expectation was that school should equip a child for wage employment outside the village; they regarded farming as a skill which all children should be taught by their parents.

(11) The final point made by the teachers was of a very practical nature, and that was that the roof of the Hall in the Primary School was leaking and should be repaired. This Hall was divided by a screen during school hours and was used by Primary Forms 1 and 2. It served as a Church on Sundays and a general meeting place for other occasions. The people promised to put this matter in hand.

The teachers having had their say, it was then the turn of the parents to raise questions:

(1) The townspeople wanted an official "Open Day" when they could see the work of the school. It was considered that some "big people" could be invited to inaugurate such an occasion.

(2) The town wanted the school band revived. It was interesting that these were the first two points mentioned, although perhaps no particular significance can be attached to this.

(3) Teachers should check the neatness of children more carefully. Parents

go to farm before their children leave for school and therefore could not be expected to take sole responsibility for their appearance.

(4) Teachers should not arrive late, or go absent frequently. This seemed to be a counter to the teachers' complaints about the absenteeism of pupils.

(5) The practice of making brooms in Handicraft periods should be watched, as a lot of the work was too hard for the children and their hands became sore. The teachers promised to look into this.

(6) Pupils sometimes went into hiding when they should have been at school. Teachers should check registers more carefully to avoid this practice, as it was not possible for parents to know what was happening once they had gone to farm. This was put forward as an additional reason for the degree of absenteeism claimed by the teachers. In other words, what they were suggesting was that the non-attendance of children was not only the result of parents keeping them away to help them in the house or on the farm.

(7) When children were away sick teachers should visit them in their homes.

(8) When children have to attend hospital teachers should write notes for them to take, as most parents were illiterate, so unable to do this.

(9) Teachers should discourage Middle School pupils from drinking ar.d smoking, habits which the townspeople alleged were increasing.

(10) The cutting of bamboos for school purposes should be supervised by teachers, as damage could easily be done to the plants.

(11) The question of corporal punishment was raised, and led to a heated discussion. Some were strongly in favour, others equally strongly against. Evidently some parents actively encouraged teachers to beat their children, whereas others protested vehemently at the practice. In fact little corporal punishment was used. Children were given order marks for misdemeanors. If they had "too many" (the actual number seemed to be flexible) at the end of the month they might get a few strokes of the cane. The discussion ended inconclusively, but at least everybody had plenty of opportunity to air their views on the subject.

(12) Teachers were appealed to, to make a good name for themselves. It was alleged that some of them went to people's houses to beg for food and that this put parents in a very difficult position. It was felt that teachers did not always set a good example, and that they should pay more attention to their behaviour, realizing the influence that they had in the community.

The meeting was lively, and people were outspoken, but it was generally agreed that it was useful and constructive. Despite what might appear to be abrasive remarks, the atmosphere was certainly not hostile. The Akan people are great talkers and ceremonies of any kind are an occasion for eloquent pronouncements. Points are put with great forcefulness, and what to outsiders might seem a bitter battle of words and gestures often ends in laughter and great good humour.

A lot of the arguments and counter-arguments are characteristic of Parent Teacher Meetings all over the world. Parents expect a lot from schools and hope that they will make up for some of their own inadequacies. This is particularly true with a largely illiterate or poorly educated population, as they see the teacher as someone who has had the opportunity of further education, who consequently should be able to make a very special contribution. Roberts (1972) in her study of "The Teacher and the Community in a West African State" speaks of the elders' "ideal type" teacher, who should, for example, visit the children in their homes, live in the village and respect the elders. She found that parents refused to answer questions on the subject of teachers. The parents of Konkonuru had no such inhibitions.

Teachers, on the other hand think that they do not always get enough support from parents, and that they cannot operate entirely on their own. They feel that too much is expected of them, and little allowance is made for human frailty, that their problems are not understood and that, after all, they are poorly paid for their efforts. The dedicated teacher may feel rewarded by the results of his labours, and by the esteem in which he is held, but even for him he would appreciate some more solid token of his worth. In developing countries he has his own educational problems. He has perhaps been more successful than the majority and has had four years post-Middle School further education at a Teacher Training College. But this is often looked upon as a stepping stone to other opportunities, and he may have seen some of his colleagues continuing to University and to careers in the Civil Service. Many Primary School teachers spoke to me of their ambitions and frustrations. They by no means looked upon their careers with equanimity, or regarded being a teacher as a mark of success. It must be remembered that the gap between Primary and Secondary school teachers, and again between those and teachers in the University, is much greater in developing than in industrialized countries.

The presence of a school in a rural community is bound to increase the pace of change in attitudes. In Konkonuru it has led to greater social mobility and has made people more conscious of the world outside, bringing in fresh ideas and influences. Along with other aspects of socio-economic change, it has led to new dissatisfactions with their lot and new aspirations for their children. The older generation may not understand much about the content of the formal educational system and may regard it as totally irrelevant to their daily needs, but they realize that for their children it is important that they should go to school. Although now there are more of the over 40s living in the community who have attended school, there does not seem to be much change in their perceptions. They do not see education so much as an influence which could change their own community and its way of life, or act as a dynamic agent in rural areas, but rather as an opportunity of improvement for members of their family, which will yield a return in the long run, both in terms of cash and prestige.

Living in Konkonuru one is struck by how much of the traditional way of life has survived, and what a small impact formal education seems to have made on it. But when people's attitudes are considered, and they express their views about life, one realizes that there have been fundamental changes amongst those of the younger age groups. These are likely to accelerate the pace of change as the younger generation takes over the leadership of the community. Already in Konkonuru leadership is now in the hands of those with formal education. In their official roles they still adhere to traditional patterns of values and behaviour. The fact that these leaders commute between Accra and their home town, must affect people's perceptions of their role. It should lead to higher expectations of the part these new leaders can play in promoting the development of the community and in improving standards of living. It is too early to assess whether this is indeed so. Nor is it easy to assess to what extent these changes are due to the impact of formal educational institutions, although their contribution is undoubtedly considerable.

Chapter 8

THE DOMESTIC GROUP

The individual's life is greatly influenced by the domestic group in which he happens to live. This is the core of what he considers as "home", where his daily needs of food, shelter and companionship are met. But there is a great deal of variation between societies in the openness of domestic organization. Akan society is an example of one in which the system shows a high degree of openness, both physically and in terms of social relationships. Compounds and households are not closed off, individuals constantly circulate to eat and to sleep, so that when considering residence patterns the total community always has to be taken into account.

This openness is a striking feature of Konkonuru. Everybody wanders in and out of other people's compounds. In walking through the town one takes short cuts straight through a courtyard without any qualms, merely greeting anybody who happens to be around. Even one's room is not a very private place. Children are always peering in to see what is going on, sharing in one's activities. Even in the Chief's compound during a meeting in his parlour it is usual for the windows to be lined with interested faces watching the proceedings. Occasionally they are bustled away, and certainly there are times, such as when the elders meet, when such intrusion is not admissible. But on the whole it is a community where everything is everybody's business and there are not many closed doors. It is in strong contrast to the Muslim societies of Northern Nigeria, where every compound has a single entrance and life inside is not exposed to public view (Hardiman 1974b; 1976a).

What then are the important aspects of domestic organization underlying this apparent fluidity? To what extent is there a stability in the residence patterns of the individual? In view of the extensive kinship network of all those living in town, is the compound an important focal point, retaining its identity over a period of time, and an objective symbol for the identity of the family? Or is it just a location of temporary convenience, somewhere to shelter, to cook, and to keep one's possessions? And if it is important, what is the basis of its composition? Is there a discernible norm, with a bias towards patrilocal patterns, or those based on matrilineal ties? (Schneider and Gough eds. 1961, Goody 1959; 1969).

Studies of Akan society have shown the close relationship between the rule of matrilineal descent and the organization of the domestic group. The conflict between a wife's conjugal obligations and her matrilineal ties are a reflection of a duality which permeates the whole of the Akan social structure, and is especially relevant to the consideration of residence patterns. Tufuo and Donkor (1969) stated that "all wives and children stay in the husband's home except by consent with a good reason." This seems to be a statement of a normative ideal, probably from the husband's viewpoint, rather than an account of what is found in practice.

Fortes (1949) referred to this in considering the methodological problems of studying domestic organization in modern Ashanti. He contrasted the continuity in time of the matrilineage, the localized, corporate group which is the basis of all political, jural and ceremonial institutions, with the more ephemeral existence of domestic and family groups based on ties of marriage and affinity, as well as kinship. These groups are subject not only to the developmental cycle, but also to changes in individual relationships and in the wider society. Even if in the past there was greater homogeneity in domestic organization this was certainly not so at the time of the Ashanti survey in 1946, resulting in a situation which Fortes described as one where there appeared to be no fixed norm. It was for this reason that Fortes placed so much emphasis on numerical validation of the incidence of different household patterns.

Fortes found that in a relatively stable community 40–50 per cent of the population were living in matrilineal households under female heads, and that only about one third of all the married women resided with their husbands. In another community, which had been more affected by social change, the bias was in favour of conjugal ties, but even there nearly half the women, even at the peak of their childbearing years, seemed to prefer to live with their own matrilineal kin.

Since the Ashanti Survey of 1945–1946 other studies of Akan societies have shown the persistence of the influence of matriliny in the domestic domain, although no such detailed, extensive surveys have been undertaken. There are now few relatively stable communities left, and socio-economic change has been observed to weaken the strength of matriliny with respect to inheritance (Douglas 1969). It would seem to follow from the tendency for a father to wish to pass on property to his children that this would be reflected both in household structure and in the strength of competing kinship ties. Fortes (1949: 140) noted that already by 1945 there had been "noticeable shifts in values in response to the new political, cultural and economic forces released by the imposition of British sovereignty, the advent of schools and literacy, and the rapid development of gold mining, cocoa farming, transport, trade and urbanization." But he went on to say that "among the great majority of the people the basic principles of their traditional and familial and also political ideologies and patterns of organization stood firm." Uchendu (1969) also referred to the ways in which social change was modifying inheritance patterns, although traditional ideology still emphasized that family property must pass through the mother's line. The tendency for changes in the domestic domain to lag behind changes in other domains is a feature of many societies, as for example was found in Maiduguri (Hardiman 1974b) and other towns in what was at that time the North-East State of Nigeria (Hardiman 1975 and 1976a).

This study considers the domestic group in a matrilineal Akwapim community, which although of a different tribal group from the Ashanti shares the same basic principles of social organization. Their own account of the formation of the settlement shows that it was founded on matrilineal lines, and they have, as far as they are concerned, always followed a matrilineal system. Although it cannot be directly compared with data from other Akan communities in order to establish trends, many of the forces of change are the same.

Konkonuru retains much of the traditional in its social structure, despite processes of change that have been going on for many years. This was certainly true in 1970, and although some significant changes have occured since then it is still true today. In considering how persistence and change are reflected in domestic organization there is, however, a further problem in the lack of previous data for this particular area, so that no statistical comparison of residence patterns can be made with the past beyond 1970. Djan (1936) describes the matrilineal system of the Akwapim but has little to say about the domestic group. All that can be done is to describe the situation in 1970 and 1990, and to record and discuss the observations of informants as to the differences that they have perceived during their lives, although there are some changes that can be more objectively assessed, such as alterations in the demographic structure, which by 1970 had resulted in a very high proportion of women in the over 18 age group. A particularly significant finding of the 1990 survey was a reversal, to some extent, of the balance between the numbers of men and women.

At the time of the 1970 household census of Konkonuru a sample survey was made of households in Aburi, and discussions were held with the Adontenhene and his officials. Although so close to Konkonuru, Aburi is a more sophisticated community, much influenced by missionary activities and by its role as an important local market and trading centre. It is a busy, bustling place on what was for many years the main road from Accra to Kumasi. As a centre of the Basel Mission activities the differences between the practices of the Akwapim and the Akan, as described by Oppong (1974) are much more apparent here than in the surrounding villages, particularly with regard to inheritance. The secretary to the Adontenhene in 1970, E.P.Nelson, said that a few years previously a Committee had been set up to discuss questions of inheritance and succession. The Committee recommended that inheritance should become patrilineal, while succession remained matrilineal. But when this recommendation was referred to professional lawyers in Accra, all of whom were originally from Aburi, they considered that this was not feasible. It cannot be imagined that, even today, such a proposal would emanate from Konkonuru, however much there have been changes in this direction in practice, as was mentioned in Chapter 4 with regard to the inheritance of cocoa farms.

In order to consider the data collected in Konkonuru and in other studies of Akan society, it is necessary to define the "household". The definition of a household has always proved difficult in Akan society. The Ghana Trial Census in 1969 used a definition similar to that used by Fortes in the Ashanti Survey of 1945–1946 (Fortes 1949), namely that "the domestic group is essentially a house-holding and housekeeping unit organized to provide the material and cultural resources needed to maintain and bring up its members." Central to this concept is the provision and preparation of food; "home is where the hearth is" (Nukunya 1992). But it is only partially correct to say that it is where one's food is prepared and domestic services performed that seems to be the primary focus of one's allegiance, since a person may have claims to more than one hearth place. For example, polygamous husbands whose wives are not co-resident have by this definition two or more "prime allegiancies". A husband may live in one household, but have his food brought to him by different wives in rotation. Or he himself may circulate between different households at different periods. In this case should the husband be regarded as head of several different households, or alternatively of none? Domestic obligations cut across physical boundaries.

Cases of this sort were comparatively few at the time of the 1970 survey, although those that existed are significant of the women's perception of their position. Of the 136 women household heads there were 14 married women who regarded themselves as household heads whose husbands were living in another part of town. Most women household heads were either widowed or divorced, or had husbands living in other parts of Ghana. The responsibilities of these 14 women in this category were obviously different from the point of view of domestic roles from the widows, divorcees and those whose husbands were elsewhere, so it is doubtful whether they can be considered as based on matrilineal principles.

More difficult is the question of relationships within the compound, and whether a valid distinction can be made between the compound as a whole and household units within it. Depending on which criteria are used, very different patterns emerge, and in making comparisons between the findings of the Konkonuru survey and others it is not always clear just what account is taken of these distinctions.

Before carrying out our 1970 household census we discussed these problems in the first place with individuals and finally at a meeting called by the Gyasehene, which was attended by most of the adult members of the community. It was found that they made a clear distinction between the head of a compound (ofi panyin) and the head of a cooking group (kuw panyin). There was a good deal of argument over the position of husbands living in different compounds from their wives, as mentioned above. The women considered that in these cases the wife should be regarded as head of her cooking group, and it was finally agreed to accept this definition as indicative of the economic independence and responsibility of the women concerned.

The case of single person households was also discussed. The people themselves were quite clear in putting both men and women into this category where they were individually responsible for providing their own food, although in many cases, particularly with men, they were known to eat with other groups.

This rather lengthy discussion of problems of definition is necessary in order to evaluate our findings and their comparability with other surveys. For example, if the household (kuw) is taken as the base a high proportion in 1970 were headed by females or consisted of nuclear families with male heads. If on the other hand the compound is used as a base most of the groups were extended, and there were considerably more male than female heads. In the first case (households) 73 per cent consisted of two generations only, whereas in the second case (compounds) 75 per cent consisted of three or more generations. In the Ashanti survey the overall figure for three generation households in Agogo and Asokore was 55 per cent.

The 1970 survey gave much more detailed information about household composition than it was possible to collect in the short period available for the 1990 survey. Hence most of this analysis is devoted to a discussion of the 1970 material, including some material from the Aburi sample survey. After this some comparative data is given from the 1990 census of Konkonuru. Although the 1990 census was less detailed it is possible to draw some conclusions from differences between the two periods reviewed.

To start with the compound; 49 of the 70 compounds in 1970 (this figure excludes the three outlying Ewe compounds and the two empty compounds) were owned by men. The average age of their owners was 52 years, compared with an average age of 66 years for the 21 women compound owners. Women in Akan society have always been able to acquire property but these figures show that men seem to have a better chance of ownership and at a younger age. This is emphasized even more strongly when the demographic composition of the town in 1970 is taken into account, as at that time 66 per cent of those over 18 years of age were women. Of the 21 women owners, 12 were widowed or divorced, and this, as well as their age, is a reflection of the phase which they had reached in the developmental cycle of the domestic group.

Compounds with male heads were larger and contained on average more household units than those with female heads. The 41 resident male compound heads were those with the largest households, with an average of nearly eighteen members and a range of from one to twenty. Women compound heads had on average the next largest number of members in their households, at 4.8, but the range was smaller from two to nine. The size of household units, other than those of compound heads, averaged 3.7 members, and there was no significant difference between those headed by men or women. The range in each case was from single person households to those with ten members.

The average number of resident members in compounds with male heads was 17.5, as against 13.7 for female heads, and the range was from 1–45 and 1–25 respectively. The number of resident household units in a compound averaged 3.9 in compounds with male heads and 3.1 in those with female heads.

There was a significant difference in the internal relationships between compounds with male and female heads. Table 39 shows the relationship between compound and household heads, and Table 40 shows the relationship of all compound members with the compound head. The lineage and non-lineage categories cover a wide range of relationships; for example, there were 18 varieties of non-lineage household heads in compounds owned by men.

Table 39

Relationship of Resident Household Heads to Compound Heads — December 1970

Relationship of Household Head to Compound Head	In Compounds with Male Heads		In Compounds with Female Heads		All Compounds	
	No.	%	No.	%	No.	%
Non- lineage	74	50	0	0	74	38
Lineage	61	41	45	96	106	54
Miscellaneous	14	9	2	4	16	8
TOTAL	149	100	47	100	196	100

Table 40

Relationship of Resident Compound Members to Compound Head — December 1970

Relationship of Compound Members to Compound Head	In Compounds with Male Heads		In Compounds with Female Heads		All Compounds	
	No.	%	No.	%	No.	%
Non-lineage	660	81	42	16	702	65
Lineage	143	17	227	84	370	34
Miscellaneous	14	2	0	0	14	1
TOTAL	817	100	269	100	1086	100

Table 41

Distribution of Households by Household Type — December 1970

	Male Household Heads			Female Household Heads	
	No	%		No.	%
1. Single Person	27	21.6	1. Single Person	28	19.9
2. Father,wife/wives, own children only	61	48.8	2. Mother & own children	67	47.5
3. Nuclear core with other kin	18	14.4	3. Woman with or without own Children/other kin	35	24.9
4. Husband & wife only	2	1.6	4. Woman with husband/own children	5	3.5
5. Father & children only	12	9.6	5. Sisters only	1	0.7
6. Miscellaneous	5	4.0	6. Miscellaneous	5	3.5
TOTAL	125	100.0		141	100.0

Details giving specific relationships of members within resident households can be found in Appendix 3.

The striking feature of these Tables is the predominance of matrilineal relationships in compounds headed by women, where nearly 96 per cent of the household heads, and nearly 85 per cent of the compound members fall into this category. In compounds with male heads only 18 per cent of all the members are matrikin, although the proportion increases to 41 per cent for heads of households within the compound. There will be a further discussion of the significance of these findings after consideration of the composition of the smaller domestic group, that is the household (kuw).

It has already been mentioned that it was within the smaller domestic unit that nuclear family patterns predominated. Particulars of different types of households are given in Table 41. If single person households, and those not possible to put into a specific category, are excluded, 67 per cent of households with male heads were nuclear in type, and just under 20 per cent were extended. Both these fall into the first category of domestic unit as classified by Fortes (1949), that is, a household grouped around a husband and wife. In households with women heads only five fell into this category.

Within these different types of households the relationships of members to the household head are also significant. Table 42 shows the distribution of members with lineage and non-lineage connections. This Table is presented in the same form as in the Ashanti survey (Fortes 1950), and compares the findings from Konkonuru with those from Agogo and Asokore. Greater detail of relationships of household members in Konkonuru are given in Appendix 2.

Table 42

Distribution of Members in Households with Male and Female Heads
1945–1946 and 1970
Percentages

	Male heads Lineage kin			Non-lineage			Female Heads Lineage			Non-lineage			Total living with Male Heads			Female Heads		
	As	Ag	K	As	Ag	K	As	Ag	K	As	Ag	K	As	Ag	K	As	Ag	K
Males	9	12	T	20	10	27	16	15	18	2	4	1	28	22	27	17	19	21
Females	7	16	T	26	17	30	18	22	22	3	5	1	33	32	30	22	27	22
TOTAL	16	28	T	46	27	57	34	37	40	5	9	3	61	54	57	39	46	43

T = Trace
Numbers of sample: Asokore, Ashanti   711
                 Agogo, Ashanti   965
                 Konkonuru, Akwapim 890

Fortes (1949) stated that the general picture is "clear and that there is good agreement between the samples", that is between those in Agogo and Asokore. For comparative purposes it is instructive to take each of the points Fortes makes in interpreting his table:

(1)   A substantially larger proportion of people of both sexes lived in households under male heads than in households with female heads. As can be seen in Table 42 the proportions for Konkonuru in 1970 were very similar, falling between the Agogo and Asokore figures. Fortes considered that a point of special interest was that the balance between the sexes in the domestic sphere was almost equal in the more traditional stable community of Agogo whereas it was less so in the newer, less stable one of Asokore. This, he concluded, was consistent with the greater strength of lineage solidarity in Agogo.

(2)   A striking feature in both places was the very small proportion of non-lineage kin living under the jurisdiction of female heads. This, Fortes said, was in keeping with Ashanti kinship and jural values. For a man to live in his wife's house was considered to be contemptible, and only five cases occurred in his sample, all the result of peculiar circumstances. Konkonuru findings closely follow this pattern; the proportion of non-lineage kin living under female heads in Konkonuru in 1970 was even smaller than in Ashanti. It was also true in Konkonuru that only in exceptional circumstances did a husband live in his wife's house. Reference is made to these cases later in this chapter. Fortes goes on to say that it is no disgrace for a man to live in his mother's or his uterine sister's house, as there is no tie so fundamental and strong in Ashanti as that of mother and child. Not only does it have the sanction of customary law, on account of the principle of matrilineal descent; it is also thought of as an ultimate and irreducible moral and psychological fact which needs no sanctions, and these ideas are graphically expressed in many Ashanti proverbs and maxims (Rattray 1914).

(3)   Households under male heads presented a different picture from those under female heads. At Asokore they had more than twice as many non-lineage as lineage kin among the male members, and nearly four times as many among the female members. At Agogo the two classes of kin were about equal. In remarking on the contrast between the two towns Fortes, once again, emphasized the much greater strength of the matricentred unit in the more stable community of Agogo. The position

of Konkonuru in this respect is extreme; hardly any lineage kin were found in households headed by males. This bears out the situation, discussed later, in which a strong preference was expressed by the people for parental type households.

(4)   The key relationships in male-headed households were those of husband and wife, brother and sister, father and child, uncle (*wofa,* i.e. mother's brother) and sister's child. Evidence for this comes from further tables in the Ashanti Survey, which show that in Asokore the preponderant stress was on conjugal and parental relationships, whereas at Agogo there was practically an equal balance between these and ties with sisters and their children. But in both places the structure of the household under a male head was the result of the balance struck between these two classes of social bonds, and this was, and still is, the case throughout Ashanti. The Table in Appendix 3 shows that in Konkonuru in 1970 the conjugal and parental bonds were paramount in these households. The sister's child was practically non-existent in households with male heads, only one case appearing in the census.

Table 43

Distribution of Members living in Compounds with Male & Female Heads —
December 1970
Percentages

| | *Relation of Members to* | | | | *Total of all Members* | |
| | *Male Heads* | | *Female Heads* | | | *under* |
	Lineage	*Non-lineage*	*Lineage*	*Non-lineage*	*Male Heads*	*Female*
Male members	7	29	8	2	36	10
Females	6	33	13	2	39	15
TOTALS	13	62	21	4	75	25
Numbers =	143	674	227	42	817	269

These comparisons are between households, as Fortes does not make the same distinction between the household and the compound as in the Konkonuru census. If, instead of the household, the compound is taken as the basis of comparison a different picture emerges. In discussing this with Fortes he agreed that this would be a more meaningful comparison as in his survey he did not distinguish between *ofi* and *kuw*. The only reservation to this is that the Fortes household corresponds more closely in size to the Konkonuru *kuw* than to the *ofi*. It may be that separate households were distinguished in some cases, even though they shared a common courtyard with others. This problem does, however, make numerical comparisons difficult. If the Konkonuru compound is used as a basis the strength of lineage ties in compounds headed by men is greater than those ties in male-headed households. The use of the compound rather than the household, also increases the total number of the population living under male heads, as is shown in Table 43. This tips the balance, shown by Fortes, in two directions. On the one hand it strengthens the lineage connection in male-headed compounds. For example, the sisters' sons, who were hardly represented in the household analysis, now figure more strongly. There were 17 full sisters' sons in male-headed compounds, 16 of whom were heading households of their own within their maternal uncle's (*wofa's*) compound. There were in addition 35 sons of full sisters' daughters. On the other hand it accentuates the dominance of male heads in terms of the proportion of the population living in their compounds. Households headed by males in Konkonuru in 1970 accounted for 57 per cent of the population, whereas for compounds the proportion rose to 75 per cent. In other words, these findings show that although more people in Konkonuru lived in compounds with male heads, many of these members were in the smaller household units under female heads, altogether accounting for 45 per cent of the resident population. Only 20 of the members in households headed by women were not of the matrilineage, which demonstrates the strength of matrilineal ties amongst women. As far as men were concerned, most of them, unless widowed or divorced, had at least one wife living with them. There were only three households with more than one wife resident; two of these with two wives, and one with three. Most women who were still married and whose spouses were in Konkonuru were living with their husbands; out of a total of 130 still married women, 89, or 68 per cent, were living in the same household as their husbands. In Agogo only about 30 per cent were living with their husbands, and in Asokore about 50 per cent. In terms of changes in the domestic structure, resulting from socio-economic developments, this reflects a move towards a greater emphasis on the nuclear family. Fortes drew attention to this trend in comparing the data from Agogo and Asokore. This data was collected many years ago, and unfortunately there has not been a later study of these two towns, although Fortes did visit Ghana in 1970 and some attempt was made to instigate a repeat study. In the meantime the towns had grown greatly in scale and complexity, and the task proved too difficult for the resources at Forte's disposal .

Table 41 summarized the way in which households are distributed by house-hold type. If single women are excluded the remaining women household heads are divided as follows:

(1) Married women with husband in another compound in Konkonuru   14
(2) Married with husband away   27
(3) Divorced   26
(4) Widowed   36
(5) Married with husband in same household   5
(6) Category not identified   5

                                                                    ───
                                                                    113

    One of the expected differences between the composition of these differ-ent groups is in their place in the developmental cycle. A more detail analysis of the data shows that the average age of widowed heads was 64 years and that in only about half of their households did they have any of their own sons or daughters. They were more likely to be caring for the young children of their sons and daughters, and this came out strongly in a survey, made in 1971, of the sleeping and eating patterns of schoolchildren.

    The average age of divorced women heads was younger, at 43 years, than that of widows, and more of them still had children living in their house-holds. The still married women heads were younger still, with an average age of 35 years, and only four of them had any children other than their own living with them.

    The proportion of household members with a filial relation to the head were high. It amounted to just over 70 per cent for households under both male and female heads. But the proportion of sons and daughters varied according to the sex of the head. Male heads had more sons living in their households, and females had more daughters. There were five married daughters living in their parental households with their husbands, and four married daughters living in households headed by their mothers. Seven divorced daughters were in their mothers' households and one in her father's house. Two married sons were living with their wives in their paternal household.

    A higher proportion of children, other than sons or daughters of the head, were found in households headed by women. They accounted for about 20 per cent of the membership, against about 9 per cent in households headed by men. So that as far as children were concerned about half were living in households with women heads. These figures correspond closely to those from the Ashanti survey.

A survey of the sleeping and eating practices of a sample of school children, carried out from March to July 1971, showed that 66 per cent were living with their mothers, either in patrilocal or matrilineal households, but the expectation that patterns of behaviour would change after puberty was only partially fulfilled. Boys did show a tendency to move out of the parental house for sleeping purposes, half of the middle school boys having made alternative arrangements. But none had moved into the household of his mother's brother (*wofa*) and most of them continued to eat in their mothers' compound. A more marked difference was the move away from the grandmother's care as the child grew older. Their role in caring for young children was great; 34 per cent of the primary school children in the sample were living with grandmothers, but none from the middle school. Tables 44 and Table 45 give details of the findings of the survey.

Table 44

Distribution of Children according to Eating Arrangements — March to July 1971

School Form	No.	Mother & Father %	Mother only %	Grand-mother %	Others* %	Total %
Primary 2	27	33.3	29.6	29.6	7.5(2)	100
Primary 6	17	11.7	47.1	41.2	—	100
P2 & P6	44	25.0	36.5	34.1	4.4	100
Middle 3	17	29.4	58.8	—	11.8(2)	100
All children	61	26.2	42.6	24.6	7.6(4)	100

Matrilineal eating group = 68.9%   Paternal eating group = 31.1%
*Others consist of: Father only (P2 boy, Mother's sister (M3 girl), Father's brother (P2 boy, Father's house for midday meal and grandfather's for evening meal (M3 boy)

Table 45

Distribution of Children according to Sleeping arrangements — March and July 1971

School Form	No.	Mother & Father %	Mother only %	Grand- mother %	Other* %	Total %
Primary 2	27	33.3	29.6	29.6	7.3(2)	100
Primary 6	17	5.8	41.2	41.2	11.8(2)	100
P2 & P6	44	22.7	34.1	34.1	9.1(4)	100
Middle 3	17	29.4	58.8	—	47.1(8)	100
All children	61	21.1	34.4	24.6	19.9(12)	100

Matrilineal sleeping group = 60.7% Paternal sleeping group = 26.25 Others = 13.1%
*Others consist of:- 2 Father only (1 P2 boy & 1M3 boy); 1 Mother's sister (M3 girl);
1 Father's brother (P2 boy); 8 Friends (5 M3 boys, 1 M3 girl, 2 P6 boys)

    A statistical analysis of a household census, based as it is on numerical incidence, is as Fortes (1949) maintained, a necessary part of understanding different household patterns; it is particularly relevant to a consideration of ideal and actual norms. But it cannot convey the infinite variety of patterns in individual compounds. In Konkonuru, as in all Akan communities, domestic arrangements varied widely; no two compounds were the same, although those headed by women followed a more homogeneous pattern. As an illustration of the different composition of compounds, three are described as they existed in 1970. I returned to Konkonuru briefly in 1972 and again in 1977, and for a rather longer period in 1990. By the end of this period, two of the compound heads had died, although the same families were still living there. Two of the compounds had male heads and one had a female head.

1.   Kwamena Asamoah's Compound.

The compound in which I had a room was owned by Kwamena Asamoah, the Asafosupi, an old man of 84 years in 1970. This was his given age, but the fact that he was still alive in 1990 raises some doubts. He was an Abrade, related to the Gyasehene, and he held usufructory rights over a considerable amount of land in Konkonuru, as well as owning cocoa farms at Asamang. The compound was probably built between 1920 and 1930 by Kwamena's father, from whom it was transmitted to him. It was one of the most substantial and best built compounds in Konkonuru. A central courtyard was completely surrounded by buildings, an ideal to which people aspire, but do not usually attain. In the corner of the courtyard a water tank had been built which was fed by gutters collecting water from the roofs. When it rained the tank filled very quickly, testimony to the efficiency of the system. As this saved the task of fetching water from the spring, obo kofi, some distance down the hill, it was a great asset, and it seemed surprising that more compounds did not install such a system. The capital cost was relatively expensive, but even most of the richer heads had not built water tanks in their compounds.

Despite his age, Kwamena was still an active farmer who went out to work every day except Friday, the non farming day, and Tuesday, which was the day of his birth. Only a few of the older farmers in 1970 observed their name day as a day of rest. His wife, Akua Adowah, was an Ashanti from Kumasi, a member of the Asona abusua (clan). She was a very active, birdlike little woman of 65 years in 1970. Having a "foreign Akan" wife is a significant feature of this compound; it means that their children have no other kinship roots in the community other than through their father. Akua also farmed, but her main interest was in trade. She kept the only shop in town, a small room at the front of the compound, in which she sold matches, paraffin, sweets and tinned goods. She made frequent expeditions to Kumasi, none of them of great length. In 1972, when I returned to Konkonuru, she had built an improvised kitchen of sticks and palm fronds in front of the shop. She found this more convenient than using one of the kitchens behind the compound, and in it she cooked on a charcoal stove, an indication of her comparatively affluent status,as charcoal was not produced in Konkonuru, and therefore had to be bought for cash. She did not prepare any food for sale, only for her own family. In 1977 she was still running her shop and using her kitchen in front of the compound. But by 1990 she had given it up. She was by then very frail, although still her cheerful self, but Kwamena was in an extremely poor state of health, and since then he has died.

When I was working at the University in Kumasi in 1990 one of Akua's grandsons came to see me, as he was employed as a messenger in the Department to which I was attached. He had heard from Isaac Ohene Osae in Konkonuru that I was there. He told me that his mother lived in a compound just outside the entrance to the University, and I was, of course, asked to visit her there. She ran a wine bar on the main Accra-Kumasi road, not far from her compound and that was where we met. She proudly took me to see her domaine, which had been bought for her by her mother, Akua. It was an even bigger compound than that of her father's in Konkonuru, a testimony to the entrepreneurial skills of Akua. Her husband was not living with her, and she and her children, all of them grown up, only occupied a few of the rooms. Most of them were let, a very profitable business in Kumasi.

When we carried out our household census in December 1970 we included in our count all those members of the household who were living away for most of the year. The total number enumerated in this compound was 51, all of whom except wives and lodgers were born in the town. Only 14 of these were normally resident, and two of these were schoolteachers renting rooms at 2 cedis a month (about one pound sterling at that time). I was also renting a room, which was slightly superior, and for which I paid three cedis a month, but I did not count myself in the census.

Most of the resident members lived in the compound head's household. Besides his wife there was a full brother's son of 16 years, two daughters and one son of Kwamena's sisters, aged 15, 14 and 14, a son's son of 4, and a son's daughter of 16. Apart from the little boy of four all the children were attending school. They were a jolly, well fed bunch and my constant companions, coming in and out of my room as they pleased, sitting chatting on the verandah, and accompanying me around the town. Akua kept a gentle but firm control over the children and saw that they helped with household chores such as fetching water, sweeping out the courtyard and verandahs, which needed constant attention as the compound was shared with Kwamena's goats and chickens. The girls helped to cook, usually preparing their own midday meal when they came home from school.

The parents of these children, all of whom were enumerated in our census, but who were living away, visited the town several times a year, notably for the Odwira festival in October. Five of them were farming in other parts of Ghana where they had acquired cocoa farms, and all but one of these, a son's son, were in their 50s and had had no formal education. Two sons were contractors at Kade, and they had both been in school until Middle Form 4 (ten years of schooling). Four sons were working in Accra, two as drivers, one as a trader, and one as a mechanic; the drivers had no formal education; both the others had completed Middle School Form 4.

Four of the remaining five resident households in the compound were of single people, two of the teachers had already been mentioned. The other two were widowed full sisters of the Compound Head. Although in their seventies and crippled with rheumatism, they still regularly went out to their farms. They lived very independent lives, each one cooking for herself, although Akua from time to time sent them in a few delicacies, such as freshly cooked corn on the cob.

The fifth household occupied a building which looked like a separate little house. Its head was a son of Kwamena Asamoah's aged 36 years, who worked as a driver in Accra and came home every weekend. His wife, aged 27 years, was an Ashanti from Kumasi and was permanently resident in the town with her daughter. She farmed her husband's, land, and he helped her at weekends, mostly at the time when the bush was cut and burnt. She was a relation of Akua's and like her also did some petty trading, but on a very small scale.

The composition of this compound was characteristic of the bigger, more prosperous ones on Konkonuru, owned by the older members of the community. The compound head's own household no longer contained any of his own sons or daughters as permanent residents, but he and his wife were caring for children related to them by kinship or marriage. Most of them did not belong to the same abusua as the head, as they were either the children of his own sons, or of patri-sisters with the same father, but a mother from a different abusua. Moreover, those notionaly regarded as members of the compound, but absent for most of the year, were also patrilateral relatives and their affines. The unusually large number of patri-relations was probably due to the compound heads wife being an Ashanti, with her roots outside Konkonuru.

In 1990, although the compound was still in fairly good repair, it presented a rather different social scene. It was still one of the bigger compounds in terms of numbers, but there were only four resident households. Kwamena and Akua, his wife, lived in a household on their own; they were no longer caring for the children of relatives. The second household, headed by a son, consisted of ten members, six of whom were children. The other two households were headed by elderly widows with their children and grandchildren; there were 14 people in these two households, bringing the total numbers in the compound to twenty-six. There were no longer any lodgers, and many of the rooms lay empty.

2. E.K.Owusu's Compound

Another of the better built compounds was of special interest as it was owned by the Methodist Catechist, E.K. Owusu, a very different type from Kwamena Asamoah. He was 60 years old in 1970 and his main occupation was farming; but he spent a lot of time on his duties as a catechist. He was also an Abrade and he inherited his house from his mother's brother (*wofa*), Moses Addo, the former catechist, who was a strong personality and did so much to improve the town before he died in 1968. It was due to his efforts that a Henderson Box was built to catch the water from the spring, obo kofi, that gutters were dug down each side of the road leading up the hill from the chief's house to the school, and that the school was kept in good repair. Sadly, after his death, these and other improvements, were not maintained.

E. K. Owusu's family had the largest number of educated members of any families in Konkonuru at that time, and many of them had left the town to seek their fortunes in the world outside. One brother of Owusu's was a lawyer in London, a brother's son was a big contractor in Tema another was a civil servant in Accra, and one had a successful modern poultry business near Ayimensa, having learnt his skills in England. I met several of the absentee members of the family and found them critical of the "backwardness" of Konkonuru. They were very "modern" men, believed in the conjugal family and the inheritance of property through the paternal line. This may have been sour grapes, as they themselves had not inherited. It was in contrast to the prevailing opinion at the home base, as Owusu did not hold this view about property. Not only had he inherited his house through the matrilineage, but also his food and cocoa farms. But as far as views about the town were concerned he was equally critical, mainly it seemed because he did not consider that most of the people were good Christians, and he thought that they failed to bring up their children properly. He felt that they did not correct them sufficiently, resulting in much more petty delinquency than in the past, such as children stealing pineapples from other people's farms. He was critical of the lack of interest of many parents in their children's education, being content merely to send them to school and expect the teachers to do the rest. Owusu's house was the only one in which more than the odd book could be found. He had a great advantage as being one of the few of the older generation who had formal education, so he was better able to take an intelligent interest in the education of his children and grandchildren.

In 1970 there were 25 people living in the compound, divided into eight households. Three of the heads were full sisters of Owusu, one was a full brother, one a full sisters daughter, one a brother's son, and the other the husband of a full sister's daughter. So relationships between the compound and household heads were mainly matrilineal and all the heads in this category were either widowed or divorced. It was a good example of the support given by the matrilineage to its members, and this by one of the least "traditional" families in town. Unlike some other cases in our survey the husband of the sister's daughter was regarded as head of his household, even though he did not belong to the town and lived in the house of his wife's kin. His wife, Beatrice Addo, was a particular favourite of Owusu's. Neither she nor her husband had any formal education, but they had attended adult education classes and were both able to read and write and to speak some English. They had four sons and two daughters; the eldest son and the elder daughter attended the Adonten Secondary School at Aburi where they lived during the week with a relative. At weekends they came home and helped on the farms. They were all keen members of the Methodist congregation, Beatrice being a leading light in the women's choir.

Although substantially built with a cement courtyard, surrounded on all sides by living rooms, and with one of the only two concrete water tanks in town, there were only eight living rooms. E. K. Owusu and his family occupied two of these so the others were very crowded. It was never clear how they all fitted in, but probably some of the children slept elsewhere. It was always a busy, cheerful place to visit and Owusu's own room was the grandest in town, with a large centre table covered with a cloth, plenty of chairs, a splendid array of portraits of distinguished members of the family, a bookcase and a mass of other knick-knacks.

E. K. Owusu had died by 1990 and the new catechist was now occupying his house. He is the nephew of the late Chief Bediako; evidently Bediako was baptised after he stood down as chief, but never attended church.

3. Abena Boakyewa's Compound

The third compound to be described was one which was entirely composed of a segment of the matrilineage. The compound head, Abena Boakyewa, was the Gyasehene's mother, and she built this compound for herself in 1957. At first the construction was wattle and daub, later it was plastered with cement and sand mortar. In 1970 the building was only in fair condition, although all the rooms had cement floors which were in a reasonable state of repair. There were four living and sleeping rooms, an inside stove, a kitchen constructed of bamboo and sticks, an additional open kitchen and a bathroom.

There were 17 resident members of the compound, divided into three households, and relationships within the compound were characteristic of those owned by women heads. Abena Boakyewa was a widow in her late 70s in 1970, and she was living in a household with one of her daughter's daughter, and two daughters' sons, all of whom were attending school in Konkonuru.

The head of the second household, Akua Oye, was a daughter of Abena's whose husband, K. Asamoah, spent most of his time on his cocoa farm in Akim Oda in the village called Konkonuru, described in Chapter 4. Akua also owned cocoa farms there, and her husband looked after them for her, although she visited them herself about eight times a year. Her husband had another wife, a Fanti woman, who lived with him near his cocoa farm, and Akua's son, Stephen Asamoah, spent a lot of time there helping his father. Stephen was very attached to his father's Fanti wife as well as to his own mother. Besides Stephen, Akua had two other sons and four daughters living with her, and all except the youngest were attending school.

The third resident household was headed by Abena Twumua, the compound head's daughter's daughter. Her husband lived in another compound in town and served food to him there. Three sons and one daughter were living with her.

All the members of these households were born in Konkonuru, and they all belonged to the Abrade abusua, the royal lineage in this town. The same held true for those recorded as absent for most of the year with the exception of one of Akua's daughters who was born in another town in the Eastern Region and who was attending a Teachers' Training College at Akropong.

This compound was entirely composed of the matrilineage, covering four generations. In 1970 there was only one male over the age of 18 years living in it, Stephen Asamoah, and he had only recently left Middle School. He was greatly relied upon by his mother and grandmother, but he had ambitions to obtain work in the modern, cash sector of the economy and was frequently absent on trips to Accra, seeking work. In between these trips he did a little food farming and made regular visits to his father's and mother's cocoa farms, where he had recently been given a farm of his own.

By 1990 Abena Boakyewa had died and the other households in her compound had dispersed. Her grandson, Stephen Asamoah, after spending some years in a variety of jobs in Accra, had returned to live in Konkonuru. He had established his own compound in another part of the town, where he was living with his wife and four children. He had married a Konkonuru girl and his children were at that time between six years and six months old. His mother, Akua, was still alive, living on her own. His father had died and Stephen was the largest owner of cocoa farms in Akim Oda, described in Chapter 4. He had taken on the role of Secretary to the local branch of the Cocoa Marketing Board, previously occupied by his father.

These accounts of three compounds give some idea of the variations in residential patterns in 1970. They demonstrate a characteristic of traditional Akan society that there was considerable freedom of choice as to where and with whom one lived. This freedom might be limited by circumstances, one might have to accept accommodation where one could, but at least there were no rigidly applied norms to which the individual had to conform. It was perfectly acceptable for a wife to choose to live in her mother's or brother's compound rather than in that of her husband, although for most the preference was expressed for a parental domestic group. As in other Akan studies this flexibility showed up neatly the "dialectic" between a high degree of individual autonomy and the various links and connections through mother, father, household head, place of birth, etc. The one common principle about residence in a compound was that some kinship link was exploited, which leads to the question whether this was necessarily so, or whether it was a result of the community being kinship based in its whole structure.

The 1970 data about household composition will first be considered before looking at the extent of continuity and change indicated by the data collected in 1990. In considering the 1970 data, in addition to numerical findings, observations made as a result of living in the town, and the results of a small sample survey to investigate the roles of men, women and children in the domestic group will be included. These matters were the subject of much discussion with people in the town and it was interesting to note to what extent there were different views held by the older and younger generations.

A key question was to what extent the findings showed a bias towards patrilocal residence patterns. Asked about the household arrangements they preferred, most men and women said that the ideal arrangement was the parental household, possibly sharing with other kin. This preference was even more marked in Aburi, where no women said that they preferred to live alone with their children, whereas in Konkonuru a few did still prefer this type of household. In both towns they expressed the opinion that this led to more peace in the family. Divided residence reflects the opposed pulls of two sets of matrikin, but this could also be an allusion to witchcraft. Because of the demographic structure of the community in 1970, although most men did live in parental households, a smaller proportion of women enjoyed this ideal. Foster children were accepted as part of a parental household, but where brothers, sisters, fathers, mothers and other kin or affines shared the compound it was considered that they should maintain separate households, often with the ultimate aim of building their own compound.

Although polygyny is still fairly widely practised, a good deal of doubt was expressed as to its suitability in "modern times", not only by women. It was said to lead to friction, particularly when a man had to divide his responsibilities between the children of different wives. The problem was seen as an economic rather than a moral issue. So long as there was no formal education and children followed their parents' footsteps into farming there was little difficulty in a man having many wives, for after all to a large extent they maintained themselves. But now that school fees had to be paid, and aspirations to acquire more material goods had increased the pressure on a man to be fair to more than one wife could be great. An Ashanti proverb says "wo yere apem a, wo asem apem", which means "when you have a thousand wives you have a thousand palavers" (Rattray 1914). In passing, it should be noted that the reference made to school fees could be misleading; Primary and Middle School education are free, but parents have to pay a small sum for registration, to cover the cost of books and other expenses, and school uniforms have to be bought, as children are not admitted unless they come in uniform. There is also the withdrawal of children from farming activities to be considered as a cost.

Fathers showed a strong attachment to their own children, not only when they were very young. An indication of this was the number of fathers who consulted me about jobs for their sons. Furthermore, there was certainly a strong desire to pass on property to sons where it was possible, that is when it was privately acquired by the father. Many houses had been transmitted in this way, and more cocoa farms than in the past seemed to be handed down from a father to his sons, and also in some cases to his daughters, during his lifetime. A detailed study of the ownership of cocoa farms in the village of Konkonuru, Akim Oda illustrated this practice. Some farms had passed through the patrilineage for as many as three generations. If transfer was left until after the death of the owner there was a risk that the matrilineage would assert its claim.

An Ewe student from Legon, who visited the town on several occasions in 1970 and 1971, thought that the community showed strong patrilateral tendencies. In discussing this with members of the community they did not agree with him, possibly because they were thinking along different lines. The Ewe student was stressing the importance of domestic arrangements and the ties between fathers and children, whereas the townsmen were holding fast to the principle of matrilineal inheritance and succession, particularly as it applied to land tenure in Konkonuru itself. Matrilineal kinship obligations were said to be strong, but in practice the mother's brother seemed to have become a rather unreliable figure, particularly when he had many children of his own. This was, and twenty years later is still more so, increasingly felt by those, such as civil servants, who have moved into the modern sector of the economy and are limiting family size in order to give their children a better start in life. These men may have sisters who continue to conform to traditional ideals about family size and who expect their brothers to honour their kinship obligations. This is a frequent cause of ill-feeling in today's socio-economic climate (Nukunya 1990). As far as household arrangements in Konkonuru were concerned if, in 1970, compound membership was taken as a criterion it was true that obligations to the matrikin were evident, but this extended mainly to the provision of house room.

The difference between the household position of men and women has already been mentioned. The women's position was more complicated. Most of those who were still married and whose husbands were living in town were in patrilateral households. The majority of household heads who were women were either divorced or widowed, or had husbands living out of town. For the 14 women household heads whose husbands were in Konkonuru, it was difficult to consider them as heads in a significant sense. Many of them were co-wives with husbands enumerated in the same household as another wife. The fact that women said that they were heads, and largely provided for their own children, is a normal feature of Akan society, where women are expected to be independent, at least in farm produce. A husband has a duty to see that his wife and chldren are well fed,and the "meat money" which he provides is intended for this purpose. Probably, the reason why so many women in Konkonuru said that they were the main providers for their children was because they represented the majority of farmers in the community. Fortes (1949) argued that the incidence of matrilineal households in Agogo and Asokore showed that women seemed to prefer to live with matrikin. But, in the case of Konkonuru, over twenty years later than the time of the Ashanti survey, it would seem to be less a question of preference than a result of the demographic structure of the community. Certainly the more prosperous households and those in which the contents of the cooking pot seemed to be most nutritious, were on the whole headed by men. Moreover, unattached women were keen to acquire new husbands and to live with them in the same domestic group.

The compounds headed by women were strongly matrilineal in composition, and women, like men, attached importance to the ownership of property. So the matrilineal ties of women living on their own remained strong. But it was questionable how much support these women were getting from the male members of the matrilineage, such as from their brothers and their sons. On the whole these women were in poorer compounds, where standards of living appeared to be lower. Women did get the use of farm land from their matrikin as well as from their husbands. There were strong values attached to alienation of land from the matrilineage, a question which is complicated and goes beyond the immediate concern of this chapter with the domestic group.

The overall impression was that when a man was rich, politically powerful or eminent he attracted to himself patrilateral dependents, whereas without these attributes, even if educated, he stuck to matrilineal norms. This fits two Akan ideas, one that fathers must provide for the education and setting up in life of their offspring and secondly that a man's most reliable support, and this particularly applies to an office holder such as a chief, comes from the sons' sons who will benefit from his wealth and position during his lifetime, and will not cause him trouble since they cannot succeed him according to customary law.

The ties between a mother and her sons and daughters remain strong and so do those between brother and sister. But these ties do not exclude close relationships with fathers, nor with patrikin. Another Ashanti proverb says "agya mma nya mepe; ena mma nya a, mepe papapa", meaning "when my father's children get anything I like that; when my mother's children get anything I like that even better" (Rattray 1914). The father-son relationship, always strong, seems to be of growing importance, and it is now more possible to translate this in economic terms owing to the increasing importance of privately acquired property. This may not yet spell doom to matriliny, but it must surely weaken its hold. In 1970 the basic traditional patterns of kinship relations, for example as between matrilateral and patrilateral "pulls" on children, remained amazingly firm in Konkonuru.

In what ways did the 1990 household census indicate changes in the composition of the domestic group? It has already been said that there were significant changes in the demographic structure of the community, resulting in a more even balance between adult men and women, a higher proportion of the population of 57 years and over and fewer in the under 18 years age group. (see tables 15, 16, 17 and 18). Although the overall population had not increased to the extent expected by the people themselves there had been a significant increase in the number of compounds, which may have led the people to think that their numbers had grown. It is interesting that despite these demographic changes, which might suggest that more compounds would be headed by men, the proportions for 1970 and 1990 were almost identical, as is shown in Table 46.

Table 46

Distribution of Male and Female headed Compounds and Households
1970 and 1990

| | Male headed Compounds | | | | Female headed Compounds | | | | Total Compounds | |
| | 1970 | | 1990 | | 1970 | | 1990 | | 1970 | 1990 |
	No.	%	No.	%	No.	%	No.	%	No.	No.
Cpd, Heads Female	49	70	61	69	21	30	28	31	70	89
Hsehld. Hds. Male	84	60	48	41	57	40	69	59	141	117
Hsehld.Hds.	114	91	124	83	11	9	25	17	125	149
Total Households	198	74	172	65	68	26	94	35	266	266

In 1990, as in 1970, there were overall more households in male headed compounds than in female, but to a lesser extent. There was a shift in the balance between male and female as regards the average number of households in a compound; in 1970 there was an average of 4.0 households in compounds headed by males and 3.2 in female headed compounds. In 1990 male headed compounds averaged only 2.8 households and females 3.4 households. This finding reflects the observation made above that many of the new com-

pounds were headed by the younger generation of men, and were built specifically for the nuclear family; few of these compounds contained more than one
household.

As in 1970, male heads of compounds had, on average, larger numbers
in their own households in 1990 than female compound heads; that is 5.7
members, against 2.8. A higher proportion of the whole population still lived
in male headed compounds, although the proportion of 69 per cent in 1990
was slightly less than the 76 per cent for 1970. As can be seen in Table 46,
there was a significant increase in the number of households in female headed
compounds and this included more households headed by men, some of whom
were living on their own.

The most interesting differences between the two years are in the distribution of household types, as is shown in Table 47. The proportion of households with only a husband and wife living in them had increased, as had all
households based on a parental relationship. This illustrates the trend towards
an increasing preference for parental type households. There was a significant
drop in the number of households headed by women living only with young
children, or with young children and other kin. There was also an increase in
the number of women living in single person households, or with other women
over 18 years of age. There was also an increase in the number of men living
in all male households.

So, although it is not possible to make exact comparisons between the
two years in respect of the extent of matrilineal and patrilateral relations within
compounds and households the data collected, as well as discussions with
people in the town suggest that the trend is towards more emphasis on the
nuclear type household. It will be interesting to see, if the plans for rebuilding
the town on a new site materialize, whether dwellings will be built in the traditional compound style, or as smaller household units.

Another aspect of the domestic group is the way in which duties and
responsibilities are divided between different members of the household, and
the implications of this for different household types (Moock ed. 1986). Also
relevant is the question to what extent these duties and responsibilities are
shared between households within a compound. A great many of these activities
can be observed just by living in the town as part of the daily round, such as
sweeping the compound, cooking, fetching water and firewood,or washing
clothes. Decisions about who pays for household items and clothes, or how
family affairs are decided and dealt with are less obvious. In order to supplement
observations on these questions, and also to collect comparative data, questions
were added to a survey which was carried out in Aburi in July 1971. These
questions were first tried out in Konkonuru, where they could be assessed

Table 47

**Distribution of Household Types in Male and Female headed Households.
1970 and 1990**

	Male Household Heads					Female Household heads			
	1970 No.	1970 %	1990 No.	1990 %		1970 No.	1970 %	1990 No.	1990 %
Single Person	27	21.6	20	13.4		28	20.0	35	29.9
Husband & Wife only	2	1.6	10	6.7	Women & Children only	67	47.5	44	37.6
Husband & Wife & Children	61	48.8	74	49.7	Women & Children & others	35	24.8	25	21.4
Husband & Wife & Children & Others	18	14.4	31	20.8	Women & Husband & Children	5	3.5	—	—
Father & Children only	12	9.6	—	—	Women over 18 years only				
Men only	—	—	14	9.4					
Not identified	5	4.0	—	—		5	3.5	5	4.3
Totals	125	100.0	149	100.0		141	100.0	117	100.0

against information already collected in a less formal way. Details of this survey can be found in Appendix 1. The figures for Konkonuru are small, but the results have nevertheless been given in percentages for purposes of comparison.

As far as division of labour in the domestic group was concerned there were no great differences between Konkonuru and the more sophisticated environment of Aburi. The divisions were much as expected, in that the main burden of household duties fell on the wife, helped by her children. Boys and girls played equal roles in most activities, although washing clothes was considered women's work, whereas ironing was done by boys and husbands. Both husbands and wives went to market, although undoubtedly women took a major share in the selling of farm products, whereas men operated more strongly in the cocoa market; most of this, however, took place in Akim and other parts of Ghana, as very little cocoa was grown in Konkonuru in 1971, and now there is none. Men often commented that women controlled the cash obtained from sales of farm produce, just because they did the marketing. If they were selling their husbands' or sons' produce they could decide how much they gave them, keeping for themselves what they thought was appropriate commission.

Decisions about buying household goods and clothes were also shared, as were those concerning family affairs, although in Konkonuru women claimed that they took most of the decisions at home, even when the husband was living in the same household. As regards the arrangement of marriages it was interesting to note that most of the respondents in Konkonuru had, had their first marriages arranged by their fathers, although this was not the case in Aburi. However, it was strongly believed in Konkonuru that their own children should be free to choose their own partners. In Aburi there was more doubt about this, as also about the question whether young people should have boy or girl friends before they married. This was generally considered a good thing in Konkonuru, but rather less so in Aburi. The answers on the issue of polygyny show little difference between Konkonuru and Aburi, despite what might have been expected on account of the more Christian ethos of Aburi. Roughly a quarter in each case favoured a man having more than one wife, nearly two-thirds thought it inadvisable,the small number remaining saying either that it depended on circumstances, or that they did not know. There was little difference between the sexes in answers to this question. The reasons given in Konkonuru have already been mentioned, where it was considered more of an economic than a moral issue.

From these findings it is self evident that a woman spends more time and effort on household duties than a man. As women are also active farmers this means that they have an extremely long working day. A previous study in Brong-Ahafo (Hardiman 1974a) found that women spent from six to seven and a half hours away from the village on farming activities on an average of four days a week. Added to their household duties this amounted to about a ten hour working day. Living in a village one is conscious that it is the women who get up before dawn, sweep the courtyard, get the children up, prepare the breakfast snacks, and on their return from the fields, after taking a bath, start to cook the evening meal and get the young children to bed. On non-farming days, some of which are devoted to taking produce to market, there are many duties to perform, such as washing clothes, not to mention the role they are expected to play in communal labour. It is not surprising that when asked who organized the activities of their children the general response was that these were looked after by the children themselves.

In the Brong-Ahafo paper, it was concluded that "social change so far does not seem greatly to have benefitted women in rural areas. Migration has taken many adult males away from the village, higher education has favoured boys more than girls, rural social services have lagged behind those in towns. Whereas in urban areas there is a trend towards the greater importance of the nuclear family unit, in the villages change has tended to leave the woman, particularly the older woman, in the position of holder-together of the household, and often, as well, of the family farms" (Hardiman 1974a: 121). These women said that they were beset by many problems and they were probably more aware of these problems than in the past. They were conscious of their burdens and frequently talked about them. They wished that their husbands or their brothers would give them more support, that they would work harder and spend less time and money on drinking. Social change had brought new anxieties, many of them due to the disappointment of their expectations. They had made sacrifices to educate their children and found that the jobs they had hoped that they would get were not available, and that education had, had a negative result in terms of the younger persons' unwillingness to settle down to farming. As mentioned in Chapter 5, education was not seen as relevant to the improvement of village life.

These views were also expressed by women in Konkonuru, especially by those who were heads of households; these women were widowed, divorced or living apart from their husbands. If they were old and living alone they did usually receive some help from relatives, either within their own compound or from outside. Children would fetch water and firewood, daughters would send round the odd meal, visiting relatives would bring the odd gift in cash or kind. But nevertheless the standard of living of such women could, in most cases, be observed to be poor. The younger women household heads who had children or other relatives in their household, also had a struggle to maintain a reasonable standard of living. Their households were not on the whole in the better-off category, although no detailed study was made of incomes, such as that by Stern *et al,* in Palanpur, India (Sharma and Dreze 1990). Many of the older women suffered from chronic ill-health, and although they carried on with a tasking way of life they were perpetually suffering from backache, headaches. stomach pain and so forth.

Returning to Konkonuru in 1990, to what extent had demographic change altered the domestic group? The differences in the balance of household types has already been recorded. The larger proportion of adult males in the population should surely have raised standards of living. It is possible only to give an impressionistic answer to this question as time and resources did not allow for a more detailed study of the many factors involved. Farming was by all accounts, and from observations on the ground, taking place on a larger scale, and the younger generation of adult males were active farmers. The shorter period of fallow between cutting the bush may have contributed to what was said to be poorer yields although the main explanation given was a decrease in rainfall. This was recognized as probably due to deforestation, which was immediately apparent on entering the town. As there had been no significant increase in population the extent of deforestation was at first surprising. However, the greater energy of the younger male farmers had led to more land being cleared; there had,in addition been some bad bush fires a few years ago. But these things in themselves do not seem to afford sufficient explanation. Firewood is a much sought after commodity, and the existence of a better access road to the town meant that it was easier for traders to collect it . This may have led some people to exploit this source of income by cutting trees beyond their needs either for making farms or firewood for their own cooking.

Despite the greater activity in farming, and the good prices received for surpluses marketed, the first impression on entering the town was that living conditions had not greatly changed. If anything the buildings were more dilapidated, more of them seemed to be letting in water when it rained. The younger generation of men were dressed in more up-to-date clothes and possessed more consumption goods, such as radios and cassette players. Their houses, however did not contain conspicuously more furniture, although they were more likely to possess beds, chairs and cupboards. Because this younger generation tended to live in one household compounds the gap between their standard of living and that of the older women who were widowed or divorced appeared to be greater.

The town still lacked electricity and the cost of connecting it seemed to the people to be prohibitive, although the Development Committee had plans to collect sufficient funds over a period of time. No doubt without these efforts Government programmes will in due course extend to provision in this Region,as already has been done for Brong-Ahafo and parts of Ashanti. Communal labour still took place on Friday, the non-farming day, but despite the presence of more working men it did not seem to have achieved more than previously. The expectation that overseas aid would come to their assistance in building a "new town" on a site donated by lineage members probably accentuated the lack of enthusiasm for improving existing houses. Little effort was being made to deal with dilapidations. Swish construction was in any case considered out-of-date, which it has been, in practice, ever since the return of the Ewes to Togoland.

Chapter 9

SUMMARY AND CONCLUSIONS

The case study of Konkonuru is of a rural community which for many years has had contacts with the outside world, yet remains extraordinarily self-contained in certain respects. It produces all its staple food needs, with surpluses for sale in the market, maintains its own property, looks after its own environment, is responsible for law and order in its own territory and provides social security for its members. The only full-time government-paid personnel are the teachers and the sanitary labourer, although other public servants visit from time to time.

Value is attached to self-sufficiency in staple crops, but this does not preclude participation in the wider economy. Both at home and abroad the people have exploited opportunities of selling their produce; estimates made at the time of the household censuses and farm surveys indicated that about half the food crops were marketed, mainly by the women. Firewood is a profitable by-product of bush clearance, akpeteshie is a lucrative consumer good for those who run the distillery, and cocoa, all of which is now grown on land acquired in other parts of Ghana, is a major source of cash.

Migration, and the decline in infant and child mortality, have affected the demographic structure of the community. By 1970 this had resulted in a relatively small proportion of the population consisting of adult men permanently resident in the town. By 1990 the balance had to some extent been redressed, although the adult population still consisted mainly of women. Most of the migration, which has taken more men than women away from the town, has been to other rural areas in Ghana, where people are residing on their cocoa farms. This is a phenomenon probably peculiar to Akwapim resulting from the early introduction of cocoa to this area. The enterprising farmers realized the profitability of this cash crop, and in order to increase production beyond what was possible on their own territory sought to acquire land in other areas. Despite the predominance of rural-rural migration,the numbers migrating to urban areas has also been substantial; Of the total number of "citizens" recorded in the 1970 census 10 per cent, or 220 people, were living in Accra and other large towns.

Migrant citizens retain strong ties with their home town and aim to return at least once a year; many of them send remittances in cash or kind to relatives at home, and young children are frequently sent to live with their grandparents. Migrants when they visit the town express an intention to return home in their old age and there are members of the older generation in

Konkonuru who have certainly followed this pattern. On the other hand, the household census of 1970 showed that there were many of that generation who had not returned and were by then unlikely to do so. Since then, as described in Chapter 2, more men have returned to farm as a result of lack of employment opportunities in the wage sector of the economy. It is still too early to say whether an upturn in this sector of the economy would reverse this situation. Moreover, although some have returned the large number of non-resident citizens recorded in the 1990 census suggests an even larger flow of out migration, and the probability that the proportion returning will decrease. Many of these non-resident citizens were children, by no means all of them born in Konkonuru. Amongst migrants it seems that less importance is attached to a woman giving birth in her home town, and this practice may well spread to women resident in the town as medical facilities improve, and this in time will no doubt affect the strength of ties of the younger generation.

Those who were back farming in 1990 seemed reasonably contented with their lot, and considered that their incomes from the sale of farm products were better than what they had been able to earn in wages, even when they were in full-time employment. But to those who had returned the disadvantages of rural life were more apparent than to those who had always lived in this environment. They particularly missed electricity, not least because it meant that running their radios and cassette players on batteries was extremely expensive. And they no longer had easy access to cinemas and other forms of entertainment.

Many traditional values and patterns of behaviour persist, although over the past twenty years there are some indications that the younger generation are becoming more critical of traditional authority. The Chief and his elders are still looked upon as leaders of the community and their authority is recognized, despite the questioning of some members of the community. They represent Konkonuru to the outside world, both in the traditional and modern sectors, and control the entry of strangers. Land is held on matrilineal principles and permanent alienation of territory from lineages is considered unthinkable. Within this system, however, there is great flexibility with regard to usufructory rights. All members of the community, including strangers who are for the time being resident in the town, have, in practice, access to land, although the extent, accessibility and quality varies. This underlines the significance of proposals to change land tenure systems, with different schools of thought supporting alternative solutions. One view is that traditional systems, based on lineage, inhibit the development of modern agriculture, as land cannot, under the present legal system, be used as collateral for loans, and there is little incentive for an individual to improve land over which he only possesses usufructory rights. On the other hand the present system does at least mean that nobody is landless, and this provides a very real sense of security and identification with the community in which one lives.

Tradition persists in behaviour patterns connected with birth, marriage and death. A woman is expected to bear her children in her home town, and proper rituals must be observed, such as the outdooring and naming of the new born child. In 1970 there were no cases recorded of women who were resident in town having given birth in hospital, and all were attended in their confinements by traditional midwives; even in the 1990's this continued to be the case. There is still a preference for marriage between members of the community, but rules of clan exogamy are expected to be observed, although the large proportion of Abrade in town makes this difficult in their case. Traditions surrounding death are retained more strongly than those surrounding birth or marriage. Migrant citizens when they die are brought home for burial and there is strict observance of funeral rites. This entails great expense for the family, as drink and food have to be provided for many people over an extended period.

The domestic group is the focal point of an individual's life. As in all Akan societies the composition of this group demonstrates the pull between matrilineal systems of succession and inheritance on the one hand and ties of paternity on the other. In compounds owned by men , and even more so in the compound head's own household, non-lineage members predominate; the reverse is true in the case of women compound heads. Both men and women expressed a preference for a paternal type of household and most men had achieved this ideal. For women the situation is more complicated. Those who are still married and have husbands living in the town usually live with them and with their children. So the majority of women household heads are widowed or divorced or have husbands living in other parts of Ghana. The demographic structure of the town results in there being more women than men in these categories, and this accounts for the large number of women household heads, although the proportion was somewhat less in 1990 than in 1970 due to changes in the demographic structure of the population.

Ownership of house property is greatly valued, and everyone aspires to having his or her own compound. Women as well as men are able to own houses in Akan society, but they are less likely to achieve this ideal, and, if they do, only at a later age. Compounds owned by women are strongly matrilineal in composition, with few non-lineage members. This is yet another reflection of the domestic cycle, in which a woman tends to live with her husband during her childbearing years, and only move to her own compound, or to one owned by her matrikin, after she is widowed or divorced. Although these tendencies are a feature of all Akan societies the strength of paternal ties are probably more strongly demonstrated in Konkonuru, and Akwapim as a whole, than in some other areas.

How then is social and economic change affecting a community such as Konkonuru? How is it adjusting to life in modern Ghana? And to what extent do these adjustments erode traditional value systems and patterns of behaviour? In all societies economic and social change present people with a wider range of opportunities. In what way can they make use of these opportunities, how can they exercise choice between alternatives, and in doing so what conflicts ensue for individuals and the community as a whole? Has Independence improved the position of people living in rural areas, or is there evidence of a new type of colonization, the exploitation of rural people by the urban elite, as examined by Lipton (1977) in his analysis of why the poor remain poor? Nukunya (1990) advances the thesis that in a situation of change traditional institutions give direction to what becomes the resulting position. Changes in matrilineal societies will therefore differ from those in patrilineal societies.

The people of Konkonuru are wrestling with these problems, both consciously and unconsciously. They still have a fierce pride in their home town and traditional way of life, contrasting it with the harsher, more impersonal relationships in modern cities. They are, for example, shocked by the information that some old people in England end their days in institutions rather than amongst their own kin; they see this as a symptom of an uncaring society, devoid of the security offered by kinship obligations. In the course of a discussion with some women one of them said that in western society the individual was not valued. This came as a surprising statement in view of the strong emphasis on individualism in industrial countries. But this woman's interpretation of the meaning of the importance of the individual was very different. She explained that in their society every member was a vital part of the whole community, playing his or her part for the greater good of all.

But retention of these values does not mean that they do not want to enjoy many of the benefits of modern amenities. Their knowledge of the outside world makes them see their town as old fashioned, lacking the amenities of electricity, piped water or a metalled road, and their consciousness of the discrepancy between their position and that of those in Accra and other big towns is even greater than in 1970. They want better opportunities for their children so that they can participate more fully in the modern sector of the economy, although there has been disillusionment with the perceived benefits of education since those with it have failed to secure the jobs they expected. They realize that these aspirations create problems, that there are inconsistencies between formal education and the traditional relationships of the older and younger generations. Such remarks as "In the old days children obeyed their parents, accepted their advice, whereas nowadays they want to go their own way", illustrate this ambivalence. They want their children to go out into the world, to make a success of life, while still retaining filial obligations and respect. This is a familiar problem in all societies. But living in the town one is struck by how harmonious relationships are, on the whole, between the different generations.

More problematic is the question of how to translate their aspirations into reality. As a community it is weak in its ability to represent itself to politicians and bureaucrats, although now that leadership is vested in those with formal education, and a much greater knowledge of the world outside, there should be some improvement in this respect. In 1970 it was clear that the traditional leadership was extremely competent and effective in the traditional sphere, and Konkonuru played an important role in the affairs of the Aburi stool. But understanding how to manipulate the bureaucratic machinery was a very different matter. They knew that it was possible to get assistance from Government agencies, and from time to time in the past they had succeeded in doing so, as when, for example, they were helped to build the present Primary School and the Henderson Box to store water from the spring. This was in the time of Moses Addo, who was not only a forceful character, but had also had some formal education. Without his initiative these projects would probably never have been undertaken. And since his death not only has little else been done with Government assistance, but even those that were completed have not been properly maintained. There were so many pitfalls to be overcome and the traditional leadership felt ill equipped to cope.

An example of the frustration experienced was the attempt to get the Department of Community Development to assist in improving the approach road from Jankama, a distance of about one and a quarter miles. A Community Development worker had visited the town a few years before 1970; he had promised assistance on condition that Konkonuru made a contribution to the cost. The Chief had duly set about raising the necessary money from the community, and had transmitted it to the District Headquarters at Koforidua. Since then nothing had been heard, and the Chief was perplexed at what action he should take. He was fearful of confronting Government officials on his own, and unsure that the outcome would be favourable. His misgivings were not unfounded. I offered to drive him, his linguist and a few others to Koforidua to see the District Community Development Officer. In his presence the Chief felt unable to put his case and I found myself making most of the running. There was great embarrassment as to what had happened to the money advanced by Konkonuru; ledgers were perused, members of staff were questioned, but no trace of the payment could be found. The Community Development Officer, however undertook to send one of his staff to Konkonuru to assess what could be done to repair the road. This was done in due course, and a rapid appraisal was made of what was needed. Shortly after this a bulldozer arrived on the scene, evidently the only one of its type in the District. It started churning up the surface, to the great delight of the people, although to the experienced eye it could be seen that what was being done would have disastrous consequences as soon as it rained. However, even before the work was completed, someone came from District Headquarters to tell the driver that he must return to base. This incensed the people of Konkonuru, so they decided to kidnap the driver and to hold him hostage in the town. District Headquarters was furious and rang me at Legon, telling me that I must control "my" people. After some discussion we arranged to meet in Konkonuru in a few days time, and at that meeting it was agreed that the driver should finish the assignment. Despite this victory the work was never satisfactorily completed, and the road rapidly returned to its old condition. No wonder that the Chief and his elders were sceptical about the benefits of seeking government assistance.

At that time, and even today, it seemed to the people that their only hope of receiving help lay through influential contacts, a view which is not devoid of reality. This belief had a stultifying effect on initiative, and resulted in a deep suspicion of the fairness of the society in which they lived. For example, the young men saw little point in going to the Labour Office to seek jobs unless they knew officials there, or were prepared to pay handsomely for their services. Parents believed that even if their children took the Common Entrance examination for entry to Secondary School they would have little hope of passing unless they knew someone on the Board who could promote their interests. They had a sense of powerlessness in the face of institutions which they did not fully understand. They clung to the belief that those with power were the only ones who could help them to achieve their ambitions for themselves and their children. Unfortunately so many of those who could help most in forging a link with the outside world had migrated. They had sought their own individual solution to the role conflicts created by social change, and by so doing had impoverished the community from which they sprang. This is an understandable reaction, and one which in many respects they were encouraged to make by those who remained behind. There was always the possibility that by improving their own positions in the world they might one day be able to help their fellow citizens who remained behind. This in some cases they did, but they were always wary of what they considered were excessive demands, and frequently the result of this was that they returned far less frequently to visit their home town. This bore particularly heavily on the many women who were left with so much of the responsibility for sustaining the home economy, as has been noticed in food farming systems in other parts of Africa (Pottier 1993; Leach 1991).

The question of farming systems is central to the development of rural areas throughout Africa and goes beyond the particular responsibilities faced by women farmers. It can be illustrated by the situation in Konkonuru, where it is significant that over the past twenty years, and by all accounts for many years before, there has been virtually no change in methods of cultivation. More adult men in the community in 1990 in comparison with 1970 has improved matters, but this advantage has been offset to some extent by what are reported to be lower yields, due to less rainfall, and probably to the shorter fallow period between cropping. Agricultural research has largely neglected the traditional sector, although it was encouraging to find that leucaena was being advocated by the Ministry of Agriculture, and that some trial plots had been planted in Ashanti. The planting of leuceana would enable farmers to use cleared ground for several seasons, if not indefinitely, by restoring fertility to the soil. It would also provide fodder for animals and firewood. The people of Konkonuru had not heard of this innovation, as agricultural extension workers tend not to visit communities off the main road unless pressed to do so by the people themselves. When told about it they expressed interest and the District Secretary at Nsawam, himself a Konkonuru man, promised to follow this up. But like so many ideas there is no evidence that eight years later any progress has been made.

Pottier (1993) reports that "involvement based on learning with farmers and taking a process-focused participatory approach to research, is becoming increasingly applauded and refined (Cernea 1990), although in Africa this involvement is just beginning". He considers the need for this in order to help improve the nutritional status of the poor. This certainly is an important consideration, but in places like Konkonuru, where production is adequate to meet staple food requirements, there is also a need to improve the quantity of food for sale, and marketing facilities, as cash is increasingly seen as not only necessary to meet basic needs, but also desirable in order to raise living standards. It is only through greatly increased farm incomes that a rural community can improve its infrastructure, as Government funds are limited for these purposes. It has already been mentioned that Konkonuru has for many years wanted electricity connected. This is seen as a major step towards bringing the town into the modern world. But with present incomes the people are unable to meet the relatively heavy costs involved.

Pottier also mentions that the "gradual phasing out of once-taken-for-granted male inputs is a problem revealed in the way husbands increasingly fail or refuse to accept duties for household food provision. In many food systems the husband's role was previously fulfilled as part of the cultivation cycle" although "husbands were not directly involved in securing an adequate food supply for their households". This subject was dealt with in the chapter on Food Farming, where it was found that many women farmers were having to pay young men for clearing the bush for their farms. This is still the case, even with more adult men in town, although perhaps not quite to the same extent. In Konkonuru, land is not yet in such scarce supply as in many parts of Africa, so those adult men who have returned are able to concentrate on extending the size of their own farms. All members of the town still have access to land, and this is a great safeguard, although, as mentioned before, this varies in location and quality. The comparatively favourable situation of Konkonuru does not obviate the need for a much more dynamic approach to the development of traditional farming in areas where, because of the terrain, mechanical agriculture is not a viable alternative.

As Haswell and Hunt (1991) point out, there are "two-way relationships between technology and technological change on the one hand, and other key elements of rural change — demographic, economic, social, cultural, political — on the other". They consider that among the most important of the variables involved are "household size and composition, child school enrollment, the farm enterprise mix, the full household range of economic activities, the stock of natural resources, the role of livestock, the man-made physical infrastructure (most notably roads, health facilities, water supplies, also electricity, telephone connections,etc.) and, of course, the actual production methods used in different branches of rural economic activity". Causal relationships between these are still imperfectly understood. The contributors to the book on "Rural Households in Emerging Societies (Haswell and Hunt eds, 1991) were invited to explore one or more of three themes. The first was the need in sub-Saharan Africa for rural technologies that are both environmentally sustainable and can support rising populations at higher income levels, as well as the need to recognize the value of local knowledge and initiatives in developing such technologies. The second theme was the need to plan and appraise technical innovations in the context of full household economic systems. The third theme concerned the search for (varying degrees of) autarky by African rural producers in the face of market failure,cash constraints and other pressures. The focus at the workshop convened to discuss these papers was on "change" rather than "development". This recognized that altering circumstances of rural life brought both successes and failures and not a steady progression from "backward" to "developed". But what constitutes the assessment of change or development depends on the values and personal preferences of both outside observers and the rural people themselves.

This study of Konkonuru has touched on many of the points raised by Haswell and Hunt. It has looked at how much of the traditional persists in the face of socio-economic change in the wider society. Konkonuru is now in much closer touch with this society, through the media, by the return of migrants from cities, and the phenomenon of a commuting chief and his assistant chiefs. So far these wider contacts do not seem to have resulted in greater assistance from national or international sources, with the exception of the housing project, which is not yet under way, and which, by itself, cannot significantly improve incomes.

The next few years are critical for Africa. Unless greater attention is paid to the needs of rural people for the improvement of their lives standards of living will fall to an even more unacceptable level. Greater operational inputs are needed in order to close the gap between town and county. The question of how material improvements will affect traditional social structures, and what will be the consequences of such changes, are other aspects to consider. It has already been seen in this study that, for example, there have been changes in the composition of the household and that more families prefer the paternal model, and that there is an increasing wish by fathers that their own children should inherit some of their property. Matrilineal principles and values are still strong in Konkonuru but are likely to be increasingly questioned by the younger generation. It is significant that members of this generation when they marry try to establish independent compounds as well as households.

The people of Konkonuru certainly desire changes which they perceive as beneficial. It is questionable whether they consider in what ways these changes will undermine much of what they value in the social system. Kinship is still the basis for the organization of rural communities (Nukunya 1990). It determines the rules, duties and obligations of individuals, and the groups in which they interact, to determine such matters as how property is transmitted, who succeeds whom, where a couple will live after marriage or who should worship at a particular shrine. Kinship obligations act as a safety net in countries where State social security systems are undeveloped. Kinship also acts as a mechanism of social control. Changes have led to more flexibility in the principles, rules and modes of operation, leading, according to Nukunya (1990) into some decline in the centrality of kinship as a means of articulating social relationships. But it is still of paramount importance in rural areas.

It is tempting to conclude that social change has not benefitted rural communities, that resources have not been expended on them in proportion to their numerical strength. But equally it would be wrong to paint a picture of increasing misery. Konkonuru is still a viable community and possesses the material and human resources , not only to survive, but to improve its way of life. It has much inner strength and has shown the ability to adapt to changing circumstances in the past, to make use of opportunities, such as the adoption of cocoa farming, while retaining traditional values which sustain its members and provide them with the security that they need. One is left with the striking impression that in a community which is so near to Accra, by no means isolated, and which for so many years has had a great deal of contact with the outside world, so much of the traditional remains.

What then are the lessons that can be learnt from this particular case study of Konkonuru? Some of these are of a general nature, others are more specific. The questions regarding infrastructure are widely applicable, as also are questions concerning land tenure systems, and appropriate technology for the production and marketing of small farmers' agricultural produce. The future of shifting cultivation is specific to those areas still practising this mode of production. In the case of Ghana this still applies to a very large number of farmers, who still produce a large proportion of the food needs of the nation.

Infrastructure

A striking characteristic of rural areas in developing countries is the poor quality of the infrastructure in most of them, such as the provision of access roads, water supply and electricity. This study drew attention to this at the outset, so it will not be discussed in great detail as a conclusion. It does, however, emphasize the need to redress the balance, which Lipton (1977) and others pointed out many years ago. It is significant that in those countries where this has to a greater extent been done there have been benefits, not only for the rural population, but also for the economy as a whole. A prime example of this is Malaysia, for which some relevant data were given in Chapter 1, in Tables 1, 2, 3 and 4.

A similar stricture applies to Social services, such as health and education. Although attempts have been made to improve services, there is still a marked gap between urban and rural provision, and this is reflected in social indicators, for which illustrations were given in Chapters 1 and 2. Bringing standards up to those in towns would be a costly business, and in Africa to-day the economic situation of most countries South of the Sahara means that it is unlikely to be achieved in the foreseeable future, unless either considerable amounts of overseas aid are devoted to this purpose, or systems are introduced which make more effective use of existing resources. For example, in remote areas it is not possible to provide hospitals, or even clinics, within easy reach of all communities, but much more could be done by enlisting the co-operation of the people themselves, as has been done in Sierra Leone in the programme of the Mulaba Hospital, or in India by the work of the Aroles in Jamkhed. In both these cases people have been taught skills to counter the effects of disease and disability. As a result infant and maternal mortality have declined, the birth rates have fallen, and there has been a general improvement in the health of the people. But an important lesson learnt from these projects is that it is not enough to replicate them on a wider scale unless there are good referral systems and committed doctors and nurses to oversee them. One of the problems here is that professional people are understandably reluctant to live in rural areas where infrastructure and services are poor, particularly where families with young children are involved. In developed countries many professional people prefer rural assignments, where living is more pleasant and yet equally good provisions exist for health, education and other services.

Agricultural Systems

The method of shifting cultivation practised in Konkonuru is widespread in Africa. Much more research and experimentation needs to be directed towards improving output in these areas. A great deal of the terrain involved is not suitable for large-scale mechanical cultivation, the slopes are often precipitous, and even where less steep there are dangers of erosion if tree roots are removed. The introduction of small scale mechanical equipment suited to the needs and within the financial reach of farmers working such lands could greatly assist their productivity, and relieve the often back-breaking work involved. The Appropriate Technology Group has experimented with small scale equipment, as it did some years ago in Sierra Leone, but the invention, development and production of suitable implements for small farmers continues to be a problem. Even with such implements shifting cultivation would continue to be labour intensive, but for the effort entailed better returns could be achieved.

As population increases there will be increased pressure on land, and traditional fallow periods will inevitably be reduced. This has already happened in parts of Africa, although so far not seriously in Konkonuru. Alternative methods need to be found to maintain fertility which are suited to the particular conditions. Inorganic fertilisers are not only expensive, but not always effective, as was demonstrated in a small way by the experiments of a farmer in Konkonuru. Alley farming, using *Leucenia*, seems to offer one possibility, but its potential has not yet been adequately tested or exploited in Ghana. Other ways of maintaining soil fertility need to be researched and developed with regard to the topographical and soil conditions where shifting cultivation has been practised for many years.

A related question concerns land tenure systems, which were considered in Chapter 5. In Konkonuru, as in much of West Africa, traditional systems have secured the rights of the individual for access to land. But when farming becomes more commercial and profitable there is a danger of alienation taking place, leaving some as landless labourers. This has been demonstrated, for example, in India in areas where the so-called "Green Revolution" has introduced hybrid strains of wheat and rice. There have been spectacular gains in productivity, which have undoubtedly benefitted the country's economy, but this has been accompanied by an increase in landlesssness. The inputs required for cultivating the new strains are not scale neutral, so are beyond the means of small farmers; as a result they are forced out by competition, and often end up by selling their holdings of land to bigger farmers.

Traditional Akan systems of land tenure no doubt have disadvantages in terms of land improvement, as they are said to act as disincentives (La-Anyane 1963). Matrilineal   inheritance means that a man cannot pass on his abusua land to his children, as on his death it will go to his matrikin. He may as a result fail to take a long term view about expenditure on improvements. This does not apply to women to the same extent, and does not in any case affect privately acquired land for cocoa farms, as was illustrated in Chapter 6. Another problem is that land under this system cannot, at present, be used as a collateral for a loan. This problem should be investigated by the Government with regard to schemes for helping farmers to improve their productivity. There is bound over time to be some erosion of traditional systems, but it is questionable whether there should be deliberate steps taken to accelerate change.

Another area where work needs to be done is on the possibilities of greater diversification of production. This could involve the introduction not only of new crops, but also of livestock for subsistence and for sale. The scope of expanding production for sale depends on accessibility to markets, which in turn relies on good roads and transport as well as on marketing systems. To what extent, for example, are co-operative societies a viable solution in order to enable farmers to share the cost of equipment and marketing facilities? Although Co-operatives have not had a very happy history in Ghana, for a variety of reasons, the principle behind co-operation is highly relevant to the development of better systems of production and marketing.

It is hoped that this study has brought out not only the need to redress the urban-rural bias in development, but in doing so to respect the traditions of the people involved, to understand their ways of life, and to consult them about changes which they perceive as desirable. Rural people, whether or not they possess formal education, have a great knowledge in depth of their land and how best it can be cultivated under present conditions. They also have aspirations to improve their levels of living, without destroying that which they value in their customs and social relationships. Government plans and programmes, if geared to appreciate this, are more likely to receive a positive response from those who are ultimately responsible for increasing the productivity of the country and securing a better life for all her citizens.

Appendix 1

METHODS OF STUDY

This appendix explains how the study was made and why Konkonuru was chosen.

I was looking for a village within easy reach of the University of Ghana at Legon, Accra, but outside the commuting catchment area of the capital city. I particularly wanted to study a matrilineal society, as this presented certain aspects of change which seemed to be of special interest. As I was teaching at Legon it was not possible for me to spend long, uninterrupted periods in a village. It was therefore a question of choosing a location with reasonably easy access. But I did not want a village on the main road, nor one in which there had been much inward migration. A friend in the Social Welfare Department ,with whom I discussed my needs, suggested that his own village might suit my requirements, and he took me there to meet the Chief and consider the possibilities. This was in July 1970. I was immediately attracted to Konkonuru as we approached it along the dirt road, and this feeling was reinforced when I met the Chief and his elders. My introduction by Godfried Addo was, of course, a great advantage.

My association with the Department of Social Welfare and Community Development had implications which it is important to mention. I was teaching in the Department of Sociology at the University of Ghana, with special responsibility for the Social Administration Unit, which ran in-service training courses for serving officers in the Department. At this time we were planning a programme of fieldwork assignments for students during their final year, and it was suggested that a few students could come to Konkonuru to work in Community Development. I had doubts about the advisability of carrying out my own research alongside a fieldwork assignment, but as the Chief was very keen on the idea I thought that the advantages would probably outweigh the disadvantages. The people of Konkonuru were familiar with Community Development and had received considerable help from the Department some years ago. But since the death of Moses Addo, who had acted as the home-based link, and had taken the main initiative for securing their services, the Community presence had been withdrawn, and no-one from the village had seriously tried to make contacts. This was puzzling in view of the fact that they did not lack advice from their migrant citizens in Accra. Godfried Addo, my friend in Social Welfare, frequently visited the village and was able to tell them who to approach. It was he who had put them in touch with the Regional Headquarters at Koforidua, with a view to obtaining assistance with improving the access road, which was in a very bad state of repair. There was an Accra-Konkonuru Association, of which he was a leading member, and they were concerned with improving their home town, and had no doubt contributed to the funds collected for the road and the Middle School.

The problem uppermost in the minds of the people of Konkonuru, and on which they required assistance, was the reconstruction of the feeder road from the main Accra-Aburi road at Jankama. The people had some time back collected £300 (600 cedis at the rate of exchange when Ghana adopted the metric system), and had deposited it at the Eastern Region Community Development Office at Koforidua. Since then they had heard nothing. They were also anxious to build a new Middle School, as their present buildings were totally inadequate. For this, too, they had collected funds and purchased a quantity of concrete blocks which were rapidly disintegrating on the edge of the playing field. Some approaches had been made to the District Education Office at Akropong, but no agreement had been reached. It appeared that the District was not prepared to assist unless a new school should be provided for the joint use of Konkonuru and Jankama. These villages were about one and a quarter miles apart and both of them wanted the school to be near to them.

I explained to the Chief and his elders that if the students came for fieldwork assignments we could discuss these and other problems, and do what we could to help them achieve their aspirations. I made it clear that we had no money to offer, no material resources. Ultimately the development of Konkonuru would depend, as it had in the past, largely on the efforts of the people themselves.

Already a Town Development Committee existed, which had been a statutory requirement under the Nkrumah regime. The Chairman was the Asafohene, Kwasi Osae, and the Secretary was his son, Isaac Ohene Osae, who had recently completed Middle School. There were 12 other members of the committee, including three women. The Chief was not a member, but he was always free to attend meetings. It was not clear to what extent by 1970 the committee ever met, or, if they did, what subjects were discussed. Certainly no action seemed to have been taken on the problems with which they expressed themselves to be concerned. Perhaps this was because, at that time, the workings of bureaucracy were perceived by them as beyond their grasp. There were no resident members of the community who felt able, or who had the energy to tackle Government officers. When I returned to Ghana in 1972, and again in 1977, the committee appeared to be defunct. In 1990 it had been revived and reconstituted under the present Chief. It met regularly and was actively discussing plans to rebuild the town, with the help of an overseas aid project, and to connect a supply of electricity.

In October 1970 I acquired a room in the house of the Asafosupi, Kwamena Asamoah, and I spent weekends there. As the fieldwork day was on a Friday this made it a reasonably long weekend. My position was, in fact, not unlike that of several members of the village who worked in Accra during the week and returned home at weekends. I became one of the circulating members of the community, a weekly boarder at Legon. During vacations I was able to spend longer periods, and even in term time I often managed to put in extra days during the week. My husband sometimes joined me and helped in many ways with the preparation of maps, and advice on technical matters.

I returned to England in September 1971. In July and August 1972 when I revisited Ghana on a Hayter Award from the University of London I spent most of my time at Konkonuru. I also visited one of the areas in Akim Oda where citizens of Konkonuru had acquired land for cocoa farming.

The question of the identity of the researcher is a crucial one in any study. It is inevitable in a village setting that one is fitted into the network of relations, and one is looked upon accordingly by different members of the community. As it is only possible to conduct research through the good offices of the leaders it is also inevitable that one is to a large extent identified with those leaders, and that one's closest contacts lie in this circle. It is important to be clear about this rather than to seek to avoid altogether one's expected role, and it may be helpful to record my own position. I was, as I have explained, introduced to the village by a friend; he was not of the Chief's lineage, but he was a member of an important village family, with connections by marriage with the Chief (it is probable that all families in Konkonuru have some connection by marriage with the Chief as a result of the rule of clan exogamy, and the strong preference for finding one's partner within the village community), and he himself was held in considerable respect, not only because of his status as a senior Civil Servant, but also because, as previously mentioned, he maintained contact with the village, was a leading member of the Accra-Konkonuru Association, and through the warmth of his personality was known and liked by all. His mother still lived in the village and was at the time looking after his youngest son. I therefore started out with some of his reflected glory, and was immediately looked upon as having concern and affection for Konkonuru, which of course had its disadvantages as well as advantages.

At an early stage I met Kate Asare, who immediately declared that I was her village sister. Kate was my constant friend and counsellor; she was a strong and at the same time a sensitive person, highly emotional and temperamental, characteristics which were controlled by her great good sense and high degree of intelligence. During the time that Community Development workers had been running classes for women in the village she had acted as the women's leader, and this role she also fulfilled in respect of the traditional obligations of women to take part in communal labour. She assembled them on Fridays, organized them to do their share of work, and she was an exacting taskmaster.

Reciprocal relations present problems when they are between individuals from different cultural backgrounds. To an Akan the importance of kinship is paramount, overriding all other obligations. Therefore, it is expected that a kinsman will do everything in his power to further the interests of his kinsfolk, and one of the most pressing interests is that of employment. This was borne in on me at an early stage, and I had to make it clear that it was not within my power ("mentumi" became a frequent expression) to secure jobs for people. I am sure that in this I did not live up to what was expected of me, particularly as it was known that my husband was Executive Engineer of the University of Ghana at Legon, and therefore must have innumerable jobs within his gift. But this role conflict with which I was confronted served the useful purpose of making me appreciate the force of the value systems related to kinship, in that I felt the conflict personally as well as recognizing it intellectually. Not that the people of Konkonuru ever pressed me unduly or appeared to blame me in any way. They accepted my explanations with great courtesy.

No stranger, especially a white stranger can ever melt into the landscape, nor expect not to alter the situation in some way. Inevitably there are expectations of the benefits his or her presence will bring, either in terms of payments for services rendered, or influence with outside sources of aid. Because from the outset I had expressed my interest in the welfare of the village I was very conscious of these problems. But my welfare role was institutionalized, limited to specific purposes, and my research interests in their way of life were, I think, reasonably well understood. The fieldwork assignment for Legon students was of limited duration, and finished in March 1971. We really achieved very little in material terms, for a variety of reasons. For the rest of the time my presence in the village was looked upon as a personal affair. I stayed over the weekend, as far as they were concerned, to rest, because I liked the hills, and was interested in their way of life, particularly in their farming activities. In these matters I wanted to learn from them and they were willing teachers. They taught me how to farm and were impressed by my achievements. They patiently tried to teach me the proper pronunciation and tonal values of Akwapim Twi. They enjoyed coming up to my room for a chat, a cup of tea or a snack, and talking about village affairs. They always welcomed me into their compounds, liked to show me around, and to instruct me in ways of preparing and cooking food. They freely discussed their customs, were inquisitive about how we ordered our lives in England. Their comments on both ways of life, and the comparisons they made, were extraordinarily perceptive.

A rather different viewpoint was provided by the village teachers, most of whom commuted daily from Aburi and none of whom was a citizen of Konkonuru. They regarded the village as too hide-bound by tradition and lacking in understanding of the needs of modern education. Most of them were unwilling to live in the village, particularly those with wives, who felt that the atmosphere was alien to an educated woman. This caused some resentment from the people of Konkonuru, as mentioned in the Chapter on Education.

Methods of Collecting Information

In addition to general observation, the keeping of a daily journal, and discussions with informants, systematic collection of data was made in the following ways:-

1.   The Household Censuses

The first census was carried out in December 1970, and formed the basis of any subsequent samples for further surveys. A sample of compounds was surveyed in 1972, and in 1990 a second census was carried out, covering all compounds. The household census was designed to establish the composition of households and compounds, and to provide information on the distribution of the population by sex, age marital status, tribe, clan, education, main and secondary occupation, religion, place of birth, location at time of census, reason for absence, number of months residence in previous year, and the ownership of farm land in other areas of Ghana. Information was also collected on the physical characteristics of compounds, i.e. the type of building construction, the number of living and sleeping rooms, kitchen, bathrooms, storerooms,etc.

Before the census was taken a great deal of preparatory work was done and in this the four Legon students assisted. Discussions were held with the Chief and the Town Committee on the questions to be asked, and it was as a result of this that we decided to record all citizens of Konkonuru, whether they were absent or not. It was the Chief who first suggested this, as he was anxious to know the strength of citizenship on a global basis. We also discussed the question of what we should use as the basic unit of the domestic group and arrived at an accepted distinction between the larger unit of the compound (ofi) and the smaller household unit (kuw). It was agreed that before proceeding further the Chief should call a meeting of the whole town to explain what we were doing and to elicit their views. This took place on 27 November 1970 and lasted for nearly two hours. Godfred Addo came up from Accra to attend this meeting, which took place round the Osofo shrine, and was attended by a large proportion of the resident adult population.

After the usual greetings and pouring of libation we explained our mission and went through the schedule which we had prepared. This gave rise to an enormous amount of discussion, the men doing most of the talking. There was an extraordinarily extrovert attitude to asking personal questions and no demand for anonymity or confidentiality. The proposal to record absent members gave rise to heated arguments as to who exactly should be included. For example, if a man was living away and his wife was not a citizen of Konkonuru should his children be counted? Some people felt that as they were not members of his matrilineage they should not be included unless they were living in Konkonuru at the time of the census or had been born there. In the end it was left to respondents to tell the interviewers the names of all those whom they regarded as citizens. This rather vague decision means that too much importance cannot be attached to the data about absent members. In the event we found that most people enumerated all the children of absent fathers, whether or not they had Konkonuru wives. Because of the preference for marriage within the community this may not have made an appreciable difference to the results.

On the question of the distinction between the household and the compound there was fair agreement. But a good deal of argument ensued over the designation of household head, and on this the men tended to take a different view from the women. Men considered that they should be regarded as head of a wife's household, even if they were not living in it, whereas women took the opposite view. In the end the women's counsel prevailed. In fact the numbers involved who were in this situation turned out, when we did the census, to be small (14 households), but it gave rise to a lot of controversy at the meeting.

When the Chief asked us to carry out a census we asked him to allocate some helpers from the town. By the time of the meeting he had chosen five young men who had recently completed Middle School, so our next task was to train them. A sixth presented himself as willing to help while he was on leave from the Army. We decided that all the household interviews should be done by these town volunteers, and that the Legon students should help with the collection of data on the physical characteristics of compounds. In any case the students could not be present during the whole period of the census. The whole task of checking the schedules was to be done by me and my room became the centre of operations. I was there continuously for the first three days and thereafter made daily visits until the work was completed, often visiting compounds with the interviewers to verify data. On farming days most of the work had to be done in the late afternoon.

The village assistants proved most competent. They possessed the great advantage of knowing the people intimately. An equally great advantage was that they had none of the sophistication of student interviewers, and were only too ready to ask if they did not understand, or to say that they did not know an answer and would go back to find out, rather than inventing data on the basis of their expectations. I checked every schedule with the helper who had filled it in, and this gave me a chance to ask additional questions and to make notes on points of interest which lay outside the strictly quantifiable.

While the census was proceeding I did some quick hand tabulations in order to get out preliminary results as soon as possible for the village. The people had shown so much interest and had co-operated so well that we decided to have a little ceremony to mark the successful completion of the exercise. So on Saturday, 12 December 1970 we invited everybody to a gathering in the Primary School. The Chief was away visiting his cocoa farms, so his place was taken by the Asafohene. It was meant to be a short meeting, but so many people decided to make speeches that it lasted for about two hours. We made small presentations to our town assistants; each of them was given a book and a certificate saying that they had assisted in the census, and one cedi. These were handed out ceremoniously by my husband. I told the people about a few of our findings, such as the numbers of men, women and children, and the total number of citizens in residence and elsewhere, and then we served soft drinks and groundnuts.

I had already discussed data analysis with Dr. Nelson Addo, at that time in charge of the Demographic Unit at Legon. He had been most helpful in planning the census, as he had, had a great deal of experience of similar work throughout Ghana. I was also assisted by Mr. Odai of the Institute of Statistical, Social and Economic Research at Legon, who worked out the computer programme for me, and did so with real interest and understanding of what I wanted. Dr. Addo very kindly lent me two of his research assistants to do the coding of the data. For all these facilities I was most grateful as without this help the task of processing the material single handed would have been great.

The second census, in June 1990, was carried out by Isaac Ohene Osae, Jacob Ayesu and Stephen Asamoah, all of whom had not only assisted in the 1970 census, but had also helped with the other surveys described below. As I was working in Kumasi I was not able to be resident in Konkonuru while the survey was being carried out. At first I suggested that we should work on a greatly simplified schedule, concentrating on the collection of data on compound and household numbers, by age and sex, and only recording resident citizens of the town at the time of the survey. However, my assistants were not satisfied with this and insisted on collecting data in the same form as in 1970, which included such items as occupation, education and place of birth; they were also insistent on recording information about non-resident citizens. There were fewer details about household relationships, and no count was made of cocoa farms owned in other parts of Ghana.

I was only able to visit Konkonuru to discuss the progress of the census on a few occasions, so it was not possible to check schedules daily; so the responsibility for this had to be left to the enumerators. I spent my last week in Ghana in Accra; so my assistants brought the results to me there, and we were able to go over any problems encountered; in appropriate cases they were able to recheck information when they returned to Konkonuru. By the time that I left I had tabulated most of the main findings, so that the results could be told to the people of Konkonuru.

My assistants had expected the resident population to have been larger; the reasons that they had thought this to be the case are discussed in the main text, and were principally based on the existence of a sizeable number of new compounds, mostly lived in by the younger generation in nuclear households. Most of these compounds only had one or at most two households, so average numbers were smaller than in those of the older, more established compounds.

The numbers of non-resident citizens had, however, doubled, suggesting that during the intervening twenty years there had been a lot of out migration. Whether this was so or not is questionable, as a good deal of the increase may have been due to the enthusiasm of the enumerators. On the other hand, in discussing this phenomenon with informants they did think that a large number of school leavers had migrated to urban areas. This was an interesting observation in view of the fact that there were 40 year olds in the community who had returned as a result of not being able to get satisfactory employment in Accra or other cities. It was not possible from the 1990 data to establish to what extent increased migration, if it had taken place, was rural-urban or rural-rural; the 1970 data had shown a majority of migrants moving to other rural areas, mostly to places where they had interests in cocoa farms. Nor was it possible from the 1990 data to estimate fertility or infant and child mortality rates. If this could have been done it would have given some indication as to whether an increase in population due to, for example, longer life expectancy and lower infant mortality, had not resulted in greater numbers in Konkonuru, because of an increase in migration. During these twenty years there have been significant improvements in health indicators, so this explanation has some credibility.

Another aspect that the 1990 census did not cover was the schedule recording the physical aspects of the compound, such as building types, number of rooms, location of kitchens. Therefore, the statement in the text that densities of occupation were lower in 1990 than in 1970 was based solely on the larger number of compounds.

Results of the census are described in the main text, so will not be discussed here.

2.   The Farm Survey

The purpose of this survey is discused in Chapter 5. I was helped by two of the assistants who had taken part in the census, Isaac Ohene Osae and Jacob Ayesu. After outlining my ideas on what we might try to find out we discussed these in the light of their experience and, having agreed on our objectives, decided on the survey design. I then worked out a preliminary schedule and we tested it out with a few farmers. In addition to the schedules we planned to visit all the farms of our respondents, to measure them and to follow the progress of operations from bush clearance through planting to harvest.

I selected a stratified random sample of farmers from our census, using the compound as the first unit of stratification. I then listed all those with farms of their own in the compounds selected in the first round and again used random tables to select one from each compound. I did not stratify by sex, although subsequently I thought that this might have been advisable, as women farmers were under-represented in the sample in proportion to their numbers in the population as a whole; however it was probably in line with the proportion of women who owned farms, as against working on those of their husbands. The procedure we used resulted in a sample of 17 men and 11 women farmers, 28 being the number with which we had decided we could deal.

We based our survey on a map traced from the master copy at the Cocoa Division office at Mampong, which was on the scale of 1:7920 (approximately 8 inches to the mile). No detailed survey had been made by the Cocoa Division of farms at Konkonuru, so the map only gave us very basic information on the site of the settlement, the lie of the approach road, the main bush paths and streams.

We started by talking to our sample farmers in their homes, and made arrangements to visit their farms. When we went with them to their farms we traced in the bush paths from the town as accurately as we could and paced out distances. This was not a full cadastral survey, but it served the purpose of giving an idea of the layout of farms in relation to the settlement. Different parts of Konkonuru territory are given distinct names and my two assistants were absolutely clear about these boundaries, and of those between their land and that of surrounding settlements. This helped us to place individual farms.

We started the farm study in March 1971, and in the first few weeks visited all the sample farms. Having reached a farm we recorded the different crops planted, the dates of planting, their state of growth,and any other relevant details for the farm in question. We measured the size of each farm with a tape and drew its shape. As farms were often irregular in shape the acreage calculated can only be considered as approximate.

Throughout the months from April to September we revisited farms and recorded the harvesting of crops. We asked about quantities sold, and quantities consumed within the household, or by other members of the extended family. We then priced the value of produce in both these categories at the rates currently received in the market; these rates were lower than the retail prices, which meant that a family buying food would have had to pay considerably more for the produce they consumed.

Having collected the data for 1971, we discussed the possibility of repeating the survey in 1972, in order to assess variations between years. I had planned to return to Ghana in 1972, but was not able to arrive until July. Isaac and Jacob were, however, confident that they could do the preliminary work on their own. In the course of the year Jacob got a job in Accra, but his place was taken by Stephen Asamoah, who had also helped with the census. We kept in close touch by correspondence and the day I arrived in Ghana Isaac came down to Legon to greet me. He brought his notebook and the farm map and was most businesslike in his approach. He had measured all the 1972 farms, had made notes on planting times, growth, disease problems, etc. This was a big task in view of the fact that ,in accordance with the practice of shifting cultivation, these were all new farms, in different locations from those in the 1971 survey. So the 1972 study was undertaken mainly by my assistants. I visited some of the farms, checked through the schedules, and had further discussions with the farmers, but the main work was theirs.

Isaac and Stephen were keen to carry on for a further year, although I said that I would not be able to return to Ghana in 1973. It was agreed that they should continue with the study and in due course I received the results of their work.

3.   *Sleeping and Eating Practices of Schoolchildren*

When we took the household census I was struck by the difficulty of allocating some of the children to specific households. We also found that a large number of children were living with grandparents. Although this is not an unexpected situation in Akan society it seemed of sufficient interest to follow up. I therefore decided to take a sample of schoolchildren and discussed this with the headmasters of the Primary and Middle Schools. They were willing to co-operate and themselves volunteered to help with the task. Instead of a random sample we took all the children in the second and sixth forms of the Primary School and the third form of the Middle School. This was an administratively simpler arrangement and gave a good age spread. The average ages of children in these three groups were 9.4 years, 12.8 years and 16.1 years, respectively. A record was kept of where they slept and where and what meals they ate during three periods of three days each, at two monthly intervals, from March to July 1971.

Results of the survey are given in Tables 44 and 45 in the main text. As can be seen there, for the majority of Primary School children their eating and sleeping locations were the same; only one girl and four boys out of 44 children were sleeping and eating in different places. In the Middle School, however, five boys and one girl, out of 17 children ate in one place and slept in another. The problem encountered in the census of not being able to locate children in a specific household was thus found to be different for the older and younger age groups. For younger children the confusion had largely arisen in cases where a mother had a kitchen in a different compound from the one in which she slept, so that the children's lives centred around one place in the daytime and another at night. In any case the perception of the significance of spatial relationships is very different in Akan society from that in our own.

4.   *Livestock Census*

I did not plan to take a complete census of livestock, although questions about animals were asked in the farm survey. However, in May 1971, at the beginning of the rainy season, people were losing animals and did not know what was the matter with them. After consultation with the Gyasehene, I approached the Department of Animal Health in the Ministry of Agriculture, where the Principal Veterinary Officer, Dr. G. A. Oduro, was keen to help. He suggested that we should make a complete census of livestock and said that he would detail one of his field assistants to undertake any necessary treatment.

He himself came to Konkonuru with two assistants and after meeting the Gyasehene, he had a look at some of the affected animals. He found evidence of serious worm infection in the sheep. The worms cause enteritis and can also affect the lungs. He said that the sheep's feet needed paring and that many of them were suffering from the damp and lack of adequate shelter in the compounds. He was not happy about their method of castration and told them that better, more humane methods were available.

One assistant was left behind to carry out the census and to treat any animals affected by disease. Dr. Oduro also suggested that all the dogs in the town should be given antirabies injections, and that some castrations should be performed to demonstrate the improved method. This programme was eventually carried out. According to the count there were 107 sheep and 242 goats in the town; it was impossible to count the hens and chickens and no attempt was made to discover all the dogs. Those found were given injections, but not much interest was shown by the people in bringing along their animals. A rough estimate was that there were 20 dogs in town. The people were keen that their sick sheep and goats should be cured, but were content to leave it at that. They were not persuaded that better husbandry would benefit their flocks, apart from one or two people who already looked after their animals better than most.

Although the number of livestock is considerable they do not form an important part of the economy. Their treatment is casual, not many are killed for eating or sale, and they wander round the town, in and out of compounds, scavenging whatever food they can. The Department of Animal Health solved our problem in the short run, and in 1972, when I returned to Ghana, no further serious problems had occured. The animals looked in better condition, but husbandry continued to be casual. Paul Addo, a Konkonuru man, who runs a poultry farm at Oyarifa, a village on the Accra plain, on the main road from Aburi to Accra, told me in 1971 that he had tried to improve livestock husbandry in his home town, and had offered to give them stock for breeding purposes. But he became discouraged by the lack of response and gave up the unequal struggle. Twenty years later, with the presence of a younger generation of literate farmers, it might have been expected that more interest would have been shown in developing what could be an useful additional source of income. However, there was not much evidence that this was the case.

5. *Domestic Roles*

In 1971 I carried out a survey on Household Composition and Domestic Roles at Aburi, in order to collect comparative data. Aburi is a busy market town with a population in 1971 of about 5,000. Since the 1820's it has been a centre of missionary activity, and although only a few miles from Konkonuru it has a very different atmosphere. When I was working out the interview schedule and translating it into Twi I decided to try it out in Konkonuru. I already had the household information and through observation and discussion had been studying domestic roles. I knew most of the respondents personally, so there are certain respects in which this could bias the information from a comparative point of view, as the Aburi interviews were a one-off exercise. However, as far as my Konkonuru studies were concerned the information I obtained added to what I had collected in a less formal way. The respondents selected in the sample were eager to discuss questions, finding it a good opportunity to express their views.

The Konkonuru sample consisted of 27 households. In 18 of these they were headed by husbands living in the same households as their wives. Of the 9 households headed by women, 3 of them were still married, but had husbands living in other parts of Ghana, 3 were divorced, 2 widowed and one turned out to be single; at first we thought that she was a widow or divorcee, but she claimed never to have been married, although she was 30 years of age, an unusual case in rural Ghana. An interview situation in a village is rarely a private affair; when a husband is being questioned wives and other members of the family join in. Different views are expressed by different parties, although in the end, after much discussion a consensus of opinion was usually reached. Where this was not the case the main respondent's view was recorded, but note was taken of the views of dissenters. The Aburi sample consisted of 112 respondents. A smaller proportion of these households consisted of husbands and wives living together, as there were proportionately more widows and divorcees heading households in Aburi than in Konkonuru.

Most of the information appears in Chapter 8 in a descriptive form. Some of the statistical findings are given here. Responses are given as percentages for purposes of comparison, although as the Konkonuru sample was so small significance cannot be attached to marginal differences. The overall picture did, however, bear out observed differences between the two communities.

1.   Age Distribution of Sample

Age Group	Konkonuru %	Aburi %
Under 30 years	4	15
30–39	22	28
40–59	48	29
60 years & over	26	22
Not stated	—	6
Total	100	100
N=	27	112

2.   Type of Marriage

Type	Konkonuru %	Aburi %
Amane* (customary	92	71
Mpena aware (mutual consent)	—	6
Asore (kristofo) nyird (church blessing)	4	17
Ordinance	—	—
Not stated/ not applicable	4	6
Total	100	100

* Those put in this category were respondents who only had this ceremony.   Those who had a church blessing had usually gone through customary rites.

3.   Present Marital Status

Marital Status	Konkonuru %	Aburi %
Still married	78	59
Widowed	17	19
Divorced	11	18
Not stated or not applicable	4	4
Total	100	100

4.   Place of Birth

	Konkonuru				Aburi			
	Self	*Spouse**	*Mother*	*Father*	*Self*	*Spouse**	*Mother*	*Father*
	%	%	%	%	%	%	%	%
Survey town	85	78	89	89	71	54	51	45
Other Akwapim	—	4	7	4	4	10	12	13
Other E. Region	11	7	4	7	13	14	6	5
Other Ghana	4	4	—	—	11	6	13	13
Other Africa	—	—	—	—	1	16	—	—
Not stated	—	7	—	—	—	16	18	24
Total	100	100	100	100	100	100	100	100

* Refers to latest spouse only

5. Time spent in Survey Town

Duration	Konkonuru	Aburi
	%	%

A. Born in Town

All life	33	9
Since birth, but spent periods away	52	62

B. Born elsewhere

20 years or more	11	5
10–19 years	—	6
5–9 years	4	5
4 years or less	—	12
Not stated	—	1
Total	100	100

6. Education

Standard reached	Konkonuru	Aburi
	%	%
None	85	56
Primary	11	14
Middle	—	22
Teacher Training	4	5
University	—	1
Adult	—	1
Not stated	—	1
Total	100	100

7. Who arranged First Marriage

Relationship	Konkonuru %	Aburi %
Father	70	14
Mother	—	5
Father & Mother	7	33
Uncle (wofa)	15	4
Other relative	—	4
Self	4	33
Other/ not stated	4	3
Total	100	100

8. Who pays for maintenance of children?

Relationship with child	Konkonuru %	Aburi %
Both parents	4	17
Mother only	44	23
Father only	22	10
Other relative	7	12
Not applicable*	23	38
Total	100	100

* This applies to cases where no children remained at home

9. Who do you think takes most of the decisions at home?
(Married couples living together only)

Person	Konkonuru %	Aburi %
Husband	5	20
Wife	53	30
Both	42	50
Total	100	100
Number=	19	70

10. Should children choose their own marriage partners?

Answer	Konkonuru %	Aburi %
Yes	89	70
No	4	23
It depends	—	5
Don't know	7	2
Total	100	100

It is interesting to compare these responses with those in Table 7. A distinction was made between "choice" and "arrangement". In other words, most parents felt that a child's wishes should be respected, but that the final arrangements should be made by parents. Attitudes in Konkonuru in this respect seem to have been more liberal, although the smallness of the sample has to be considered. The differences do, however, bear out observations and discussions with a wider range of people than just those in the sample. This impression is borne out by the answers in Table 11.

11.   Should young people have boy/girl friends before marriage?

Answer	Konkonuru %	Aburi %
Yes	89	61
No	4	33
It depends	—	2
Don't know	7	4
Total	100	100

12.   Should a man have more than one wife?

Answer	Konkonuru %	Aburi %
Yes	26	25
No	63	64
It depends	7	7
Don't know	4	4
Total	100	100

13.   Which domestic arrangements do you prefer? And which do you have?

Type of domestic group	Konkonuru		Aburi	
	Prefer %	*Actual* %	*Prefer* %	*Actual* %
Husband, wife & own Children only	56	33	77	32
These, plus brothers/ sisters, with or without their children	18	26	4	—
These, plus mother, & or father	15	15	17	1
Alone with children	—	18	—	26*
Single person	—	4	—	6
Other (including lodgers)	—	4	—	35
No clear reply	11	—	2	—
Total	100	100	100	100

*This reflects the high proportion of widowed and divorced women in the Aburi sample

14.   Division of labour in the domestic group

This is not presented statistically as it would involve lengthy and rather meaningless tables.   The trend is clear.

i.	Cleaning the house	Wife,* or woman living on her own, with the help of children. In some cases the children do all the cleaning
ii.	Cooking	Same as i.
iii.	Fetching water	Children: both boys and girls.
iv.	Fetching firewood	Wife, sometimes helped by children & mother if there.
v .	Washing clothes	Wife and girls, and mother if present.
vi.	Ironing clothes	Boys, Husband.
vii.	Going to market	Husband or wife or both.
viii.	Paying for bought items of food	Husband if present or both at different times.
ix.	Buying clothes	As for viii.
x.	Paying for clothes	As for viii.
xi.	Buying household goods	Wife, and mother if present
xii.	Paying for household goods	Husband if present
xiii.	Looking after young children	Wife
xiv.	Organization of day-to-day activities of children	Children themselves
xv.	Helping children with schoolwork	Mostly left to children. In Aburi some mothers and fathers helped. Only one case of this was found in Konkonuru. This reflects the higher standard of literacy in Aburi.
xiv.	Dealing with family affairs,	Both or wife only. Where mothers are in the house-

deciding contributions to   household they take a large share of responsibility
funerals, etc.

* For subsequent items wife includes woman living on her own.

Appendix 2

TRADITIONAL ORGANIZATION IN 1970

1. Office or Stool Name   Name of Occupant

Office or Stool Name	Name of Occupant
Chief	Kwadwo Bediako, Gyasehene to Adontenhene
Osiahene	Kwame Baah, alias Obuobi III
Opanyin	Kwasi Kumah
Abusuapanyin	Obeng Kwaku
Asafosupi	Kwabena Asamoah
Asafohene	Osae Kwasi
Asafo Okyeame	Yaw Bediako
Ohemmea	Afua Kae
Mmerantehene	Osae Kwaku
Okyeame	Ahwireng Kwaku
Opanyin	Osae Kwadwo

2. Names of Quarters

    Aboagyawe
    Ahen brong
    Kenkuase
    Sraha

3. Special Festivals

Odwira	August
Awukudae	Once every 42 days
Akwasidae	Once every 42 days
Wato eburow	At beginning of maize harvest

4. Shrines

Tutu	Atia Yaw
Fofie	Opiri
Gygyafo	
Otaapem	

5. Stool Regalia and Relics

Horns.   Sound — Dodow na eye ade
Drums: Kyenesin   Sound — Mmere beho da bi (coated with sheep's
                          annually at Odwira)

Appendix 3

Relations of Members within Resident Households Konkonuru 1970

| Relation to Household Head | Percentage Distribution | | | | | |
| | MALE HEADS | | FEMALE HEADS | | ALL HEADS | |
	% of all members	% excluding heads	% of all members	% excluding heads	% of all members	% excluding heads
SELF						
Single Person households	4	—	5	—	5	—
Other heads	15	—	21	—	18	—
Total Self	19	—	26	—	23	—
OTHERS						
Wives	13	17	—	—	7	10
Husbands	—	—	1	1	Trace	Trace
Sons	33	40	24	33	29	37
Daughters	25	31	29	39	27	34
Son's son's	2	3	2	3	2	3
Daughters son's & daughters	4	4	15	20	9	11
Other patrikin	3	4	1.5	2	2	3
Other matrikin	1	1*	1.5	2	1	2
Sub Totals						
Household Members	81	100	74	100	77	100
Heads	19	—	26	—	23	—
TOTAL	100	100	100	100	100	100
Number =	630	510	516	380	1146	890

* In only one case was a sister's son in the household

REFERENCES

Abbey, K. S. 1996. *Personal communication.*

Adamako Safo 1971. Unpublished paper for seminar at the University of Ghana, Legon

African Development Bank 1998. *African Development Report.* London: Oxford OUP.

Appiah, K. A. 1992. In *My Father's House.* London, Methuen.

Arhin, K. 1968. "The Missionary Role on the Gold Coast and in Ashanti." *Institute of African Studies Research Review,* Legon. Vol.4, No.2.

Assimeng, Max. 1981. *Social Structure of Ghana.* Accra: Ghana Publishing Corp.

Bardhan, Pranab. 1997. *The Nature of Institutional Impediments to Economic Development.* Working Paper No. 96066 Center for International Development and Economic Research. University of California: Berkeley.

Bartels, F.L. 1965. The Roots of Ghana Methodism. Cambridge: C.U.P.

Barth, F. 1967. *Economic Spheres in Darfur, in R Firth (ed). Theories in Economic Anthropology.* London: Tavistock Publications Ltd.

Bauer, P.T. 1954. *West African Trade.* Cambridge: CUP.

Becker, G. 1965. A Theory of the Allocation of Time. *Economic Journal 75.*

Beckett, W.H. 1944. Akokoaso: A Survey of a Gold Coast Village. *L.S.E. Monographs on Social Anthropology,* No. 10.

Benneh, G. 1976. *Unpublished Report on a Conference on Land and Economic Development,* held at the University of Science and Technology, Kumasi.

Benneh, G. 1973. Small-scale Farming Systems in Ghana. In *Africa* no. 43 pp 134-146

Bentsi-Enchill, K. 1964. *Ghana Land Law: an exposition, analysis and critique.* London: Sweet and Maxwell.

Blay, P.K. 1972. *Geology, in D.Brokensha, Akwapim Handbook,* Tema: Ghana Publishing Corporation.

Bohannan, P. 1959. "The Impact of Money on African Subsistence Economies" in *The Journal of Economic History,* 19: 491–503.

Boserup, E. 1970. *Woman's Role in Economic Development.* London: George Allen and Unwin.

Brokensha, D. ed. 1972. *Akwapim Handbook.* Tema: Ghana, Ghana Publishing Corporation.

Brown, C. K. 1986. *Rural Development in Ghana.* Legon, ISSER.

Brush, C. K. & D. Sabinsky 1995. *Valuing Local Knowledge: Indigenous People and Intellectual Property Rights.* Washington D.C.: Island Press.

Buhr, Ales. 1998. *The price incentive to smuggle and the cocoa supply in*

Ghana 1950–1996. Washington D.C.: IMF Africa Department.

Buller, H. & Wright, Susan 1990. *Rural Development. Problems and Practices.* Aldershot: Avebury.

Busia, K. A. 1951. *The Position of the Chief in the Political System of the Ashanti.* International African Institute.

Caldwell, J. C. 1969. *African Rural-Urban Migration.* Canberra: A.N.U.P.

Caldwell, J. C. 1989. "Population Change and Rural Transformation in Ghana," in *Ghana Population Studies* No.2. Legon: University of Ghana.

Cardoso, F. H. 1972. "Dependency and Development in Latin America", in *New Left Review,* No.74, 83–95.

Castro-Leal, Florentia, Julia Drayton, Lionel Demery & Kalpana Mehra. 1997. *Public Social Spending in Africa. Do the Poor Benefit?.* Working Paper. Poverty Reduction and Economic Management Network. Poverty Division World Bank, Washington D.C.

Cernea, M. M. ed. 1990. *Putting People First; Sociological Variables in Rural Development.* (2nd. edition) Oxford: OUP.

Chambers, R. 1969. *Settlement Schemes in Tropical Africa.* London: Routledge and Kegan Paul.

Chambers, R.; A. Pacey and L. A. Thrupp, eds. 1989. *Farmer First: Farmer innovation and agricultural research.* London: ITP.

Christaller, J. G. 1881. Second Edition 1933. *Dictionary of the Asante and Fante Language, called Tshi,* with a geographical appendix. Basel: Basel Mission.

Demographic and Health Surveys. 1994. *Socio-Economic and Health Indicators for Subnational Areas.* Calverton: Maryland: Macro Internat. Inc.

Diaw, Kofi *et al.* 1990. *Effects of Volta Lake Resettlement in Ghana: a reappraisal after 25 years.* Hamburg Institut fur Africa kunde in Verbund der Schifter Deutsches Ubersee Institut.

Dickson, K. B. & Benneh, G. 1969. *A Historical Geography of Ghana.* London:

Djan, O. S. 1936. *Sunlight Reference Almanack.* Aburi: Ghana.

Dos Santos, T. 1973. *The crisis in development theory and the problem of dependence in Latin America,* in H. Bernstein (ed) Underdevelopment and Development 57–80. Harmondsworth: Penguin.

Douglas, M. 1969. *Is Matriliny Doomed in Africa?,* in M. Douglas and P.M. Kabbery (eds). Man in Africa. London: Tavistock Press.

Dutta-Roy. 1969. *Household Budget Survey. Eastern Region.* Legon: ISSER.

Eisenstadt. 1963. *The Political Systems of Empires.* New York: The Free Press.

Elliot, Charles 1980. *Equity and Growth — Unresolved Conflict in Zambian Rural Development Policy.* Geneva: ILO.

Epstein, T. S. 1962. *Economic Development and Social Change in South India*. Manchester: Manchester University Press.

Ewusi, Kodwo 1978. *Planning for the Neglected Rural Poor in Ghana*: A Report to the UN Research Institute for Social Development (UNRISD) in Geneva, January 1978. Accra: New Times Corporation.

FAO 1997. *Production Yearbook*. Rome: FAO.

Feder, Gershon 1991. "Land Tenure and Property Rights: The Theory and Implications for Development Policy." *World Bank Economic Review* 5(1): 135–53. World Bank: Washington D.C.

Fei, J. C. H., & Ranis 1961. *A Theory of Economic Development*, in American Economic Review 1961.

Field, M.J. 1960. *Search for Security: an Ethno- Psychiriatic Study of Rural Ghana*. London: Faber.

Firth, Rosemary. 1966. *Housekeeping among Malay Peasants*. London: Athlone Press.

Firth, R. 1970. *Human Types*. London: Sphere Books.

Fortes, M. 1949. *Time and Social Structure: an Ashanti Case Study*, in Studies presented to A. R. Radcliffe-Brown. Oxford: Clarendon Press.

Fortes, M. 1950. *Kinship and Marriage amongst the Ashanti*, in African Systems of Kinship and Marriage. A.R. Radcliffe & Daryll Forde (eds). Oxford: OUP.

Frank, A. G. 1967. *Capitalism and Underdevelopment in Latin America*. New York: Monthly Review Press.

Furtado, C. 1970. *Economic Development of Latin America: A Survey of Colonial Times to the Cuban Revolution*. Cambridge: CUP.

Gil B. and Omaboe E.N 1966. Internal Migration Differentials from Conventional Questionnaire Items in Ghana. *Proceddings of the 1963 Session of the International Statistical Institute*. Ottawa.

Gluckman, M. 1955. *Custom and Conflict in Africa*. Oxford: Clarendon.

Goode, W. J. 1963. *World Revolution and Family Patterns*. New York: The Free Press.

Goody, J. 1959. "The Mother's Brother and the Sister's son in West Africa", in *Journal of the R.A.I.* 89. 61–88.

Goody, J. 1969. *Comparative Studies in Kinship*. London: Routledge & Kegan Paul.

Goody, J. ed. 1977. *The Domestication of the Savage Mind*. Cambridge: C.U.P.

Greenstreet, M. 1981. *Females in the agricultural labour force and non-formal education for rural development in Ghana*. Accra.

Grillo, R. D. & Rew 1985. *Social Anthropology and Development Policy*.

London: Routledge.

Groves, A. T. 1978. *Africa*. 3rd edition. Oxford: OUP.

Gubbels, P. 1993. *Peasant Farmer Organization in Farmer First Agriculture: New Opportunities and Constraints*. London: ODI.

Hardiman, M. 1974a. *A Preliminary study of the Role of Women in Akan Rural Society*, in Domestic Rights and Duties in Southern Ghana. Legon: Institute of African Studies.

Hardiman, M. 1974b. *Report on the Household Survey of Maiduguri, Nigeria*. Nigeria: Max Lock Group.

Hardiman, M. 1975. *Women in Maiduguri: some aspects of their lives*. Nigeria, Max Lock Group.

Hardiman, M. 1976a. Report on the Household Survey of Six Towns in *the N.E. State of Nigeria*. Nigeria: Max Lock Group.

Hardiman, M. & G. Nott 1976b. *Social Aspects of Development*, in Report of ULG Consultants to the Government of the Kingdom of Swaziland and the African Development Bank. Warwick: ULG.

Hardiman, M. 1977. *Konkonuru: A Village in the Akwapim Hills of Ghana*. London: London School of Economics. (mimeo).

Hardiman, M, & J. Midgley 1982. "Social Planning and Access to the Social Services in Developing Countries", in *Third World Planning Review*, Vol. 4, No. 1 February 1982.

Hardiman, M. & J. Midgley 1982, revised edition 1989. *The Social Dimensions of Development*. Aldershot: Gower.

Harris, J. ed. 1982. *Rural Development: Theories of Peasant Economy and Rural Change*. London: Hutchinson.

Hart, K. 1982. *The Political Economy of West African Agriculture*. Cambridge: C.U.P

Haswell, Margaret and Hunt, Diana. eds. 1991. *Rural Households in Emerging Societies: Technology and Change in Sub-Saharan Africa*. Oxford: Berg Pub.

Hill, P. 1963. *Migrant Cocoa Farmers of Southern Ghana*. Cambridge: C.U.P.

Hobart, Mark (ed.) 1993. *An Anthropological Critique of Development*. London: Routledge & Kegan Paul.

Hoselitz, B. F. 1960. *Social Factors in Economic Development*. New York: The Free Press.

Institute for Resource Development & Ghana Statistical Service, 1989. *Demographic and Health Survey 1988*. Maryland, USA: Colombia Press.

International Fund for Agricultural Development. 1994. *Interim Evaluation Report*. Rome: IFAD.

Jaffee, D. 1998. *Levels of Socio-Economic Development Theory*. Westport

CT. Praeger Pub.

Johnson, M. 1972. "Migration", in *D. Brokensha. Akwapim Handbook*. Tema: G.B.C

Kang, B. T. and Reynolds, L. 1989. Alley Farming in the Humid and Sub-humid Tropics; *Proceedings of an international workshop*, held at Ibadan, Nigeria, 10–14 March 1986.

Kaye, B. L. B. 1962. *Bringing up Children in Ghana*. London: Institute of Education.

King, Elizabeth & M.Anne, eds. 1993. *Women's Education in Developing Countries: Barriers, Benefits and Policies*. Baltimore Md.: Johns Hopkins University Press.

Kulick, D. 1993. "Heroes from Hell", in *Anthropology Today*, Vol.3. June 1993.

Kwamena-Poh, M. A. 1972. "History of Akwapim", in *D.Brokensha. Akwapim Handbook*. Tema: G.B.C.

La-Anyane, S. 1963. *Ghana Agriculture*. Oxford: O.U.P.

La-Anyane, S. 1969. "Issues in Agricultural Policy". In *Proceedings of a Seminar*, organized by the Faculty of Agriculture, University of Ghana, Accra, Liberty Press.

Lawson. G. & A. A. Enti 1972. "Vegetation", in *D.Brokensha. Akwapim Handbook*. Tema: G.B.C.

Leach, M. 1991. "Locating Gendered Experience: an anthropologist's view of a Sierra Leone village". *Sussex, IDS Bulletin* 22(1) pp.44–50.

Lewis, W. A. 1955. *The Theory of Economic Growth*. London: Allen and Unwin.

Lipton, M. 1977. *Why Poor People Stay Poor: Urban Bias in World Development*. London: Temple Smith.

Lipton, M. and R. Longhurst 1989. *New Seeds and Poor People*. London: Unwin Hyman.

Long, N. 1977. *An Introduction to the Sociology of Rural Development*. London: Tavistock

Mair, L. 1965. *An Introduction to Social Anthropology*. Oxford: Clarendon.

Mamdani, M. 1972. *The Myth of Population Control*. New York: Monthly Review Press.

Meillassoux, C. 1972. "From Reproduction to Production", in *Economy and Society* I(1) 93–105.

Mikell, Gwendoline. 1989.*Cocoa and Chaos in Ghana*.

Moock, J. L. ed. 1986. *Understanding Africa's Rural Households*, Boulder, Colorado: Westview.

Moore, W. E. 1963. *Social Change*. Englewood Cliffs, New Jersey: Prentice-

Hall Inc.

Murinde, Victor. 1993. *Policy Modelling for Developing Countries*. Aldershot: Avebury.

Myers, Robert A. 1991. *Ghana: a bibliography*. Oxford: Clio Press Ltd.

National Archives. *ADM, 32/1/6*.

National Research Council 1984. *Leucaena: Promising forage and tree crop in developing countries*. BOSTID.

Nsiah-Gyaboah, Kwasi 1994. *Environmental Degradation and Desertification in Ghana*. Aldershot: Avebury.

Nukunya. G. K. 1969. *Kinship and Marriage among the Anlo Ewe*. London: The Athlone Press.

Nukunya, G. K. 1990. *The Social Structure of Ghana*. Papers prepared for lectures at The University of Ghana. Legon, Accra; later published as a book.

Nukunya, G. K. 1992. *Tradition and Change in Ghana: An Introduction to Sociology*. Accra: Ghana Universities Press

Okali, C. and R. A. Kotey 1971. Akokoaso: A Resurvey. *Technical Publication* Series No. 15, Institute of Statistical, Social and Economic Research. University of Ghana: Legon,

Okali, C. 1983. Cocoa and Kinship in Ghana. London, Kegan Paul.

Opoku, A. A. 1970. The Odwuira Festival In Ayisi E. D. 1972. *An Introduction to the Study of African Culture*. London, Heinemann.

Oppong, C. 1974. *Marriage among a matrilineal elite*. Cambridge: C.U.P.

Osae 2000. *Personal Communication*.

Parsons, Talcott. 1971. *The system of modern societies*. Englewood Cliffs, New Jersey, Prentice-Hall Inc.

Peppy Roberts 1972. *The Teacher and the Community in a West African State*. Unpublished Cambridge thesis.

Pottier, Johan 1993. African Food Systems under Stress: Research Priorities, In *Anthropology in Action*, No. 14 Spring 1993.

Prebisch, R. 1950. *The Economic Development of Latin America and its Principal Problems*. New York: United Nations.

Rattray, R. S. 1914. *Ashanti Proverbs: The Primitive Ethics of a Savage People*. Oxford, Clarendon Press.

Rattray, R. S. 1923. *Ashanti*. Oxford: Clarendon Press.

Rattray, R. S. 1929. *Ashanti Law and Constitution*. Oxford: Clarendon Press.

Ray, Debraj. 1998. *Development Economics*. Princeton N.J.: Princeton University Press.

Republic of Ghana 1970. *A Socio-Economic Survey: Eastern Region*. Rural Planning Department. Accra.

Republic of Ghana 1984. *1984 Population Census: the Gazeteer*. Accra.

Republic of Ghana Statistical Service 1989. Special Report on localities, by *Local Authorities*, based on 1984 census. Accra.

Republic of Ghana and UN Children's Fund 1990. *Children and Women of Ghana: A Situation Analysis 1989 90*. Accra.

Republic of Ghana, Ministry of Finance and Economic Planning. 1991. *Public Investment Programme 1991–1993. Vol. 2 and 3*. Accra.

Republic of Ghana Statistical Service 1993. *Quarterly Digest of Statistics*, No.1 March 1993. Accra.

Roberts, P. 1972. *The Teacher and the Community in a West African State*, Unpublished PhD Thesis: Cambridge .

Robertson, A. 1987. *The Dynamics of Production Relationships*. Cambridge: C.U.P.

Rostow, W. 1960. *The Stages of Economic Growth: A Non-Communist Manifesto*. Cambridge: CUP.

Rostow, W. 1963. *The Economic of Take-Off into Sustained Growth*. London: Macmillan.

Rourke, B. 1971. Wages and Incomes of Africultural Workers in Ghana. Paper prepared for the ILO. August 1970. Published in *Technical Publication Series*, Vo.13. Institute of Statistical and Economic Research. Legon: 1971.

Sahn, David ed. 1996. *Economic Reform and the Poor in Africa*. Oxford: Clarendon.

Schneider, D. M. and K. Gough (eds), 1961. *Matrilineal Kinship*. University of California Press.

Sharma, N.and J. Dreze 1990. *Share Cropping in Palanpur*. London: Suntory-Toyota International Centre for Economics and Related Disciplines.

Siddle, D. and K. Swindell 1990. *Rural Change in Tropical Africa: From Colonies to nation States*. Oxford: Blackwell.

Singh, S. 1985. *Demographic Patterns in Ghana*. Ghana Official Publications. WFS (12). Accra.

Smelser, Neil J. 1963. *The Sociology of Economic Life*. Englewood Cliffs, New Jersey: Prentice-Hall Inc.

Smith, N. 1966. *The Presbyterian Church in Ghana*. Accra: Ghana Universities Press.

Spencer, Herbert. 1862. *First Principles*. London.

Swift, M. G. 1965. *Malay Peasant Society in Jelebu*. London: The Athlone Press.

Szeresewski, R. 1965. *Structural Change in the Economy of Ghana 1891–1911*. London: Weidenfeld.

Todaro, Michael P. 1989. *Economic Development in the Third World,* *4th. edition,* Harlow: Longman.

Tufuo, J. W. and C. E. Donkor 1969. *The Ashantis of Ghana.* Accra: Anowuo Educational Publications.

Uchendu, V. 1969. *Preliminary Report No. 8.* Field Study of Agricultural Change. The Cocoa Farmers of Akim Abuakwa, Eastern Region, Ghana. Stanford University Food Research Institute, June 1969.

UNECA 1998. *UN Economic Commission for Africa 1995–1996.* Addis Abbaba UN.

UNDP 1994. *Human Development Report.* New York: OUP.

UNDP 1998. *Human Development Report.* New York: OUP.

UNICEF 1997. *The State of the World's Children.* New York: OUP.

Ward, W. E. F. 1967. *A History of Ghana.* London: George, Allen & Unwin.

Wilks, I. 1964. *The Growth of the Akwapim State. In The Historian in Tropical Africa.* Oxford, O.U.P.

World Bank 1980. *World Development Report.* Washington, .

World Bank 1994. *World Development Report.* New York: OUP.

WHO 1997. *The World Health Report.* Geneva.

SUGGESTIONS FOR FURTHER READING

Ardayfio-Schandorf, Elizabeth 1996. *The changing family in Ghana: proceedings of the National Research Conference, held at the Golden Tulip Hotel,* Accra from 25–27 January 1995.

Bardhan, Pranab & A. Ruda 1986. Labor Mobility and the Boundaries of the Village Moral Economy, **In** *Journal of Peasant Studies* 13(3) 90–99.

Benneh, G. 1970. The Impact of Cocoa Cultivation on the Traditional Tenure Systems of the Akan in Ghana. *Ghana Journal of Sociology.* Vol.6 No.1, 43–61.

Brokensha, D. 1966. *Social Change at Larteh, Ghana.* Oxford: Clarendon Press.

Burnside, Craig & David Dollar 1997. Aid Policies and Growth. *Policy Research Working Paper* No. 1777. World Bank: Washington D.C.

Caldwell, J. C. ed. 1975. Population Growth and Socio-Economic Change in West Africa. New York, Columbia University Press.

Danquah, J. B. 1922. *Akan Laws and Customs.* London: Routledge.

Danquah, J. B. 1928. *Cases in Akan Law.* London: Routledge.

Djan, O. S. 1945. *The Aburi.* Aburi.

Doward, A. *et al.* ed. 1998. *Smallholder Cash Crop Production under market Liberalisation.* New York: CAB International.

Dreze, Jean & Amartiya Sen. 1989. *Hunger and Public Action.* Oxford: OUP.

Durkheim, E. 1893. *The Division of Labour in Society, translated by G. Simpson.* London: Macmillan 1934.

Evans- Pritchard, E. E. 1965. *The Position of Women in Primitive Societies.* London: Faber and Faber.

Fortes, M. *et al.* 1949. The Ashanti Survey 1945–46: an experiment in social research, **In** *The Geographical Journal* 60, 4–6.

Foster, P. 1965. *Education and Social Change in Ghana.* London: Routledge & Kegan Paul.

Goody, J. 1957. Anomie in Ashanti, **In** *Africa,* 27. 356–363.

Goody, J. 1962. *Death, Property and the ancestors.* Stanford: U.P.

Goody, J. 1965. Descent Groups. Article in *Encyclopedia of Social Sciences.* Legon: Institute of African Studies.

Greenstreet, M. 1972. Social Change and Ghanaian Women, **In** *Canadian Journal of African Studies,* 6,2, 1972; pp. 351–355.

Jahoda, G. 1959. "Love, marriage and Social Change", in *Africa* Vol. xxi 1959.

Jahoda, G. 1961/62. "Aspects of Westernization", **In** *B. J. S.* Vols. 12 & 13 .

Mikell, Gwendoline. 1986. Ghanaian Females; Rural Economy and National Stability, In *African Studies Review*, Vol. 29 No. 3 1986.

Nsarkoh, J. K. 1964. *Local Government in Ghana*. Accra: Ghana U.P.

Nyanteng, V. K. and G. J. Apeldorn 1972. The Farmer and the Marketing of Foodstuffs. *Technical Publications Series* No, 19. Legon: ISSER.

Paulme, D. 1963. *Women in Tropical Africa*. London, Routledge & Kegan Paul.

Quisumbing, Agnes R.; R. Lynn Brown; S. Hillary; L. Feldstein; Hadda & Pena. Christine 1995. *Women: the Key to Food Security*. Washington D.C., International Food Policy Research Institute.

Republic of Ghana Publications 1984. *Policies and Programmes for adjustment*. Accra.

Twumasi, P. A. 1986. *Social Research in Rural Communities: the Problems of Field Work in Ghana*. Accra: Ghana Universities Press.

Vercuijsse, Emil. 1988. *The Political Economy of Peasant Farming in Ghana*. The Hague: Netherlands Institute of Social Studies.Ward, W. E. F. 1991. *My Africa*. Accra: Ghana Universities Press.

Weber, Max, translated by Talcott Parsons 1930. *The Protestant Ethic and the Spirit of Capitalis*m. London: Unwin University Books.

Westendorff, David G. & Ghaj, Dharan 1993. *Monitoring Social Progress in the 1990s (UNRISD)*. Aldershot: Avebury.

White, Landeg 1989. *Portrait of an African Village*. Cambridge: CUP.

Woodman, G. R. 1966. *The Development of Customary Law in Ghana*. Cambridge: Unpublished PhD Thesis.

Wyllie, R. W. 1964. One Ghanaian Teacher and his Profession, In *West African Journal of Education*, Vol. 8.

INDEX

Abrade, 63, 72-73, 97, 119, 187, 193
Aburi, 63, 67, 143, 176, 198
Aburiamanfo, 65
Accra, 93, 132
Acreages farmed, 111-113
Adaebutto, 76
Addo, Godfried, 10, 141, 217, 220
Addo Mensah II, Gyasehene Bediako, 10, 67, 69, 73
Addo Mensah III, 9, 93
Addo, Moses, 77, 83, 99, 190, 208, 217
Addo, Nelson, 11, 221
Adontenhene of Akwapim, 69, 176
Adult Education, 98,
Agricutural systems/technology, 46, 103, 214
Ahwireng, Kwaku, 10
Akim, 68
Akpeteshie, 87, 114, 124
Akwamu, 68
Akwapim State, 63, 68, 69-70, 133
Ansa Sasriku, Chief of the Akwamu 67
Asabidie, 142, 146
Asamoah, Kwamena, 10, 86, 187-190, 218
Asamoah, K., 141, 192
Asamoah, Stephen, 10, 91, 142, 192-193, 221
Asare, Kate, 10, 111, 126, 219
Ashanti, 60, 175
Ayesu, Jacob, 10, 91
Basel Mission, 4, 71, 77, 153, 176
Bediako, Gyasehene see also Addo Mensah II, 166.
Benneh, G., 104
Boserup, E., 2.
Brong-Ahafo, 48, 60, 150, 200
Caldwell, J.,C., 132-133
Cash crops, 13
Cassava, 42-43
Censuses of Konkonuru, 90, 134
Cernea, M.M., 210
Chambers, R. et al., 1
Children; sleeping and eating practices, 186, 224

Christaller, 71
Christianity, 8, 77-78, 95, 167
Cocoa, 4, 41, 47-53, 72, 78-79, 103, 114, 141
Cocoyam, 108
Colonial Government, 13, 32, 49, 63
Commercial Agriculture, 104, 115, 128
Common Entrance, 154-156, 165, 168, 209
Communal labour, 125, 203, 219
Cooking, 201
Danes, 70
Deforestation, 108
Demographic change, 54-55, 197, 202
Densities, 222
Densu, Kwadjo, 138-141
Development policies, 25-28, 55
Dickson, K. B. & G. Benneh, 115
Disputes, 99, 120, 139
District Secretary, 93
Division of labour, 95, 96, 114-118
Djan, O. S., 7, 176
Djan Osae, 63
Doctors (traditional), 76
Domestic group, 174-203
Douglas, M., 175
Eastern Region, 132
Education, 7, 102, 152-173
Education, Ministry of..., 154, 163-164
Electricity, 60, 93, 150
Ewes, 84, 87, 99, 119, 142, 178, 203
Extension workers, 1,
Farming, 100, 103-131
Farm survey, 222-224
Fei, J. C. H. & Ranis, 133
Field, M., 167
Firewood, 87, 114,
Friday; non-farming day, 99,
Food production, 15, 16, 18, 26, 39, 42-44, 103-131
Fortes, M., 7, 175, 177, 181, 187, 196
Fostering, 153, 194
Funerals, 206
Gil & Omaboe, 132

Goody, J., 148, 174
Government officials, 208
Green Revolution, 26, 215
Gubbels, P., 1, 128
Hardiman, M., 126, 174, 176, 200, 201
Harris, J., 129
Haswell, M. & Hunt, D., 211
Hill, P., 51, 104, 138, 142, 146
House constuction, 82-83, 142, 192, 203
Household, 177
Household census, 220-222
Inheritance, 44-45, 51, 141, 148, 176-177, 195
Intercropping, 35
Isert, H. M., 70
Jankama, 81, 114,
Kaye, B. L .B., 152
Kinship, 7, 45, 96, 197, 207, 212, 219
Koforidua, 132, 208
Kulick, D., 89
Kwamena-Poh, M.A. 69
La Anyane, S., 38, 215
Land tenure systems, 38, 45-46, 50, 103-104, 119, 205, 214
Leach, M., 210
Leadership, 90, 93, 98, 173, 205, 208
Leucaena, 127,
Livestock, 116, 128, 224
Maize, 107, 110
Malaysia, 28, 126, 213
Marketing, 87, 114-115, 128
Marriage, 133
Matriliny, 44, 51, 119-120, 141, 174
Methodism, 77, 153, 156
Methods of study, 217-231
Migration, 7, 54, 87, 132-151
Missionaries, 4, 71, 77, 153
Moock, J. L., 198
Musama Disco Christo Church, 95
National Archives, Accra. 63, 145
Nkrumah, 38, 49, 154
Nsawam, 63, 139
Nukunya, G. K., 11, 96, 105, 177, 195, 207, 212
Obo kofi – the spring in Konkonuru, 65, 76, 77

Odai, 11, 221
Odwira festival, 34, 73-76, 189
Okali, C., 50, 146
Omanhene, Paramount Chief of Akwapim, 69, 145-146
Oppong, C., 176
Oppong Tin Tin, 73
Osae, Isaac Ohene, 5, 10, 76, 91, 218, 221
Osae, Kwasi, 76, 111, 218
Osofo shrine, 67, 76
Owusu, E. K., 10, 77, 190-192
Palm oil, 108
Palanpur (India), 202
Parent-teacher association, 166-172
Patriliny, 148, 195
Patrilocal/patrilinial, 51, 142
Planning, 93-94
Plantain, 119
Polygyny, 177, 194
Population growth, 16, 18, 44
Portuguese, 13
Pettier, J., 210
Rainfall, 81, 108, 202
Rattray, R. S., 194, 196
Renting of land, 124
Roberts, P., 172
Rural services, 19, 27, 83
Rural settlement patterns, 37-41, 142-143
Safo Afamako, 146
School attendance, 159, 166, 168, 171
School teachers, 159, 163, 168, 171
Schneider and Gough, 174
Shrine priests, 167
Siddle, D. & Swindell, K. 134
Social indicators, 1, 56-59, 213
Social Welfare and Community Development, Department of..., 5, 83-84, 141, 208, 217
Soils, 8, 13, 81, 214
Succession, 45, 195
Swaziland, 126
Swollen shoot, 48, 78, 103

fe in a West

e ..